# The Hierarchy of Heaven and Earth

# THE HIERARCHY
# OF HEAVEN AND EARTH

*A New Diagram of Man in the Universe*

*by*

## D. E. HARDING

*A University of Florida Book*

**UNIVERSITY PRESSES OF FLORIDA**
*FAMU / FAU / FIU / FSU / UCF / UF / UNF / USF / UWF*
Gainesville

First published in 1952 by Faber and Faber, Ltd., London

The illustrations were drawn by the author.

BD
511
H3
1979

Library of Congress Cataloging in Publication Data

Harding, Douglas Edison, 1909—
    The hierarchy of heaven and earth.

    "A University of Florida book."
    Reprint of the 1952 ed. published by Faber and
Faber, London.
    1. Cosmology. I. Title.
BD511.H3 1979   113   79-10880

ISBN 0-8130-0640-6


Lithography by Graphic Services, Tallahassee
Printed by Bay Center Corporation, Tampa


University Presses of Florida is the central agency for scholarly publishing of the
State of Florida's university system. Its offices are located at 15 NW 15th Street,
Gainesville, FL 32603. Works published by University Presses of Florida are
evaluated and selected for publication by a faculty editorial committee of any one of
Florida's nine public universities: Florida A & M University (Tallahassee), Florida
Atlantic University (Boca Raton), Florida International University (Miami), Florida
State University (Tallahassee), University of Central Florida (Orlando), University
of Florida (Gainesville), University of North Florida (Jacksonville), University of
South Florida (Tampa), University of West Florida (Pensacola).

*It would be impossible to acknowledge in detail my immense (and indeed obvious) debt to others, and not least to those writers and friends who have generously read the manuscript and given advice and encouragement. Particular thanks, however, are due to Mr. C. S. Lewis, whose Preface might equally well be called an Introduction, and to my wife, Beryl Mary Harding, who made the book possible. I dedicate it to her.*

# Preface

## by C. S. LEWIS

This book is, I believe, the first attempt to reverse a movement of thought which has been going on since the beginning of philosophy.

The process whereby man has come to know the universe is from one point of view extremely complicated; from another it is alarmingly simple. We can observe a single one-way progression. At the outset the universe appears packed with will, intelligence, life and positive qualities; every tree is a nymph and every planet a god. Man himself is akin to the gods. The advance of knowledge gradually empties this rich and genial universe: first of its gods, then of its colours, smells, sounds and tastes, finally of solidity itself as solidity was originally imagined. As these items are taken from the world, they are transferred to the subjective side of the account: classified as our sensations, thoughts, images or emotions. The Subject becomes gorged, inflated, at the expense of the Object. But the matter does not rest there. The same method which has emptied the world now proceeds to empty ourselves. The masters of the method soon announce that we were just as mistaken (and mistaken in much the same way) when we attributed 'souls', or 'selves' or 'minds' to human organisms, as when we attributed Dryads to the trees. Animism, apparently, begins at home. We, who have personified all other things, turn out to be ourselves mere personifications. Man is indeed akin to the gods: that is, he is no less phantasmal than they. Just as the Dryad is a 'ghost', an abbreviated symbol for all the facts we know about the tree foolishly mistaken for a mysterious entity over and above the facts, so

9

the man's 'mind' or 'consciousness' is an abbreviated symbol for certain verifiable facts about his behaviour: a symbol mistaken for a thing. And just as we have been broken of our bad habit of personifying trees, so we must now be broken of our bad habit of personifying men: a reform already effected in the political field. There never was a Subjective account into which we could transfer the items which the Object had lost. There is no 'consciousness' to contain, as images or private experiences, all the lost gods, colours, and concepts. *Consciousness* is 'not the sort of noun that can be used that way'.

For we are given to understand that our mistake was a linguistic one. All our previous theologies, metaphysics, and psychologies were a by-product of our bad grammar. Max Müller's formula (Mythology is a disease of language) thus returns with a wider scope than he ever dreamed of. We were not even imagining these things, we were only talking confusedly. All the questions which humanity has hitherto asked with deepest concern for the answer turn out to be unanswerable; not because the answers are hidden from us like 'goddes privitee', but because they are nonsense questions like 'How far is it from London Bridge to Christmas Day?' What we thought we were loving when we loved a woman or a friend was not even a phantom like the phantom sail which starving sailors think they see on the horizon. It was something more like a pun or a *sophisma per figuram dictionis*. It is as though a man, deceived by the linguistic similarity between 'myself' and 'my spectacles', should start looking round for his 'self' to put in his pocket before he left his bedroom in the morning: he might want it during the course of the day. If we lament the discovery that our friends have no 'selves' in the old sense, we shall be behaving like a man who shed bitter tears at being unable to find his 'self' anywhere on the dressing-table or even underneath it.

And thus we arrive at a result uncommonly like zero. While we were reducing the world to almost nothing we deceived ourselves with the fancy that all its lost qualities were being kept safe (if in a somewhat humbled condition) as 'things in our own mind'. Apparently we had no mind of the sort required. The Subject is as empty as the Object. Almost nobody has been making linguistic mistakes about almost nothing. By and large, this is the only thing that has ever happened.

Now the trouble about this conclusion is not simply that it is unwelcome to our emotions. It is not unwelcome to them at all times or in all people. This philosophy, like every other, has its pleasures. And it will, I fancy, prove very congenial to government. The old 'liberty-talk' was very much mixed up with the idea that, as inside the ruler, so inside the subject, there was a whole world, to him the centre of all worlds, capacious of endless suffering and delight. But now, of course, he has no 'inside', except the sort you can find by cutting him open. If I had to burn a man alive, I think I should find this doctrine comfortable. The real difficulty for most of us is more like a physical difficulty: we find it impossible to keep our minds, even for ten seconds at a stretch, twisted into the shape that this philosophy demands. And, to do him justice, Hume (who is its great ancestor) warned us not to try. He recommended backgammon instead; and freely admitted that when, after a suitable dose, we returned to our theory, we should find it 'cold and strained and ridiculous'. And obviously, if we really must accept nihilism, that is how we shall have to live: just as, if we have diabetes, we must take insulin. But one would rather not have diabetes and do without the insulin. If there should, after all, turn out to be any alternative to a philosophy that can be supported only by repeated (and presumably increasing) doses of backgammon, I suppose that most people would be glad to hear of it.

There is indeed (or so I am told) one way of living under this philosophy without the backgammon, but it is not one a man would like to try. I have heard that there are states of insanity in which such a nihilistic doctrine becomes really credible: that is, as Dr. I. A. Richards would say, 'belief feelings' are attached to it. The patient has the experience of being nobody in a world of nobodies and nothings. Those who return from this condition describe it as highly disagreeable.

Now there is of course nothing new in the attempt to arrest the process that has led us from the living universe where man meets the gods to the final void where almost-nobody discovers his mistakes about almost-nothing. Every step in that process has been contested. Many rearguard actions have been fought: some are being fought at the moment. But it has only been a question of arresting, not of reversing, the movement. That is what makes Mr. Harding's book so important. If it 'works', then we shall have seen the beginning of a reversal: not a stand here, or a stand there, but a kind of thought which attempts to reopen the whole question. And we feel sure in advance that only thought of this type can help. The fatal slip which has led us to nihilism must have occurred at the very beginning.

There is of course no question of returning to Animism as Animism was before the 'rot' began. No one supposes that the beliefs of pre-philosophic humanity, just as they stood before they were criticized, can or should be restored. The question is whether the first thinkers in modifying (and rightly modifying) them under criticism, did not make some rash and unnecessary concession. It was certainly not their intention to commit us to the absurd consequences that have actually followed. This sort of error is of course very common in debate or even in our solitary thought. We start with a view which contains a good deal of truth, though in a confused or exaggerated form. Objections are then suggested and we withdraw it. But hours later we discover that we have emptied the baby out with the bath and that the original view must have contained certain truths for lack of which we are now entangled in absurdities. So here. In emptying out the dryads and the gods (which, admittedly, 'would not do' just as they stood) we appear to have thrown out the whole universe, ourselves included. We must go back and begin over again: this time with a better chance of success, for of course we can now use all particular truths and all improvements of method which our argument may have thrown up as by-products in its otherwise ruinous course.

It would be affectation to pretend that I know whether Mr. Harding's attempt, in its present form, will work. Very possibly not. One hardly expects the first, or the twenty-first, rocket to the Moon to make a good landing. But it is a beginning. If it should turn out to have been even the remote ancestor of some system which will give us again a credible universe inhabited by credible agents and observers, this will still have been a very important book indeed.

It has also given me that bracing and satisfying experience which, in certain books of theory, seems to be partially independent of our final agreement or disagreement. It is an experience most easily disengaged by remembering what has happened to us whenever we turned from the inferior exponents of a system, even a system we reject, to its great doctors. I have had it on turning from common 'Existentialists to M. Sartre himself, from Calvinists to the *Institutio*, from 'Transcendentalists' to

Emerson, from books about 'Renaissance Platonism' to Ficino. One may still disagree (I disagree heartily with all the authors I have just named) but one now sees for the first time why anyone ever did agree. One has breathed a new air, become free of a new country. It may be a country you cannot live in, but you now know why the natives love it. You will henceforward see all systems a little differently because you have been inside that one. From this point of view philosophies have some of the same qualities as works of art. I am not referring at all to the literary art with which they may or may not be expressed. It is the *ipseitas*, the peculiar unity of effect produced by a special balancing and patterning of thoughts and classes of thoughts: a delight very like that which would be given by Hesse's *Glasperlenspiel* (in the book of that name) if it could really exist. I owe a new experience of that kind to Mr. Harding.

# Contents

# CONTENTS

## PART IV

## PART V

## PART VI

# PART ONE

## CHAPTER I

# The View Out and the View In

*1. The missing head*

This book is an unconventional attempt to discover, for myself and in my own way, what I am and what I amount to in the universe.

What am I? That is *the* question. Let me try to answer it as honestly and simply as I can, forgetting the ready-made answers.

Common sense tells me that I am a man very similar to other men (adding that I am five-feet-ten, fortyish, grey-headed, around eleven stone, and so on), and that I know just what it is like here and now to be me, writing on this sheet of paper.

So far, surely, nothing can have gone wrong. But has my common sense really described what it is like to be me? Others cannot help me here: only I am in a position to say what I am. At once I make a startling discovery: common sense could not be more wrong to suppose that I resemble other men. I have no head! Here are my hands, arms, parts of my trunk and shoulders —and, mounted (so to say) on these shoulders, not a head, but these words and this paper and this desk, the wall of the room, the window, the grey sky beyond. . . . My head has gone, and in its place is a world. And all my life long I had imagined myself to be built according to the ordinary human and animal plan!

Where other creatures carry small rounded body-terminals, fairly constant in shape and furnished with such things as eyes and hair and mouth, there is for me a boundless and infinitely varied universe. It looks as if I alone have a body which fades out so that almost the only hints which remain of it above my shoulders are two transparent shadows thrown across everything. (I may call them nose-shadows if I please, but they are not in the least like noses.)

And certainly I do not find myself living inside an eight-inch ball and peering out through its portholes. I am not shut up in the gloomy interior of any object, and least of all in a small tightly-packed sphere, somehow managing to live my life there in its interstices. I am at large in the world. I can discover no watcher here, and over there something watched, no peep-hole out into the world, no window-pane, no frontier. I do not detect a universe: it lies wide open to me. These ink-marks are now forming on this sheet of paper. They are present. At this moment there is nothing else but this blue and white pattern, and not even a screen here (where I imagined I had a head) upon which the pattern is projected. My head, eyes, brain—all the instruments that I thought were here at the centre—are a fiction. It is incredible that I ever believed in them.

(No doubt something is going on here. But whatever they are and wherever they are, these aches and chafings and roughnesses, these tastes and smells and warmths, are not grey-haired and equipped with eyes and ears; they are not pink and eight inches across and ugly or handsome. In short they are not a head.)

## 2. *The head found*

A further and no less remarkable discovery follows—while I have no head where I thought I had one, I have innumerable heads where I thought I had none: heads mysteriously shrunken and variable, twisted back to front, and multiplied endlessly, in every reflecting surface. That my head pervades the region

round about is shown, first, by the fact that I have only to give any object there a polish to find my head in it; second, by the fact that if I take a box with a small hole in it (that is, a camera) and point it to the centre of the region, I find my head trapped in the box; and third, by the fact that my friends tell me that my head is present to them where they are, so that they can describe it in detail. It seems, then, that I am a decapitated body watched from the middle distance by its severed head, now made elastic, turned round to face its trunk, and hiding everywhere. Even the face with which my friend confronts me turns out to be a mask for mine: he cannot take off this mask, but he can tell me what it hides. And if he should be mistaken, at least his camera will hardly repeat the mistake: unlike him, it cannot be credited with the power of grasping what is going on elsewhere. It is honest about that part of me which it contains where it is. And if it could describe me as I really am, here at the centre, it would be a failure as a camera; for its photographs of me would show me beheaded, with itself—the camera—mounted on my shoulders.

(In fact there is precisely such a device, called the first-person camera, which is sometimes used to make a film in which the audience sees, not the chief actor, but what he sees—namely his world, including his hands and feet, and perhaps his pipe and the rims of his spectacles, but never his head. The body with which the cinema audience identifies itself is headless. The effect can be a startling realism, though few cinema-goers are aware of its source. In the film studio, either a headless dummy is used, with the camera where the head should be, or the camera is mounted close to the living subject's head so that it looks with him instead of at him.)

The many legends of loose and flying heads, and of headless monsters, are not far from the sober truth after all. Perhaps also the mediaeval fondness for martyrs who walked (even if they did not, like King Charles in the ill-punctuated sentence, talk) after their heads had been cut off, owed something to the half-conscious realization that we are all in much the same state.

### 3. The human region and its centre

There is, then, a zone where I keep my heads. Approaching observers report that, towards the inner edge of this zone, my head grows till only a part of it is registered, and that this part

gets hazier and hazier till nothing appears at all. Receding observers, on the other hand, say that towards the outer edge of
the zone my head shrinks till it is replaced by the whole body,
and this in turn shrinks till it vanishes altogether. Thus my
observers come to plot the boundaries of what may be called
my human region. My friend, entering this region, takes on my
man's body. And I take on his, for each of us is centred in the
human region of the other. The shell of my manifestations has
for kernel the shell of his manifestations, and *vice versa*. Each
of us is Brünhilda perfectly guarded by fiery rings, a magician
who casts a spell over all who dare approach, transforming
them utterly.

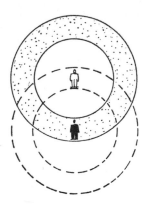

But we are not content to exchange heads. Neither of us holds
on to what is presented to him, but instead projects it upon the
other. Thus my friend insists that the head he registers is not
where he is, but here at the centre of my human region; and he
says this regardless of the fact that if he were to come here to
verify his statement he would (like Ixion embracing Hera) find
on the way things very different from my head, and then nothing. Or, if he came all the way here, he would be in a position
to find, not what he calls my head, but what he calls his own.

To push home your inquiry into my existence is to destroy it,
for I am always elsewhere, like a rainbow or a mirage. If I take
myself as I am to myself, I find presented these men, trees,
clouds, stars; and I scatter them all as if in a giant centrifuge,
leaving the centre empty. If, instead, I take myself as I am to
others, I am a host of creatures of numberless shapes and sizes;

and all of them, though they belong out there, I pull in here as if by a powerful magnet, leaving none at large. Accordingly it is impossible to pin me down either to my centre here or to the centres of my regional observers there. I am something like a game of hide-and-seek in which hider and seeker never meet because each takes refuge in the other. Everybody is out on a visit; but because no one will stay at home to be visited, there are no meetings. We all keep our distance by changing places, and live inside-out.

And one of the reasons why we can never meet is that we more than meet: we become one another. For I do not live here at this centre only, content to enjoy what is presented here and to refer it to centres over there in my regions. Equally I live out there in those centres, contemplating myself as manifested in them. Indeed I have already found that I am more at home out there observing my head, than here observing my headlessness. The view in comes at least as naturally to me as the view out. Unlike Burns, the gift I need is to see myself as I see myself.

## 4. The view out from the centre

Let me now examine, in more detail, this miscellany of objects which I find presented here. They arrange themselves in many ways, but notably according to their range or remoteness. Thus all the men I register are dispatched to my human region not many feet away; all the clouds to a greater distance; all the stars still further. I see them there, from here. If my friend is to show himself to me as a man, he must keep off; if he comes too near he is likely to be revealed as a mass of very lowly animals, and nearer still he may take on the guise of mere particles. It is as if I carried about with me a worldwide nest of concentric sieves so graded that all things from stars to atoms are caught in its meshes, and thus made to keep their proper distances no matter where I go. Always the chief class distinctions I note amongst my present guests are linked with residential distinctions. If you are a star, you can never trespass out of my star region into any other; if a man, your home cannot be far away. I allow neither slumming nor social climbing in my zoned suburbs.

My guests, then, refuse to stay. And I am not content to see them off, making sure that their baggage is properly labelled: I see them home, so that in one sense my boundaries come to include all their destinations to the furthest visible nebula. And when I get there I turn round to share their view of me.

## 5. *The view in to the centre*

Common sense suggests that this self-portrait is strange only because in beginning with the view out I am beginning at the wrong end, beginning with what is arbitrary and irrelevant and for ever changing—one moment I entertain galaxies, the next, a dust grain—whereas the view in is constant, of practical importance, and the true revelation of what I am. Does my tailor care whether I am contemplating an elephant or a mouse, or my hatter need to ask whether I am an astronomer or a philatelist?

But common sense is wrong: the view in is just as odd and as variable as the view out. To show that this is so, let me call in a really efficient observer. His first rule is to keep on the move, and take no one aspect of me as final. Thus the innumerable views he gets of me in this room—back and front and side, above and below, near and far—are all of them parts of my true portrait. But he sees no reason why he should confine his travels to this room of arbitrary dimensions, and he retires beyond it. Now his story is of a mannikin, a house, a street of houses, a town, a country, a planet, a star (a star that has developed into —or rather absorbed—a solar system), a galaxy, and in the end a spark of light that goes out altogether.

And if, finding this odd, he decides to approach me instead of retiring, his tale is equally curious and its end is the same. Whether he moves away or draws near, he finds all manner of non-human transformations regionally set out, and finally nothing. Even outside the looking-glass world there comes a point when to get to the Red Queen the observer must leave her, and to escape her he must imitate the ingenious cockroach that took refuge from the tortoise by hiding in its shell. The only way to get out of my presence is to make for its centre—the one spot where it does not exist.

## 6. *A common-sense objection answered*

To the objection that it is not I who am so transformed, it may be replied: what I am is the question at issue, and may not be prejudged. In any case, if one view of me (say the back view at twelve inches' range) is not enough for the observer in my human region, if he must move about there to find out what I am, then there seems no good reason for restricting his movements to that one region—provided he keeps the centre of all the regions in view. Again, if I, from my side, tell him that I am occupied with the inhabitants of many regions (and am indeed on visiting terms with them all), then it would be fastidious of him to ban them, ignoring their perspectives of me. Moreover if it is admitted that the near view of organs and cells, of molecules and lesser particles, is germane to my nature (and in some sense a view of *me*) despite the fact that it discloses something less than a man, then there is nothing to show why the far view, where the scene becomes more comprehensive (but no more strange), should not be equally valid. At this stage anyhow, neither can be given preference and neither ignored. For it is not as if there were some reality at the centre against which its regional appearances could be checked.

### 7. *The view out and the view in brought together*

Both my own view out and my observer's view in are so unexpected that, if either had to stand by itself, it might well be taken for an illusion. But they agree, each supporting and complementing the other. Looking in at me, and out with me, come to much the same thing—with this vital difference, that whereas the first reveals *my* head, *my* human body, *my* planet, *my* star, *my*

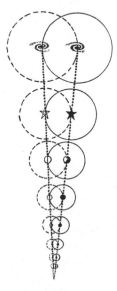

galaxy, the second reveals *other* heads, *other* bodies, *other* planets, and the rest. Thus the two accounts agree in describing me in human and planetary and sidereal and galactic terms, and differ only as to which men, planets, and so on, are in question. The view in is of a particular one of these at each stage; the view out is of the others.

And their combination, the twofold story which must now be told, is of a pair of mutual observers who, whether they go or come, keep equal rank. When one of them finds himself in the other's star region, he too is shown to be a star; when each inhabits the other's middle region, they are likely to prove men; venturing closer, they are less than men. Always their relationship is symmetrical.

All my looking, then, is looking in a mirror—in a glass which has the knack of showing me, not what I call *this* face, but its rough likeness. And it is often far from human. For most purposes my arm is too short and my hand-mirror is too small—I cannot hold it in my remoter regions to see what I am there—but all I really need is that perfectly telescopic and elastic glass, namely simple sight, to tell me in terms of others what I am.

## 8. The elastic self

Now these remarkable metamorphoses are not tricks of perspective, but really are happening to me all the while. Consider the place I call *here*. When I tell my dog to come here, I mean to this part of the room; when my friend comes here, he comes to this house; when foreigners come here, they come to this country; if one day Martians arrive, they will arrive here, even though they alight in Australia. The rule is that my *here* grows and shrinks along with my *there*.

Again, I find myself taking up the viewpoint of such diverse units as my solitary human self, my family, town, country, and even planet. And this unit that I think for, that I vaguely feel behind me, that I have for backing, is on a par with what I am facing or up against. When a man offends, this man is offended; when a nation offends, this nation—no less—is up in arms. Once more, equality. I grow at a moment's notice a 'body' to match what I have in 'mind', though it is true I can discover this body only by taking up my station in other bodies, in my regional observers who are where I keep all my property.

My regions' boundaries are the tide-marks left by my outflowing and ebbing sympathy. In fact there is nothing here at the centre but a receptacle for others—an infinitely elastic receptacle for infinitely elastic objects—and this centre is half the time swelling to include in its own nonentity the surrounding regions with their full population of observers, and half the time shrinking to extrude them again, like myriads of rabbits out of a master-magician's top hat. Thus to perceive another man is to centralize and abolish all of this man—atoms, molecules, cells, head, and total body—in his favour; thus to perceive another planet is not merely to look beyond all of this one, nor merely to incorporate it, but also to dissolve the whole of its mass into empty room (so to speak) for that planet. When mutual observers approach, thereby shrinking in each other's estimation, each produces the other from his own central void; and when they recede again, thereby growing in each other's estimation, each does so by reabsorbing the other.

### 9. Both views involve centre-shifting

An important complication is that my observer is obliged from time to time to alter slightly the direction of his gaze. He attends, say, to a cell; and then, as the cell shrinks and vanishes and a limb comes into view, his line of sight is likely to move a little. It moves again when the whole man takes the limb's

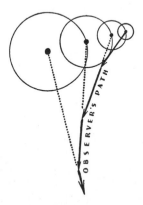

place; and later there occur shifts of direction from the planet's centre to the solar system's, and from this to the Galaxy's.

And once more the inside story confirms and completes the outside. My observer sees truly when he finds the lesser me eccentric to the greater; for when I forget my private interest and identify my well-being with that of my town, or country, or planet, I find myself acknowledging a more distant centre, and placing myself there. The larger the unit to which I am thus attached, the more remote its headquarters are likely to be. Initially eccentric, I can grow only by correcting this condition, stage by stage. My observer finds this out in his own fashion, I in mine.

### 10. Illusions of grandeur?

Here, then, are the makings of a new portrait of myself. It is not what I had reckoned for, but it is drawn from the life. But is it, perhaps, too flattering? Am I not in danger of thinking too highly of myself?

The danger may be averted by four considerations. First, that my base, which I can never cut loose from, is my merely human phase; second, that if I am more than human I am also much less; third, that it is only by sinking myself in my object that I rise to its status; fourth, that in myself I am nothing but a reception-centre for others. My life is the life they live in me. Take away these visitors of mine and I vanish; alter the least of them and I am altered. The fluctuation of a variable star is a fluctuation in me. I am different because of the cloud that is now sailing past my window: for it is not white, or swift, or beautiful, over there, but here from there. Unless they leave home and arrive in me (or in some such home-from-home) my objects, from my friend's face to a spiral nebula, can never amount to anything. Truly I forget in what my wealth and true grandeur lie, and how inexhaustible they are, and how my title to them is my absolute poverty. Plunging head-first into the sea of nothingness, I find there untold treasure.

### 11. The depth of the picture

This abundance, this wonderful universe of objects, is present to me and not absent, presented and not represented here. And indeed the slightest attention to these things discloses that they are two-dimensional, that they have breadth and height, but no depth which really succeeds in coming between us; for the radii that connect me with them (though I may make a show of reckoning them in inches or miles or light-years) are only so many points when taken end-on. Between two planets in the sky is a palpable gap, but between them and this planet is no such interval. Yet, because my objects are essentially centrifugal, there arises between us that mysterious 'third dimension' which is in fact not a dimension at all (till it is changed into one of the others). It is, as pure depth, non-dimensional, a quality of otherness (including perhaps majesty or holiness or transcendent constancy) rather than a quantity of remoteness. And this quality of otherness or thereness is itself realized *here* at the centre, along with the rest of my object's qualities.

The truth is that if I find the main conclusions of this chapter incredible, it is because, full of preconceived notions, I lack the simplicity to notice what is always staring me in the face.

*12. Relativity and the regional schema*

This centre is the spaceless bud which is never and yet always bursting into the immense flower of my many-regioned space. Now this exfoliated space is essentially hierarchical. And hierarchy is the natural development of relativity—of the principle that an event or 'thing' is the system of its manifestations to observers elsewhere. Taking this principle seriously and applying it to myself, I find that I saturate a graded space (in fact, space-time), a nest of boxes whose value varies with their size, a cosmic onion instead of a cosmic potato. Hierarchy is quantitative relativity turned qualitative, disembodied and uniform and human observers become embodied and multiform and non-human, indifferent space mapped out into something like the ancient circles of heaven and earth and hell, with all their traffic, naked and invisible light richly clothed in every garment of its hierarchical wardrobe, the light which falls off as the square of its distance transformed into the light which evolves men and universes as it advances. And already the outline of this regional constitution of mine is hinted at by the physical science which distinguishes between the Euclidean geometry of my middle regions and the non-Euclidean geometry of my nearest and furthest regions.

# CHAPTER II

# My Knowledge of the World Outside

## 1. *The scientist is called in*

Common sense suggests that, before going on with this inquiry, I should hear the scientist's account of the way I come to experience these objects of mine. It may be that, with his help, some of the surprises and paradoxes of the previous chapter will vanish, and I shall keep my head.

The first question I put to him is this: how do I see the hand that is writing these words?

## 2. *His account of vision—light*

He tells me, in effect, that a portion of a star detaches itself, travels to my hand, and bounces off it into my eyeballs, where with lightning artistry it contrives to paint two small inverted pictures of the thing it bounced off.

I find this story full of difficulties. To start with, I cannot pretend I see a *hand*, but only a surface, and not all of this. Again, since sunlight (whatever that may be) takes time to get across from my hand to my eye, I can never see the surface of the hand I have now, but only something which 'isn't really there'. Most serious of all, if the light by which I see this out-of-date surface is the light which it rejects, which it refuses to make its own, isn't the thing I see here the very opposite of the thing that is (or rather, was) over there? How can I say my hand is pink, if pink is the one colour it will have none of?

Moreover I seek in vain any comprehensible tale of what happens in the gap between my hand and my eye. If it is neither my hand nor a flock of miniature hands which flies across, if what makes the journey is quite unlike what lies at that end and what lies at this end of it, and is not starry or luminous or hand-like or pink or five-fingered, then endless doubts arise—doubts which convenient little words such as light, and waves, and photons, seem wholly unable to resolve.

### 3. His account of vision—nerves and brain

Putting all these difficulties to one side, let me consider the rest of the story. I am told that somehow there occurs at the back of my eye a picture of my hand—shrunken, upside-down, right-side-left. How do I get to know of it? The answer I am offered is, at its briefest, that no man—but only a lot of primitive animals called cells—can ever see my hand, and that each of them sees not my hand but a tiny part of it, and in fact does not see that part but tastes it, and in fact does not taste it but tastes (I should say: reacts chemically to) certain changes in a light-sensitive substance in my retinae—all of which is going on in a place remote from my hand.

Certainly it is nothing like a taste, and still less like a star or a sunbeam or a hand, which passes along my optic nerves to my brain. The story is now of electrical impulses travelling along attenuated animal bodies—as it were a communal shuddering of creatures of the humblest sort. And what happens at the terminus in my visual cortex is no less obscure. It is safe to say, however, that no surgeon operating on my brain is ever likely to find there a model of my hand; and even if he did do so, he would be a long way from understanding how this dwarfed and pitch-dark and hemmed-in version of my hand, composed of one kind of animals, can begin to do justice to the full-size illuminated original, composed of a very different kind of animals. (In fact, such a discovery would leave the investigator much worse off: his work would only begin all over again, with the added inconvenience that the object is now a hopelessly inadequate copy of the real thing, and packed into a light-tight box where I keep no sense organs to help me to perceive it. And I cannot avoid the feeling that this idea—the idea of having a second right hand, mysterious and withered and futilely groping in the dark among my brains—is much more comical and fantastic than anything in the previous chapter.)

Of course this is not the whole story—much more than retinal cells, optic nerves, and visual cortex, is involved in vision—but the point is now clear enough. It is that everything depends upon the continuity of the incoming train of events. For if this train is anywhere broken (as when the sun is darkened at night, or my eyes are shut, or my brain is injured in a certain way) then I cannot see my hand.

## 4. The unknown outside world

If the foregoing account is in the main true, I can only know what happens in a part of my brain, at the terminus of the incoming train of events. The outer world is an inference. Worse, I must confess it to be the wildest of guesses, when I bear in mind all the hazards of that long journey, with its variety of vehicles, and the business of changing vehicles so often, and above all the immense discrepancy between the universe at one end and the brain cell at the other. To believe that 'the world I see' here is anything like 'the world as it is' there, is blindest faith, making belief in the most colourful miracles of religion seem cautious realism.

Besides, the entire story from sun to cortex is itself more than suspect. For it is impossible to throw doubt upon what this apparatus is supposed to reveal, without throwing doubt also upon the apparatus itself. And so, if I take the scientist's tale seriously, I am not even left with that tale, but only with my private collection of coloured and moving shapes, which may have no relevance whatever to any universe beyond themselves.

## 5. The senses other than vision

Nor does the scientist's account of the other senses help. For in every instance his story is the same in essentials—a story of outside events, of events in a sense organ, of events in nerves and brain. And only the last, which few would claim to be like the first, is directly experienced. In short, my senses, whether taken singly or all together, are more like blinds than peep-holes. If by some fortunate chance a chink should let through a ray of outer sunshine, I have no means of telling it from the candlelight within.

## 6. Am I alone?

The world, then, may be my dream, and I its sole dreamer. And even this dreamer may be a dream within this dream. At this moment a pink patch is moving across a larger white patch, to the accompaniment of a faint grating sound; there are also certain warmths and tinglings and pressures. To be sure of much more than this is impossible.

### 7. *Shall I reject the scientist's story?*

The scientist's explanation of how he knows the world turns out to be an explanation of how he cannot do so. And from the start, by assuming the very thing that needed proof—namely his knowledge of an external sun and hand and eye and all the rest —he was deep in contradictions.

Nevertheless I do not propose, on this account, to ignore his story. For, firstly, both he and I, if we are outside a lunatic asylum, cannot help but take on trust our perceptions of the external world; and, secondly, we both believe his story to be substantially true and of the greatest practical importance.

Instead of rejecting it, then, I shall try to retell it in a way that gets rid of its inconsistencies.

### 8. *The confusion in the story*

He tells me that my world is not over there, but here 'in my head'. Now this is what I found in the previous chapter, with one all-important difference—I put only the world 'on my shoulders': he puts my head as well. He overcrowds the spot I call Here. Here I am headless, eyeless, brainless: all are turned out by my world. I keep the whole of my bodily equipment over there in my regions, for my observers to appropriate. My world and my brain will not mix; they must keep apart—for the first is central, the second regional. And this is only common sense. Manifestly my head cannot contain the sun, and it would be unreasonable of me to claim two heads here at once—my friend's and mine. And manifestly I know the sun, not a brain that knows the sun; I see you, not an eye that sees you; I smell a rose, not a nose; I enjoy fresh air, not lungs; my dinner, not a palate. I am where the sun is, not where my brains are, though it is true that they play their part in bringing about the sun's presence here: for I see what's here, with what's there. Indeed I am slightly off my head so long as it is on me.

One of the consequences of trying to crowd the world I perceive and the brains I do not perceive into the same place is that one or the other has to be sacrificed. Generally it is my world. It has to be spaceless because no room can be found for it in my head, where it is supposed to be lurking. For instance it is sometimes said that what I experience here is not my hand, or my dog, or my friend, but a 'mental image' or 'idea' or 'impression'; and that when I am looking at an elephant my 'idea' of it is no bigger than when I am looking at a pin; and that all my 'ideas' of the world in space are themselves out of space and in a world of their own—a world which copies everything in space without itself becoming infected. But I can neither find any traces of this second world, nor understand what it is and how it may be recognized. For I have only to attend for a moment to this hand and page, to see that they have all the room they want here to be their full-scale original selves. This one world will do for me. I am not driven to the desperate expedient of first doubling it, and then depriving one world of its qualities and the other of its space.

The sun I see is not shut up here in any little bone box; no hordes of unicellular animals stand in its way. Freed now from all competition and confusion with eyes and nerves and brain, my objects are at liberty to come to themselves—not copies or ideas or impressions of themselves—here at the centre. The sun is a sun and sunny, not over there in itself, but here in me and in its other regional observers. And so with the plain man I say that roses are as red and as fragrant as they seem, and the real sun is yellow and pleasantly warm and not particularly large, and marmalade and toast have a flavour that is all their own and no illusion. These colours and shapes and smells and tastes are not my way of misinterpreting the real universe, and not even useful clues to a universe which produces such effects in me; they are the facts, a fair sample of the stuff the universe is made of. And the reason why the scientist's story suggested the contrary was that it mixed the immiscibles—my brain and my world. He began with common sense and ended with paradox; I began with paradox and ended with common sense.

### 9. The revised story—the inward journey

Let me, then, retell his story thus: Light from the SOLAR SYSTEM (in particular from the sun) reaches the EARTH (in particular its atmosphere), where it is modified and passed down to my HUMAN BODY (in particular my hand), from which it is reflected to my HEAD (in particular to my eye), some of whose CELLS are specially affected. And since cells consist of MOLECULES, and molecules of ATOMS, and atoms of ELECTRONS and other particles, the story should go on (at least ideally) to show how the changes wrought in my cells are reducible to changes in and among these progressively smaller units.

Now the scientist who describes this train of events is none other than my approaching regional observer; for his account of how I see my hand is an account of his journey through my regions, from the place where he registers a star, through places where he registers a planet and then a man and then cells or a cell, to places where he registers mere particles, and in the end

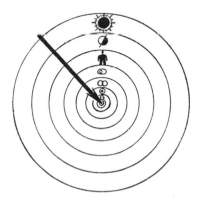

nothing definite at all. His tale is no longer of things in a row, with that mysterious abstraction called *light* leaping from one to the next, but of a nest of regional manifestations, the first of which contains the second, the second the third, and so on to the void at the centre. Of course his detailed description holds good: only its setting or framework is changed. Before, his journey was a series of unrelated movements; now it is an organized whole. Before, he merely wandered in this star (this developed star, the solar system); now he explores it. He peels this celestial fruit, stripping off a planetary rind, a human rind, and many more, till he gets to the core which is nothing.

But this tale so far is the very opposite of what is needed: it shows the universe breaking down by orderly stages to nothing here in me, whereas the question is how it is built up here. To remedy this defect, my observer must on arrival here turn round, looking out with me instead of in at me; and then it is plain that while his journey from the sun was my undoing and in the end my abolition, it was at the same time the building-up of the sun. The moment of his arrival is the moment of the sun's completion, and of my reduction to a mere receptacle for it. The same radial process which is for me centripetal and destructive is for my object centrifugal and constructive.

The only way to understand how I see something is to join in the process by which I see it, travelling from the object there to this centre here while looking at both. The efficient observer combines the attitudes of cox and crew; he is the mythical bird which flies backwards to see where it has come from, as well as the ordinary bird which has eyes only for where it is going. That is to say, the train of events which the scientist describes is a misleading half-truth unless it is read in two antithetical ways. Till he grows eyes in the back of his head he is purblind.

### 10. The inward journey, continued

But no competent observer is content to give such a bare account of me. He is out to find every kind of link between each regional manifestation and the next, till he comes to the nucleus of the system. For instance, he may note how the troubled condition of the planet as a whole affects my country, how this affects the prosperity of my district and town, how this affects my family fortunes, and how these in turn affect my condition as an individual man. He may then seek to show how the stimuli which have thus converged upon my body's surface set up nervous impulses which converge upon my brain, and upon some particular brain area, and even upon some particular synapse or gap between two nerve cells—upon the switch where some fatal connection is established, where that central decision, which is the point of the entire converging system, is irretrievably made.

But even this story, like that of my vision, is partial and abstract; it is only a thin bundle of the innumerable threads that run through the total story of my bodily scaling-down. Truly speaking there is but one stimulus—my whole effective environment for the time being—and one sense organ—the whole surface of my body for the time being, whether that body is a planet's or a man's or a cell's. For distinct trains of events, and separate afferent impulses, do not oblige the investigator by coming in one after the other, like expresses arriving to schedule at a main-line terminus. The process is spherical and unremitting, and not merely linear and intermittent; it is a circumference seeking its centre rather than one point seeking

34

another. Messages do not get through to me, but are continually replacing me.

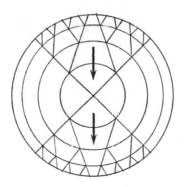

## 11. The outward journey

But the full tale is still only half told. The system of up-lines converging upon this terminus must be matched by a system of down-lines fanning out from it, otherwise all comes to a stop. I see in order to do, and do in order to see. I am anything but a mere registrar of objects. The central decision or switch-over issues in regional action, in a diverging complex of events which spreads by way of efferent nerves and muscles to my body as a whole, to my impact on my family and town and country, and my country's impact on the community of nations, and so on to the remoter regions. Thus the connection made here at the centre is at once the final outcome of a world-wide converging stimulus, and the initiator of a world-wide diverging response; and the two chambers of this immense hour-glass are inseparable. Though my observer's visit is my death and dissolution, he holds a return ticket which is the certificate of my revival.

My story is the complementary opposite of his. I declare he is nothing over there in himself, but builds up to manhood (say) or starhood here at the centre, and reduces to nothing as he returns home. He declares I am a man (say) or a star over there in my regions, but reduce to nothing here at the centre, and build up to my original status as I return there. Whereas he finds (a) me regionally, (b) nothing centrally, (c) me regionally; I find (a¹) nothing regionally, (b¹) him centrally, (c¹) nothing regionally. And this is only another way of saying that the inward journey which is the making of my object is my unmaking, and the outward journey which is its unmaking is my remaking.

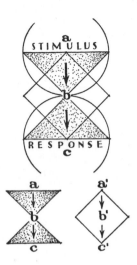

## 12. *Mind and body*

To the central station I give the name *mind*, to the regional stations the name *body*. That is to say, my mind is the view out from this centre, my body the view in—where the term *view* is given its widest and most concrete meaning.

The difference between my body and my mind, then, is firstly one of direction (of the way the observer is facing); secondly one of place (my mind is central, my body regional); and thirdly one of content (my body embraces this body; my mind, other bodies). But there is no fundamental distinction between them: they are different ways of taking the same kind of social facts.

(Of course I may abstract from the strictly indivisible mind-body complex as many part-functions as I please, and call some mental and others physical. For instance, noting in my objects here such common characteristics as painfulness, promise, interest, marvellousness, on the one hand, and such common characteristics as roundness, redness, movement, weight, on the other hand, I may feel the practical need for a distinction between the two classes. Nevertheless this distinction is not between the psychical and the physical, between mind and body, but between two aspects of the mind-body complex. For all

36

these qualities belong impartially to mind and to body, seeing that every view out from one centre is a view in to another, and there are no views which are not views out. I can find here no experience which is merely central and subjective, which has no outer location or reference, and which is not a part of the way my regional objects come to themselves in me.

Again, I may distinguish such part-functions as will and perception. But these also are equally physical and psychical, for each mind perceives the body that the other wills. The stimulus

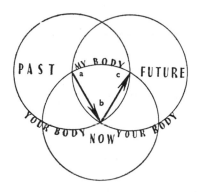

(ab), which was for you outgoing and intended and your bodily expression, is for me now incoming and extended and my mental impression; and the response (bc), which is for me now outgoing and intended and my bodily expression, will presently be for you incoming and extended and your mental impression. In short, I play the game of life from the centre of an immense circular court; and whether the ball is mental or physical, perceived or willed, is a question of whether I am now catching it from the past or throwing it into the future.)

# CHAPTER III

# Projection and Reflection

## 1. *Errors of the instrument*

Often I misread a thing, or mistake it for something else. But if the regional object is nothing over there at its own centre, and has to come here to mine to be itself, how can I ever be wrong about it?

The first half of the answer is that, as an empty receptacle for the object, I cannot distort it: the instrument here is perfect because it does not exist. The second half is that, since the object is what it is to *all* its observers, and I am not all of them, I must always distort it. But my errors are, basically, errors of omission. There is nothing in the object itself at its own centre against which regional estimates of it may be weighed and found wanting; they can only be weighed against one another. The truest view, in that case, is the most inclusive; the untruest, the least inclusive. But in the end all are valid, because all go to make the object what it is. I know the object in so far as I become all its observers in all its regions at all times.

## 2. *Errors of projection*

But even if I can never be wholly wrong about the datum here, do I not often project it upon the wrong place—as when I take the lamp on the hill for a star?

I say that there are ultimately no errors of projection, but only uncommon and private projections which we call illusions, and common and public ones which we call true; and the difference between them is one of degree and not kind. If enough observers project upon any centre a consistent content, then that content becomes what we call objectively real, for no centre is armed to keep off anything that is attributed to it. The real is what is consistently and persistently imagined—countless 'psychical phenomena' bear witness. Projections come true because they are true; they cannot fail to strike home. The tree will never again be a mere tree or the same tree, once it has for a moment been, one moonlit night, an old man with upstretched arms.

On the one hand there is a vast quantity of empirical evidence to show that no line can be drawn between 'unreal imagined objects' and 'real perceived objects'; on the other I can find none to show that there are two worlds, one of fact and the other of imagination. Rather it seems that there is one universe which is the work of countless observers of every hierarchical grade, busy projecting upon one another all their contents. The relatively unreal centres, those which are the product and the source of few and feeble and peculiar projections, differ from the others in no absolute respect. Indeed the trouble with the imaginary is that it is not half imaginary enough: waking is a more thorough kind of dreaming, a dream serial instead of dream short stories. The rats of *delirium tremens* may be more vivid than other rats, but we hear nothing of their diet or their fertile unions: they are insufficiently worked out, failures and not successes of the imagination.

### 3. *Projection and reflection*

Nor can I find good reason for sharply dividing my objects into (a) genuine observers, who are two-sided and something for themselves as well as for me, and (b) mere things, whose views in are matched by no views out. Everything suggests that a view in implies a view out, however rudimentary; that the observer, who can scarcely help attributing to the object some of his own capacity for observation, does not do so in vain; that to be two-sidedly alive is to bring others to similar life; that observation is infectious or nothing. Primitives, children, poets, worshippers, find around them a vitality which is no longer their own projection, but comes back to them as a foreign influence. The phenomena of telekinesis and the poltergeist hint that the mountains which faith moves are not merely metaphorical. When we give our mind to our work it lives and works. Thus many an author of fiction has found his characters developing an intractable life of their own, which startles or even menaces their creator.

# PROJECTION AND REFLECTION

It would seem that the universal society is a great novel, of which each of us is at once joint author, and one of the characters, and many of the characters. At every level we make one another what we are, by reciprocal projection and reflection. Indeed it is common knowledge that we get out of things what we put into them; that kings and idols, gods and ghosts, come to own the powers they are sincerely credited with; that our love and hate are returned, not as ours, but as genuinely the other's; that enthusiasm is contagious; that what we think of men, men come to think of us. Appearances, then, do matter; for reality is keeping up appearances.

Each grows aware of himself in and through his equals, without whom he is imprisoned in his own central nothingness; and his self-consciousness is not in the end a different thing from their consciousness of him. To confer on myself a body is to confer on the objects around me a mind, for only they are in a position to note my body. Thus the self-conscious man is not one but many, even if he is alone on a desert island: someone over there is watching him, and that someone is himself yet another. He is always in company, though he calls it his own.

So far from being chained to this observation post, then, I am always placing myself at others, and often establishing new ones; and so I come to enjoy, not only their varied perspectives of myself, but of all the world. But what I cannot do is to leave my observation posts unchanged and mindless: my view out from them is theirs, not a copy of it or a substitute for it. I cannot recognize you to be a man without partially identifying myself with you, without entering into your life. And it is much the same with nonhuman and even 'inanimate' things—trees, waves, mountains, clouds—I have the irresistible feeling of entering into what they are for themselves. In the pillar I stoutly thrust; in the taut rope I feel the pull. I ride in the clouds, shine as the sun, look down from the stars. I throw myself into the object's motions, I am swayed by its laws, I feel for it and with it. The pathetic fallacy is a fallacy only when I lack the vitality to make it anything else.

Nevertheless I do not leave this original centre for that one, but keep my hold on both. Thus is established a two-centred system whose subject-pole and object-pole are frequently reversed; and the two-way traffic of this system, with all its experienced content of 'mind' and 'body', is indivisible. No item or function belongs exclusively to either pole, but rather to the system as a whole. All our existence is transregional circulation.

## 4. The mirror

The other centre to which I thus attach myself may be a mirror. What happens when I look in my glass is that I, who am nothing here, place myself there where I am a man, and project him back upon this centre. Now this is only a specially lucid case of self-observation in general; my glass does for me what my friends do, only with fewer complications, for I contribute only a part of my friend's nature, whereas I am for the time being the whole life and mind of my mirror. What occurs everywhere obscurely occurs plainly here—the mirror is living, active, human, and conceivably also suprahuman, in commerce with the observers ranged about it. Between us, the glass and I achieve a man; but break the mediating radial processes of our regions (which appear abstractly in optical diagrams) and neither of us achieves anything.

## 5. Some levels of projection-reflection

If you and I are a pair of mutual observers, our hierarchical status varies with our mutual range, which in turn depends upon the vigour of our projective activities. If these are short-range, we do not amount to much; if long-range, we are more comprehensive.

Let me give some examples. (a) Where there is no projection, no second centre linked to this one, there is nothing, not even an electron. For modern physics, a particle is something only in so far as it has regional effects, or (in my terms) in so far as it projectively contributes to what its fellows are. (b) Amongst cells, this projective activity is visibly bodied forth: the dividing

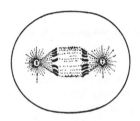

*A dividing animal cell*
(diagrammatic)

cell is organized about two centres (centrosomes) whose commerce appears as the nuclear spindle. And when this commerce ceases and division is complete, the two cells revert to a relatively unorganized condition—thus they are most themselves (with chromosomes fully formed) when they are most busy with each other. (c) As projective-reflective particles comprise projective-reflective cells, so these in turn comprise projective-reflective multicellular organisms. In sexual reproduction, the offspring is a relatively long-range and long-term joint projection of the parents; and when they rear their offspring their original projective activity is prolonged and complicated, with proportionate results. The higher the newborn creature the less self-contained it is. (d) The highest multicellular animals comprise a society of self-conscious persons who not only make one another by projection-reflection, but involve as they do so the surrounding world, animating it with life and meaning. (e) And finally such a society may come to see its internal projective-reflective activities as mere ingredients of a similar universal activity. There arises the notion of One who does not find himself in himself, but in his Other, in his projected Image; and all that exists owes its being to this, the supreme and all-embracing instance of projection-reflection, of the imagination which creates.

These examples will do to indicate that the scope and quality of what is projected tend to improve with range; and that the lower grades of projection play their part below and within the higher grades, as their substratum.

## 6. *Projection-reflection and the law of equality*

At every level we project our equals. Yet man advances by painfully finding how *unlike* other things he is, how superior to animals and trees and stones on the one hand, and how inferior to his gods on the other; indeed the surest measure of the man is the measure of the hierarchy that he finds towering above him and opening at his feet. Is the law of equality, then, a dead letter for him?

No: the law holds good. For man to survey this double and widening gap, this discrepancy between his own and his object's level, is for him to span the gap. If he had no access to the base and the apex of the hierarchy, he could never see himself as in the middle. He cannot know his very **real** inferiority without knowing what he is inferior to, and without being in some sense raised to its level. And this, subject to varying qualifications, has been the teaching of all the higher religions. We cannot know our place by staying there. The real limitation is ignorance of limitation.

We are like what we like. Knowledge of a hierarchical level is only to be had at that level, by one who joins in the projective-reflective activities which constitute it; for such knowledge is nothing else than a true part of these activities. I shall try to show in what sense this is so at the infrahuman levels explored by science, no less than at the suprahuman levels explored by religion.

Surely it would be plain to an impartial observer that the scientist is far too big, too heavy-handed, for his job: he is altogether too human. He needs to be a Proteus, infinitely mutable and elastic, capable of insinuating himself into the living tissue, into the giant protein molecule, into the electron rings of the atom, without causing the slightest disturbance. An efficient detective merges with his surroundings and never spoils the evidence; and in so far as the scientist falls short of this ideal he investigates the products of his own ineptitude rather than the data. But what, in that case, is the explanation of his wonderful success? It can only be this: he *is* just such a Proteus, such a super-detective. Automatically he is the equal of what he observes. He takes a particle's view of a particle, a cell's view of a cell; for he places himself at the spot where the object arrives at the status he accords it, and where he is necessarily reduced to the same rank. Atoms are cases of extreme myopia, infecting all their observers with the same condition. No *man* may enter the object's atom region: the radial extension, the feeler which the physicist puts out towards the object, cannot keep human status, but must conform to each of the object's regions as it traverses them.

For concrete evidence there is the scientist's apparatus—that ingenious set of telescopic ladders by which he descends deep into the infrahuman realm, while he is himself remodelled at every rung. And indeed you have only to listen to him to be sure where he is. If he is a microscopist looking at an animalcule, he has obviously been admitted to its world, for he talks of a few millimetres as a vast distance, to cover which in ten minutes is to race along. All his standards are nonhuman.

At the same time, of course, he is still a man. In fact he is distributed throughout several of the object's regions, and is himself correspondingly multiform. As human at the end where he is, say, twelve inches from the object, he describes it in terms which must be anthropomorphic, thereby raising it to his own rank; nevertheless his very human account is a description of the infrahuman life he is living at the other end, thanks to the

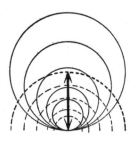

instrument which extends him to within a fraction of an inch of the object. Thus each party is assimilated to the other's rank without loss of his own, and the law of equality allows scope for any amount of inequality. And this ambiguity is typical of our investigation of all nonhuman levels.

To summarize, then, our projective-reflective activities give rise to: (a) the primitive estimate of the object as man's equal; (b) the religious estimate of the object as his superior; (c) the scientific estimate of the object as his inferior; (d) the philosophical estimate of the object as his equal and superior and inferior—with himself sending feelers towards the crown and the foot of the hierarchy, and so entering on equal terms into the life of each level.

# PART TWO

## CHAPTER IV

# The Close View

*1. The unknown body*

Part I was a rough survey of my regional constitution, which Part II will map more thoroughly.

My observer begins in the region where I am a man. He has that rare vision—a human body seen as if for the first time, by one who did not know whether to expect this flesh and blood, or machinery, or gas, or a flame; who has no idea why these limbs should not be caterpillar tracks, or why this head should not be a constellation or a dial or inflorescence. I am not often in danger of seeing myself; but occasionally, by courtesy of my travelling observer, I have glimpsed this thing called man. It is a breath-taking and memorable sight.

*2. The unknown interior*

But the science-inspired observer is not content to keep a surprised and respectful distance: he goes into matters. And he finds this smooth exterior to be a tissue-thin screen for a fabulous menagerie of live things, fed at short intervals through a hole near the top of their cage—beings which, though blind and brainless, have a wonderful way of helping one another, and of responding with exquisite accuracy and speed to their keeper-trainer's unspoken commands. And almost as curious is the fact that my observer can read to me a whole medical library, or lead me round endless museums of bottled viscera and laboratories full of amputated but still living organs, without persuading me to take seriously for a moment this wild life just under my waistcoat. In theory I accept it; in practice I find it incredible. The escapement of the watch in my pocket is immeasurably more real to me than the monstrous interior world of which it is

45

the merest appendage. The truth is that to be anything but homogeneous from head to toe and from front to back, like a stone statue, is neither flattering nor nice; and so I hide from myself this walking chamber of horrors which I am, this intimate realm which is more outlandish than the scenery of the moon or the deepest ocean bed. We are the skeletons in our own cupboards, busy hushing ourselves up in a vast game of make-believe—the game of pretending to be only human, the skin game. And part of the game is that, having put our dinners into a slit in our faces, they are gone and forgotten. More, we actually *expect* this unmentionable vacuity to stay the same temperature winter and summer, to interpret and execute faultlessly our vaguest wishes as to how it shall move, to keep the same structure and chemical composition whatever we pour into it, to carry out its own repairs and readjustments however it is used or misused.

But this is only to be expected, after all. We do not care to lose human status; therefore we keep to that region where, as men, we are skin-deep and emptied of all infrahuman contents. In so far as I live at the human level I really am eviscerated. All my organs are absorbed into the central void, which becomes accommodation for my human visitors. That is to say, whole men and organs are incompatible, for levels may not be mixed. The cynical host, reflecting upon the faeces which even his most refined guests have brought into his drawing-room, is in fact no longer in human company.

### 3. The community of organs

But at their own level my parts are real enough, and are moreover arranged in a hierarchy which is a rough model of the hierarchy as a whole. Science supports more or less the traditional view that in the human body order of height is order of importance: in particular, higher nervous centres tend to be higher in both senses of the word. Again, if in our social intercourse we are not complete men to each other, then we are busts, or if not busts, then heads.

For my cobbler I become a pair of feet, for my barber a head of hair, for the hospital staff the liver in bed 9 or the heart in bed 5, and for other observers a mouth to feed, or all eyes, or a new face. And I, from my side, confirm these descriptions. As man, I am one indivisible living thing; as lower than man, many living things—beings which may, if suitably housed and fed in a laboratory, long survive the whole. And even now I often shrink till I live the life of a single organ or set of organs—an aching tooth, a cold hand, a greedy belly—no copy of their life, but the real thing. Indeed my biography could be written in terms of the struggle between the parts of the body, for their perfect subordination to the interests of the whole is, even in health, an unrealized ideal. A small thing unmans me. My one human existence is precariously poised upon my multitudinous infrahuman existence, and is destined to collapse into it—like the puppet whose limbs alarmingly detach themselves one by one, and dance off the stage.

## 4. Cells

It is no recipe for a quiet life to be this congruent society of part-men—luxurious viscera, strenuous muscles and skeleton, impressionable nervous system—and each striving for the mastery. Yet even at their most unruly such specialists do not rank as true individuals, but as fragments. Not so the cells of which they are composed. These—there are billions of them—are distinct, self-contained animals, of many different types and ways of life. Most are sedentary, but some make their way freely about the body; and each, whatever its way of picking up a living, is born separately and dies separately, feeds for itself upon its environment, and excretes into it. And certainly there is, in the community of cells, no lack of what, at other levels, are called warfare and ruthlessness and struggle for existence.

Taking up my observer's viewpoint, I call these billions of animals *they*; here, I must say *we*. When I declare that I am writing about my cells, I mean that these creatures, by means of an unspeakably vast communal effort, are attempting this essay in autobiography: in these words they are now recording the activity by which they make that record. I may be described as an organization which a great animal population has formed to promote certain common ends and arrive at self-knowledge. But again, I do not believe in my cells. I am a king who is so wrapped up in foreign policy that he is permanently forgetful of the existence of his subjects, without whom there is neither foreign policy, nor State, nor monarch. If I hear of them and of my kingship, it is almost by accident; and the news is unlikely to rouse me from my trance of self-unconsciousness. Here is a miraculous city-on-legs rushing about the face of the earth in search of some diversion, and for ever overlooking itself.

## 5. Man into cell: cell into man

How does my intention to write this sentence issue in the concerted action of the myriads of animals now engaged upon that task? How do I get at them, or rather become them? Again (if Chapter II was right in suggesting that my sense experience is cellular before it is human) how does what they make of one another issue in what I make of my companions? How do they get at me, or rather become me?

Certainly such questions, were any cell of mine intelligent enough to put them, would be condemned by his positivist fellows as meaningless theological speculation, and the existence of any supracellular being dismissed as superstition; for a cell, however well-travelled and observant, never comes across anything superior to itself. Besides, the speculating cell would be quite unable to explain how, in stepping down one rung of the hierarchical ladder, I divide into twenty millions of millions of animals, and how, in stepping up again, they all coalesce in a single human climber. He could only plead, lamely enough, that these hierarchical or regional metamorphoses have to be accepted with natural piety. In the language of the observer who is moving radially through my regions in search of explanations, what I am as man persistently refers inwards to what I am as cells, and what I am as cells persistently refers outwards to what I am as man. This elsewhereness, this two-way radial traffic in which my observer himself is caught up, is of my essence. Though I think horizontally, I live vertically.

## 6. The cell-mesh

Each of my cells is, in effect, an observer who, by placing himself at close range, discovers me to be cellular. In the ordinary sense, it is true, my cells do not for the most part keep their distance, but are in contact. The most important part of the cell, however, is the nucleus, which is separated from the cell-wall by a zone of relatively unorganized material; and this acts as a distance-piece or fender. Thus cellular range is preserved in spite of contact, just as human range is preserved when men shake hands, and sidereal range is preserved though stars' gravitational fields overlap.

## 7. *The empty body*

My approaching observer sees me as several cells, then as one cell, then as a 'cell-organ' (e.g. a chromosome), then perhaps as a giant protein molecule, which in its turn is discovered to be a great community of atoms, elaborately patterned. Finally, the atom is analysed into a system of particles, some of which are collected in the atom's nucleus, while the rest move round them somewhat like planets round a sun. In fact, the atom is no more solid than the solar system: it is practically empty, and there is no sense in describing even its particles—circulating electrons, and nuclear protons and neutrons—as material or solid things.

My approaching observer, then, who believes that the true view is the near view of me, finds at last something like the final vision of my receding observer—something like a sky sprinkled with stars that are on the point of vanishing. And—he may well remark—the culminating marvel is that such a sparsely constellated void should yet contrive this description of itself, as something that will bear neither close nor distant inspection.

## 8. *Inside the atom*

If I really am atoms, it is worth while examining atomic structure a little more carefully. The simplest case is the hydrogen atom, which has for nucleus a solitary proton (a relatively massive, positively charged particle) balanced by a solitary orbital electron (a much less massive, negatively charged particle). The helium atom has two orbital electrons balanced by two nuclear protons, which are linked with two neutrons (uncharged particles whose mass resembles that of protons). The

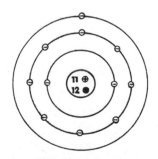

*The sodium atom*
(A schematic indication)

same general pattern is followed in all the heavier atoms: normally, the number of circulating electrons (which goes up to about 92) is matched by an equal number of central protons, and the latter are as a rule accompanied by a somewhat greater number of neutrons. In the higher atoms, the electrons are not bunched together, but are distributed in a number of distinct shells, each of which has limited electron-capacity. The innermost shell contains up to two electrons; the outermost up to eight. And atoms behave as if they preferred complete outer shells: for example, the chlorine atom, whose three shells contain two, eight, and seven electrons respectively, may fill the vacant place in its third shell with the single electron of the sodium atom's outer shell. The result of this convenient electron-sharing arrangement is that the two atoms, each with its outer shell fully completed, together make up a molecule of sodium chloride or common salt.

This summary account provides no more than a rough sketch of the atom. For instance, I have described subatomic particles as if they were ordinary bodies whose whereabouts and physical properties were determinate: in fact, however, they are full of uncertainty. The physicist cannot pin down a particle. All he can do is to state mathematically the likelihood of its being in a certain place in the atom at a certain time. Circulating electrons, then, are best thought of as diffuse rings, or 'clouds of probability'.

And the position of the electron ring depends upon the energy-state of the atom: when a unit of energy is absorbed from outside the atom, an electron springs to a wider orbit; when it is emitted again, an electron springs to a narrower orbit.

*9. The atom and the regional schema: the hydrogen atom*

Such, in outline, is my portrait at close range. But what of the portraitist? Has he suffered a like change?

Suppose he has come so close to me that I am for him no more than (say) a proton, a hydrogen nucleus. What, in that case, if this inquiry so far is on the right lines, may be expected? (i) He has come to a zone which is habitable only by an electron or something of the kind, and only as a perfectly acclimatized native is he let in. (ii) And, once admitted, he may well (as in other regions) move round this zone to get a fuller view of me. (iii) If his estimate is to be approximately constant, his motion will be more or less circular. (iv) Since how I strike him depends on where I strike him from, any notable increase in me is likely to find him at a more respectful distance; or decrease, to find him closer. (v) Experience in other regions (the sudden apprehension of a pattern, for instance) suggests that such re-estimations of me are likely to happen abruptly. (vi) But what I am and what he makes of me are the same thing, for I am nothing in myself: we are a projective-reflective couple, like the positive and negative poles of an electric cell. (vii) We are of equal status in the hierarchy, but not necessarily equal: there is no reason why one of us, for example, should not be more massive than the other. (viii) However that may be, we are both of extremely humble rank: we are unlikely, in that case, to be very efficient observers. We may well be ignorant of each other's exact whereabouts. And if we do not know them, they do not exist; for knowledge of this level is a sharing in its ignorance. The vagueness of our knowing is the vagueness of our being. . . .

I need not keep up the pretence any longer. This conjectural description of the observer who makes me out to be a hydrogen nucleus is a description, in unorthodox language, of the electron that circulates about that nucleus. At his infrahuman end, my observer reaches identity with my attendant electron. And no wonder: only particles find me to be particles: others see more in me.

About the proton in itself at the centre, my scientific observer is silent: only its regional effects are observable, and their unobservable source is scarcely so much as a necessary fiction. And I (who am at the very centre) am in a position to confirm this —what is only here is nothing.

*10. The atom and the regional schema: more complex atoms*

It is the experience of my travelling observer that while, in the long run, increase of range means increase of status, this rule does not hold in the short run. Between one of my regions and the next, the view is apt to prove less and less interesting, or even to fade away altogether. And this tendency, which I call the law of the spindle, is particularly plain at the atomic level.

I have noted that the atom's electron shells have different capacities. Now this capacity, in the more complex atoms, increases with the radius of the shell, and then falls off again. Thus the shells of a uranium atom, starting with the innermost, contain 2, 8, 18, 32, 18, 12, and 2 electrons respectively. And this is to be expected if (a) each successive shell is essentially an observation post from which the nucleus is viewed, and (b) increase of range up to a certain point adds content to the view, which beyond that point declines. Indeed the same law would

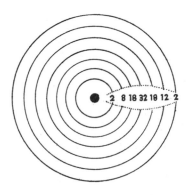

seem to regulate the nucleus itself, setting a natural limit to its compact shells of protons and neutrons. In general terms, it will become increasingly clear in the course of this inquiry that my growth at a given level leads to instability and disruption, before it is continued (and in a sense recommenced) at the next.

The fact is that, to find the regional schema clearly marked out and freed from confusing detail, the observer needs to penetrate to these extreme hierarchical levels: for here my zonal constitution, with its spindle law, its procedure of elsewhereness, its projective-reflective couples, can no longer be ignored. For example, not only does the orbital electron have for opposite number a nuclear proton of equal though unlike charge, but it is typically linked with another orbital electron of opposite spin; and the proton, in turn, exchanges identity with a neutron companion. Again, a gamma ray gives birth to a positive and a negative electron of equal mass—twins which, when they fail to keep distance, vanish. At these levels, in short, the fundamental conditions of all knowing can no longer be separated from what is known. Here metaphysics becomes physics. The physicist very properly sends out feelers towards me to find out 'what I really am'; for he comes to that austere region where we are both stripped, where we are reduced to the merest—and most revealing—outline of what we are at ordinary range, and our essential structure is laid bare at last.

## 11. The physicist in the atom

If this transformation seems incredible, it is because we are over-subtle. We have only to use our ears. Here is someone who calls himself an atomic or a nuclear physicist, and goes on to prove all too conclusively his right to that title. He says *he* is going to bombard nitrogen nuclei, and presently a stream of alpha particles—helium nuclei—hurls itself at them. He says '*I* shall smash the uranium nucleus', and neutrons advance to the attack. These are not instances of loose speaking, but rather of the rigour hidden in our common idiom.

A physicist has written a popular book in which the reader is invited to explore the atom with him—by becoming one of its electrons. And how else, indeed, can we worm our way into this little world? If the physicist is not clearly aware of what and where he is, that is only because he has made himself so very much at home in atomic circles, and learned to speak their language so fluently—the language of mathematics, and in particular of quantum mechanics. He is too domesticated to notice that he is domesticated at all. But I say: there exists, besides particles having certain mass and charge and velocity, *awareness* of particles having certain mass and charge and velocity; and I see no reason for divorcing the facts from the awareness, by relegating it to a region where, by definition, particles are out of place. Where he counts two, I count one; and it is for him to show me the need for duplication.

The electron, then, does not blindly run. But it would be silly to say that the physics which lends it eyes belongs exclusively to the electron's level. For physics itself, like its data, declines simple location: it works at the base of the hierarchy, from the middle levels. Apparatus like the cyclotron and the Van de Graaff generator, and the mathematical procedure that goes with them, are the step-ladder by which the physicist goes down to the basement floor of the universe, and all its rungs are necessary. In fact, the further we venture from the human plane, the more we come to see that no plane is anything by itself or apart from the vertical supports of the whole structure. To arrive at the nucleus, the physicist must advance radially through all its regions, conforming to the laws of each in turn; but it is his

journey as a whole which counts, which determines the outcome of his adventure. Though the arrow's shaft must always
fall short of the bull's-eye, the arrowhead gets nowhere without
it.

### 12. *The horizontal and the vertical*

A flat portrait of myself, one which ignores the many-levelled
living whole, is in fact no more than the diagram of an autopsy.
The tree of knowledge—of knowledge about my nature—
springs from the seed of nothingness at the centre, and thrusts
its branches into the furthermost regions; but branches, trunk,
and seed are one. The innumerable observers who compose it
are ultimately one observer. Or (to change the figure again) my
regions are none of them self-supporting: their very existence
depends on exports and imports. Each is the well-guarded
province of some department of science, nevertheless two-way
radial traffic unites all these zones into one indivisible realm—
the realm of that unitary or vertical science of which this book
is a prospectus: of that hierarchical science which may one day
recognize and do justice to the hierarchical scientist.

In any case we are forced to comply with the hierarchical rule
that no one shall travel far on one level. Horizontal development leads to vertical development: the two kinds alternate.
Thus my growth has two phases: (a) the horizontal, as my observer (or observer-self) attends at once to this centre and
another, so linking them; (b) the vertical, as he includes them
both in a more distant perspective. The pattern of (a) is a
lengthening system of contiguous circles; of (b), a widening
system of concentric circles.

Let me give some instances. The *atom* is built up (a) as the
electrons of the existing shells entertain new electrons, and (b)
as new shells are formed. The *molecule* is built up (a) as the
electrons of one atom attach themselves also to other atoms, and
recognize more than one nucleus; and (b) as the radius of the
molecule as a whole increases. The *cell's* development (a) requires that its materials—the chromosomes in particular—
recognize two centres; but once this duality has led to division,
then each daughter cell (b) grows up to a certain limit as a
roughly concentric system of increasing radius. In the *multicellular animal*, (a) the mere aggregation of relatively undifferentiated cells is followed by (b) 'concentric' development, as

54

cells are specialized and integrated with regard to the needs of the whole; but this in turn reaches a limit, beyond which further development means (a) the establishment of new centres in the offspring. Similarly *society* is (a) a growing population of private citizens, (b) co-ordinated for common ends. The citizen owes (a) plural allegiance to other citizens and small groups, and (b) single allegiance to the whole community as a concentric system. For his impartial travelling observer, he belongs to and so links two families (his own and his wife's) in much the same way that, on closer inspection, he belongs to and so links two cell nuclei and two atom nuclei. It is no mere coincidence that the accompanying diagram does almost equally well for me at

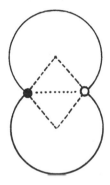

all three stages—whether I am taken to be a man that is a member of two families, or a chromosome that is a member of what will soon be two cells, or an electron that is a member of two hydrogen atoms in a hydrogen molecule.

My receding observer, then, as he comes to each new region, pauses to look around, and note a plurality of centres. For I cannot develop from one stage to the next while preserving my concentric pattern, or by the vertical method alone. In other words, at no level can I use my equals as my staircase to the next level, unless I am so used by them. Before they can fall into place in my concentric design, they must be recognized as independent centres, separate and inviolable, and no more apt than beads on a thread to merge with each other and with me. Aggregation precedes individuation; two-directional observation precedes one-directional.

Conversely, horizontal development cannot go far without

the vertical, and has often to await it. The lower is completed only in the higher. Thus the inner electron shells are not in all cases filled to capacity until the outer ones are partly filled. Thus the transuranic elements (plutonium, for instance) had to wait for man. Thus the molecule rises to greatest complexity only in the cell. Thus the cell in an animal's body is capable of many things denied to the solitary cell. Thus man-in-society is often, as an individual organism, much more successful biologically than he could ever be on his own.

CHAPTER V

# The Close View, continued

## 1. To the centre

The observer has come to where I am a proton, or something of that sort, but he has yet to make contact. What is the scenery between the station where I am viewed as one of these particles, and the terminus where there is no view—supposing that my observer is willing to jettison enough to make the journey? Perhaps science will one day resolve the proton and the electron into still more primitive particles. Yet even they would not be my true 'physical basis', but only its regional

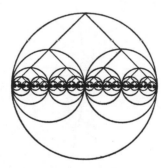

appearance. The question that naturally occurs to my observer is: appearance of what? How many boxes are there in this nest of boxes which I am, and what does the smallest contain—if there is a smallest?

The ultimate substratum would only call for further analysis if it were not uniform, a featureless unity; and if it is such a unity, changeless and inscrutable, then surely it is nothing. And this is indeed what I find myself to be, here at the central fountain of all my regional manifestations. Here the many are one, and the one is nothing, and the nothing is all. At this spot the only view is outwards: no-space, seen the other way round, is all-space. Whether I advertise it or not, this organization which I am has a vacancy for a universe.

### 2. The centre and causation

Here at the centre I act and am acted upon. Here I keep house—the rest is only portico, haunted by the innumerable but ineffectual ghosts of me. They are the hierarchical appearances of that nucleus which, though changeless, is yet the initiator and receptacle of change; which, though one, is yet the mother of endless multiplicity; which, though nothing, is yet the seed and container of all things.

Consequently nothing can touch me; or rather, *only* nothing can touch me. For to act upon me you must advance through my regions, conforming to each in turn, until you arrive here and share my central nonentity. As the area of contact of two spheres is infinitely small, no matter how large they may be, so the place where we are one is the place where we are nothing.

Each has digested the other. Here we sink our differences—or rather *we* sink, and leave our differences floating. All action is stooping to conquer, where stooping is absolute abasement. And this joint nonentity is the source of my reaction to you: every disturbance which I can be said to make in my regions begins here.

Small wonder, then, that this all-creating and all-destroying Centre (which hereafter has a capital C to distinguish it from centres in general) should be a favourite topic of numberless philosophical and psychological and mystical treatises, and the main preoccupation of much devout experience. Here I carry this *caput mortuum*, this undying death's head, this empty head which is the fountain-head of all heads, this infinitely old head on young shoulders, this head so high and so primitive that it has never fallen from paradise. Fixed at the mid-point of an endlessly elastic dome, I am the still and invisible Eye which takes in all the dome's restless and many-coloured linings from the firmament down to my eyelid. I am this infinitesimal spot on the cosmic map, with nevertheless the map in my hand; for ever caught in this traffic bottleneck, which nevertheless finds room for the bottle. My world-wide wheels can neither exist nor turn without this unmoving hub; my world-wide body has no organ half so vital as this subvital and indeed subphysical heart of hearts. Here are key and keyhole and door in one—the central emptiness which is the key of the Kingdom, the keyhole which leads to Wonderland, the needle's eye which is the gate of Heaven. Through this Point of entry I am in all the world and all the world is in me. And if, having entered, I am capable of many things, it is because capability means room; if I am a thinking reed it is because, reed-like, I am coreless. *Cogito ergo* NON *sum*. And common sense, for ever trying to salvage some miserable chattel for me, only breaks the conditions of that universal policy of insurance whereby unlimited compensation is given to those who lose all.

## 3. Action at a distance

No body can act upon another at a distance (that is, regionally) precisely because of that distance; or at the point of contact (that is, Centrally) because both are there annihilated. Only the radial process as a whole, as an unbroken lever-arm whose moment is nothing at the fulcrum and increases in each successive region, can move me. That is to say, action upon me is always *from* one of my regions, *through* the intervening regions, *to* the Centre—these three in one—and my action is the same, but reversed. Thus when I stretch out an arm to greet my friend, this end of it is in his human region and human; the other end, where I touch him, is Central to him and nothing; while the part between conforms to each intermediate region. In real, regionally organized space (in contrast to the abstract and uniform space of science) my arm reaches down from the middle of the hierarchy to the very base, and is itself transformed accordingly. And the many-regioned whole must act as one before it can be said that I—the man here—touch my friend there.

### 4. A model of the two-way vertical process

How is it that our distance is the making of us, and our nearness our undoing? How comes it that the near view of a colourless, scentless, silent, and altogether poverty-stricken collocation of particles turns out to be a man and a man's world, with its unspeakable wealth of experience? How does a universe without a whisper, without the palest tint, without a twinge of feeling, become this rich and terrifying place? How does the physicist's desire to study atoms emerge from them? Latimer was cells, and cells are primitive animals indifferent to moral considerations, yet Latimer's hand did not withdraw from the flame. Why? From what in electrons and protons does this rather contemptuous reference to them spring?

My departing observer can do little more than note admiringly the developing scenery of each zone in its turn, from the featureless desert at one end of the journey to the infinitely colourful and varied human climate at the other. Nevertheless it is only their common pattern which enables him to distinguish my regions at all. For example, at each stage of the journey he is apt to find in his field of view a unit of a given order, then several such, all of them shrinking and drawing together and losing their differentiating features, till they are lost to view altogether, and a unit of a higher order supervenes. And on the return journey this procedure is reversed: the swelling higher unit produces and gives place to several lower units which repel one another as they grow, till only one is left in the field. My observer may then conclude that the reason I became so much more interesting in my outer regions, the secret of my improvement, was that I made myself small, and was not self-sufficient, and embraced my fellows; and, conversely, the reason for my decline as he approached me was my thrusting, aggressive, repellent behaviour, my habit of crowding out all but myself.

### 5. Hierarchy, sociability, and emergence

In other words, his theory is that sociability and hierarchical ascent are two names for one thing, as also are unsociability and hierarchical descent. He calls an atom a society of particles, a molecule a society of atoms, a cell a society of molecules, a man a society of cells; and adds that to lose caste in this social hierarchy it is only necessary to push one's companions out of the way, while to gain caste it is only necessary to bring them back. There is advance from this hierarchical level to the next when the units at this level, becoming specialized in structure and function, find one another indispensable, so that there is founded a society whose qualities are not to be seen in its members seriatim. But nothing is explained by saying that these novel and unpredictable emergents—such as colour, life, intelligence, values—are the product of social relationships: this is only a way

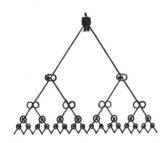

—only one way—of recording what is observed. And indeed it is not so much my higher as my lower levels, with their increasing privation of qualities, that call for explanation. The human world, lively, poignant, rich in every sort of contrast, lies wide open to me: it is real beyond doubt. Not so the world of atoms and electrons—featureless and difficult country, invaded only by the specially equipped. My continual descent into this nether world is at least as remarkable as my continual arising from it, and at least as necessary. The electrons which are my manhood lying in ruins, and the man who is their fruition and apotheosis, are inseparable parts of the many-levelled whole of me. In my observer's terms, I live by the death-dealing failure of my components to reconcile their differences, no less than by their life-promoting successes in social organization.

## 6. The two-sided members of the societies

To be social is to be social-minded. But is it likely that the humbler members of the hierarchy are minds as well as bodies, two-sided, or anything for themselves?

I am this vast hierarchy, which could not survive for a moment if its members at every level were not able to react appropriately to the subtlest changes in their environments. How are these changes registered? How does a molecule in me respect in its behaviour the position and mass of all its fellows, without ever being at a loss for information about the least or the remotest of them?

Now I know for certain how these things are done at one hierarchical level, namely the human: I have no difficulty in detecting the behaviour of my fellow men, for it is behaviour in me, the very stuff of me. Moreover I know of no other way than this way of mutual immanence, whereby interaction is possible. Until I am shown another way, then, I can only (arguing from the more known to the less known) invoke the principle of continuity, and suppose that my constitution at lower levels resembles that at higher levels, and that I am at all stages two-sided—a view out as well as a view in, a system of regional aspects of my fellows. Each of my subordinates is in itself what it is for itself, and for itself what others are for it—their present activity. All other 'explanations', such as the doctrine that disembodied spirits called Laws of Nature play each particle of me like a piece in a cosmic chess-game, seem to me to call in supernatural aid prematurely.

Of course it is true that the lower the level the poorer the view, both in and out, must be; and to apply the language of the higher orders (with its talk of social relationships) to these very humble perspectives, is apt to mislead. In my atomic capacity I am almost without capacity: my narrow-mindedness and myopia are such that I am almost mindless (in most respects) and almost nothing, either for myself or for my fellow atoms. The all-but-vacant world I inhabit is the projection and measure of my own idiocy.

Nor is this baseless speculation. I am atoms. Having inside information, I am qualified to speak for them; for they are a lower power of my being. And indeed, if I were unable genuinely to go down to their level of myself, I could never write this description of them and their world, with its lack of scenery. Knowledge about a level is only to be had by going there. And as we go down to these depths we find at every step regional observation of a Centre which is nothing in itself, by a Centre which is nothing in itself. The hard core of matter or energy, the nuclear thing which is only view in (if that) and utterly mindless, which is self-existent apart from all observation—*that* is the wild hypothesis, the myth, the fantasy. How and at what point in the evolution of matter is mind miraculously spirited from no-mind? Certainly it is—even in myth-making—too much to begin by admitting that science cannot know what particles are in themselves, then to deny that they can be mind-like, and finally to gasp at the spectacle of mind arising from them.

## 7. *The hierarchical pyramid*

I am, then, a pyramid whose cement is sociality—a multi-storeyed structure floating upon a sea of nothingness, but growing more and more substantial and ornate towards the apex. And the whole is maintained by continual building operations which make good, from the base upwards, the wear and tear that are always destroying the structure from the apex downwards.

I have already distinguished the storeys of this pyramid. Between them are many intermediate structures—units which lack integral status, which are imperfectly individuated. Such meso-forms include the organs and tissues that lie between the whole man and the cell, and the analogous structures within the cell. It is true that the two orders—integral and non-integral—cannot be sharply divided, for the criteria of individuality (such as indivisibility, independence, definition, freedom from accident) are not in practice capable of measurement. Nevertheless I think the facts support my provisional choice of true hierarchical individuals—namely subatomic particles, atoms, molecules, cells, and multicellular organisms—as distinct from mesoforms. But I must add the reminder that hierarchical status and degree of individuality are two very different matters: the first specifies the storey a feature belongs to, while the second specifies the level within the storey. And this double specification is necessary because each pyramidal stage tends, by beginning once more the task of unification, to reflect the architecture of the whole. The law of the spindle governs the entire design.

## 8. *The observer at the apex of the pyramid*

Also it must be remembered that this structure is not solid, but a castle in the air. I am the base, my observer is the apex, and between us is the pyramid of regional space. It is as if I were a ruin—or rather, the mere outline—of some boundless ancient monument, visible only from the air. The higher the archaeologist flies the more of me he takes in, and the more he .nakes of me, and the more interesting my plan becomes. But for him there is no emergence, no towering structure with himself the

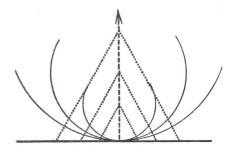

pinnacle: there is only observation. All he does is to put himself in a position to see what really exists at the base.

And in fact all experience whatever is just such an aerial survey of the substratum or base or Centre; and what we take it to be is very much a question of how high our ceiling is. No one has ever seen or heard or tasted, loved or feared or hated, anything but the Centre; yet the Centre is unknown till it is known from every elevation.

## 9. *The laws of hierarchical limitation*

Some further qualifications are needed. First, as to my *number*. My apical observer can take in only one of me at a time, or a few at most; hence he has little reason for looking upon me as 'really' an immense population of cells or molecules or atoms. To say that a man must in fact *contain* all these subordinates is to misuse that word, for the container and its alleged contents are incompatibles which belong to quite different occasions. Levels will not mix; and nobody need be put off by tales of fabulous numbers which (though they have their use) are merely theoretical extrapolations. Even the mathematician cannot deal with big numbers: he reduces the largest of them to a single pattern that can be taken in at a glance. The universe is not so teeming, neither am I so multitudinous, as common sense assumes. Our world is simple once we trust the data; its Centres of experience are not lost in a crowd. At each level there is one of me, for the individual is all-important and cannot take cover in plurality. There is no safety in numbers.

Similarly as to my *size*. The only measure, the only yardstick which covers all levels of observation, is my observer's constant field. A unit is as big as it appears in this field. And when it vanishes because of the observer's approach, it does not go on swelling in some occult manner beyond the field of view: there is no carrying over from level to level. My observer adjusts all his standards at each new frontier; accordingly no region is for him unduly crowded or out-of-scale, and no regional manifestation of me excessively large or small. In short, we are equals. The hierarchical surveyor, because his tape-measure stretches and shrinks along with the object, finds the hierarchy to be a masterpiece of moderation: its supposed excesses turn out to be little better than convenient superstitions.

Indeed it is time I believed the evidence of my senses, which tell me that the truth of one level is the lie of the next. Let me open my human eyes to see that Earth is flat after all and the Australians the same way up as I am; my terrestrial eyes to see that I am not a weevil in a cosmic boomerang, but rooted in this stable world about which the sun really does swing; my solar eyes to see that this star is daily the death of the stars, and that they can have no planets. Thus to distinguish hierarchical planes, to ask at what level (and not so much whether) a proposition is valid, is to reconcile a million conflicting views.

*10. Hierarchical limitation and organization*

To the objection that the observer's findings are not only visual, that they include other types of sensory and non-sensory experience to which the foregoing remarks may not apply, I answer that my experience (so far as I can discover) is always presented as a living whole in one field of limited spatio-temporal capacity. To distinguish different faculties and fields is artificial and posthumous work; but even so I find that much the same limitations apply to what I 'imagine' or 'conceive' as to what I 'perceive', to what I hear and touch as to what I see.

I have a special reason for respecting these limitations. I am

E 65

hierarchically organized, and the real work of every organization I have known is done by the official who deals with one immediate superior and a few immediate subordinates, instead of with all impartially. Organization abhors large numbers, and the vast and the minute. Its secret is that to each functionary, high or low, his work shall be *the* work, that on which all hangs.

If the private felt his task mean, and the general felt his responsibilities beyond him, the army would disband: unless all ranks are somehow equal there are no ranks. Subdivision does not diminish, neither does aggregation enlarge: and in this lies their use. There is a sense in which the hierarchy is not a pyramid but a cube, and the numerators and denominators of its fractions cancel out.

# CHAPTER VI

# The Middle View

## 1. The Proteus

Returning to the region where I am seen to be human, my observer makes it his first business to define the object of his study. But at once he finds formidable difficulties, for it dawns upon him that I am elastic and variable: there is no telling what monster—winged, many-footed, swifter than sound, fiendishly lethal, gifted with every sort of new ability—I shall not presently turn into.

## 2. The question of my boundaries

Common sense objects that none of the thousand things I use —my clothes, tools, house, car—can be reckoned true parts or extensions of my body, seeing that I am neither sensitive nor active in them. To which I reply: On the contrary, I am often more hurt by their injury than by an injury of the flesh at their core; through them also I am much more alive to changes in my environment than ever this unaided flesh could be; and certainly I move these outer organs, acting in them more deliberately, more precisely, more effectively, than in much of my original equipment. This vast yet fine-grained world I live in is no function of a mammal that has taken to strutting on its hind legs, but of an altogether new order of creature—a supersensitive giant, a Titan with a feather-touch. In every way the kind of life I live can only be lived by one whose body is not chiefly protoplasm, but wood, steel, brick, glass, cotton. . . .

To the objection that these things are dead, I reply that every dead thing is a disorganization of a living thing and every living thing is an organization of dead things, which are nevertheless alive as a whole. Presently I shall drink some tea and put on my overcoat, and both will live in me.

67

To the objection that they are discontinuous, detachable, impermanent, I reply that it is precisely this loose-jointedness of my outer limbs, the ease with which they are amputated and regenerated, which accounts for my more-than-animal vitality, my unmatched organic efficiency. In many ways a notable improvement upon the organ of flesh and blood, they are more a part of me for being less so. In any case, as grafting and blood-transfusion and indeed nutrition show, the core itself is anything but a fixture and inviolable. To live is to be the resurrection and the life of others. If my wrist is in any sense more mine than my wrist-watch, that is chiefly because I am always replacing it with dead material, whereas my watch needs no more than an occasional replacement of parts.

There is, then, no reason for my observer to doubt his eyes, which show him a creature able to change its species to suit the occasion—on land, on and in the sea, and in the air. And, after all, this way of looking at me is the natural one. The tools make the workman because without them he is maimed, and the clothes make the man because without them he is flayed: it is not done to see him as a live body in dead fabrics, to undress him with your eyes. And when you meet him at sea you say 'There goes a ship', not 'There go some men in a ship'. Indeed only the blind and deaf could suppose that *man* is the dominant creature in any of the elements. We know, yet contrive not to know, that they have been invaded by a new and terrible kingdom of nonhuman beings—beautiful and dangerous and exceedingly accomplished mesoforms, which might well be mistaken for the conquering armies of some utterly alien planet.

*3. Growth and amputation in my greater body*

To write this sentence I have grown on my right hand a new kind of sixth finger, which I shall amputate when I have done. Also I have six legs like a fly; but, unlike the fly, I shall leave four of them behind when I get up. The insect has rashly committed itself to a single set of limbs, and that is the chief reason why it is only an insect. A man, on the other hand, grows all the legs and wings and fins and pincers and claws and carapaces and furs of the animal world, because he also *un*grows them. The reason he can graft on to himself a bowel five miles long, and look through ten-ton eyes, and pluck the nucleus out of a cell or the heart out of a mountain, is that he has never lost the

habit of reverting, at a moment's notice, to his primitive in-
competence. He alone has grown up, because he has never
grown up.

And his growth is temporal no less than spatial: one of the
chief novelties of the well-developed human body is the manner
in which it incorporates time, so that organs enter into temporal
relationships of unique complexity. Here is a new order of anatomy, a physique that cannot be taken in at a glance, a time-
developed creature of which the many-limbed gods of the East
are a fitting diagram. Thus my soup-spoon hand, though coin-
cident spatially with my dessert-spoon hand, is removed from it
by twenty minutes; and when at night I revert to the quadru-
pedal state, my legs are eight hours as well as eight inches long.

Moreover the vital processes of this greater body are propor-
tionately long-drawn-out. The meal I am about to enjoy has in
fact already begun. It started with reaping-machine jaws forag-
ing in the field, went on to digestive processes in such preliminary stomachs as mills and bakeries and the kitchen, and will
eventually come to a conclusion at the sewage works. This
gigantic herbivore feeds and excretes upon the land like all the
rest, but in a manner all its own. Here is an organism that lies
right outside the animal kingdom, in a kingdom of its own. But
the most advanced organism on earth is one which no department of science studies or rarely suspects. Only the dismembered corpse is parcelled out amongst scores of specialists. There
is no pure science of applied science.

One unfortunate result of this oversight is the argument from
man's animal physique to his mental limitations. But in fact his
mind (or view out) is perfectly matched by his body (or view
in), both of which are organized on novel lines: his physical
superiority to the animal is no less remarkable than his psychical. It takes more than eleven stone to think this thought. Man
—grown-up man—is nine-tenths manufactured article, personality expressed as personalty, the human body prolonged and
brought to a fine edge, keyed up and exaggerated for each
special task, given point and precision.

### 4. The periphery and the core

On casual inspection—or rather, to the eye that has lost its
innocence—men are all much the same, a single sort of biped.
But the fact that they are highly social, and the further fact that

the members of other complex societies (such as the anthill) have bodies to fit their tasks, warn us to look again. And then we find that the human frame varies endlessly, from the crafts- man's little body with its overgrown right arm to the tentacled and world-wide organization of the business magnate. In fact our society is possible only because its members, though more diverse than all the animals put together, revert daily to their primitive undifferentiated state. A man sheds twenty millen- niums with his working clothes. He has not avoided the ancient penalty for increasing expertness and social habits, but only contrived that his recent and detachable outer organs shall pay it. Wiser than the ant and the termite, he has not burnt his bridges, but retreats across them nightly. The doctor may be as neuter as the worker ant, the infantryman as burdened with arms as the soldier ant, the pilot as dependent on his wings as the young queen ant; yet off duty the three men are indis- tinguishable. And to the extent that he fails to fall back upon the past, and remains consistently up-to-date, man is inhuman and deformed.

Common sense, then, has every reason for distinguishing be- tween the 'living' organ and the 'dead', for the peculiar con- tribution of my periphery lies in its contrast with the core. The tool is more a part of me for being less so. By its deadness I live; by its discontinuity I am integrated; by its variability I stay constant; by its hugeness I am spared the fate of the huge; by its capacity for piecemeal replacement I avoid replacement. What does the deadness of the outer organ mean but the choice of countless materials denied to the jelly at the centre; the use of countless inventions which that jelly could never build out of its own resources; freedom from the past for each fresh venture instead of protoplasm's cramping necessity to adapt old organs to new uses; the command of immense forces; sensitiveness nicely adjusted to each occasion, to a vastly increased range of influences, to types of influence no animal is alive to; insensitive- ness where sensitiveness would hamper; and above all the need for new skill, for much more awareness and effort than ever the living organ demanded? And what is such deadness in the part but more abundant life in the whole creature?

That these two so different layers really are—or rather, be- come—a whole organism, I can from my side confirm. Learning the use of an instrument is the practice of its incorporation. I do not grip a handle attached to a blade that cuts some wood: *I* cut wood. I do not get inside a thing which flies: *I* fly. Till I extend to my wing-tips or bumpers or keel, I am a mere beginner. The difference between the novice and the expert is chiefly one of size.

Yet it is not so much this growth as its correlated ungrowth which is the essential human achievement. I should be less and not more alive if it took a surgical operation to remove my house and my overcoat, if my piano were built of cells, if my wings sprouted from my shoulder-blades like an angel's. It is more important that the telephone and the pen should die the moment I put them down, than that they should spring to life the moment I pick them up. But too often necessity is the child of invention. If we do not keep killing our tools they will make us their tools and finally kill us. The appendage I cannot do without is a malignant growth, a shirt steeped in the poison of Nessus.

## 5. *Natural and artificial evolution*

Though the secret of their living unity lies in their disunity and unlikeness, yet the inner and the outer organ, as stages of a single development, have much in common. The new evolutionary venture does not contradict what it extends.

Let me give examples. An organ develops by *adaptation* to its environment; and so, also, does the tool which buds at the end of it. Thus my fins are prolonged into legs, and my legs into wheels and caterpillar-tracks, by progressive adjustments to conditions on land. I develop also by *integration*, as when, ceasing to be one cell, I become many specialized cells; and as when, much later, this multicellular organism expands to include a car which unites such separate specialized devices as the wheel, the spring, the internal combustion engine, and many more. Now the result of such modes of development is *variation* (the emergence of minor novelties) and *mutation* (the emergence of more important novelties) first among protoplasmic organs and then among their outgrowths. In both stages of evolution life advances by alternately crawling and leaping: there comes a moment when the improvement of the old device cannot go much further, and a new departure is needed. And variations and mutations are alike subject to *selection*—first a wasteful sifting of the unfit, giving place at last to more economical and deliberate methods: the mounting scrap-heap is the price of progress, but we have learned to throw the organ away instead of the organism. Man is the deciduous animal: acceptance of peripheral mortality is the secret of his survival. Nevertheless advance is not always assured: there is much *degeneration*. Thus only vestiges remain of my tail and fur, and all that is left of my turned-up cuff is a row of dummy button-holes. Conversely, there is *exuberance*, the tendency for organs to go on developing far beyond what is needed: the human head of hair, and its further elaboration into hats, are instances.

### 6. The natural and the artificial

Artifice, then, is nature becoming deliberate. This process, appearing first in the region of my outer manufactured organs, works inwards to my home and clothes and flesh, and outwards to my vital and cosmic environment, till none of my regions lacks its proper degree of lucidity and intention.

And, to the unprejudiced travelling observer, this spreading artifice does not merely carry on more swiftly and effectively nature's own work: full awareness of nature is nature's own regional flower, without which the Central seed (unconscious by itself, because nothing is there to be conscious of) and the radial stem (whose growth provides the spatio-temporal interval which consciousness requires) are incomprehensible fragments.

In any case, the more I call nature blind, ruthless, wasteful, and set about curing these defects, the more I disprove my point—unless, indeed, I am supernatural, an invading parachutist who has no business to land in the cosmos at all. Yet my effectuality requires that, ten hours out of the twelve, I shall look on myself as just such an intruder. Nature at her best completes the rest of nature by opposing it, by working upon it as upon alien material, till at length it is won over. As the embryo is not even an embryo without the adult, so nature is not nature without the awareness that transforms her into artifice. Those who are so fond of reminding us that she is red in tooth and claw should remember, first, that the stricture is her own, and, second, that some of the claws have grown into hands, and some of the hands have grown into scalpels and all the instruments of healing. But no wonder nature is heartless and brainless, when directly we find in her any design or kindness we call it unnatural, instead of what it really is—doubly natural.

## 7. *The total body—its expansion and contraction*

I look out upon an alien nature, on what is essentially not myself. At the same time this nature is mine, the body without which I could not live for an instant. It is a headless body, a body that is (so to say) all legs, and legs which are 'natural' up to one joint, then 'artificial', then 'natural' again, as I stretch them out into my further regions. Of no point can I say that I stop there, and my world begins. And if, indeed, the boundary of this body is not reached until it embraces a living whole, a self-contained organism, then (as will become clearer in the course of this inquiry) it includes the universe.

But how much of this body I take on, thereby dissolving it into Central accommodation, is a question of how much accommodation my object needs. Strictly speaking, I can never glimpse so much as a hair of *my* body—flesh and artefacts and outer

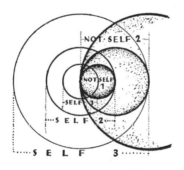

nature are either reduced to room here at the Centre, or are what fills that room. If I have one of my 'limbs' in mind, it is not mine; if in body, it is nothing; either way I am disembodied.

Briefly, then, my 'body' is (a) as much of the universe as I need to match my 'mind', and (b) all of the universe, and (c) none of it—and anything less than these three together is a dangerous part-truth.

What I see with is the measure of what I see. For me, every visible has an equal and opposite invisible. Seeing my hand, I am a head yet headless; seeing my friend, a man yet the obliteration of a man; seeing Mars, Earth yet purged of everything terrestrial; seeing Rigel, the Sun yet alone in sunless night. There is nothing so remote that I cannot make it present, so alien that I cannot make it a limb, so opaque that I cannot make it transparent, so physical that I cannot make it psychical—provided I find the object for which it becomes accommodation. In other words, I am as much of that total body, which includes every Centre, as I care to own to, as I cease to repudiate. It is for me to find that in my world-wide physique there are no involuntary muscles, no paralysed extremities, nothing unmeant, nothing merely natural, nothing that is not view out as well as view in, nothing that is something in itself, nothing that I cannot dissolve by inclusion or recrystallize by exclusion—and throughout these adventures holding fast to the lifeline of my nothingness.

Such are the reflections—developed in later chapters—which follow upon the demolition of the artificial wall that fences self from not-self.

CHAPTER VII

# The Distant View—Humanity

*1. The reticulum*

Resuming his journey, my observer reaches a height of several thousand feet. And he finds that I am presented here as a fine network or creeper whose threads ramify over much of the planet's land surface, in some places profusely and with many nuclei, in others sparsely or hardly at all. He notes its

preference for warmer climates, for rivers, for regions of abundant vegetation; its growth, here slow and there rapid; the glow of its nuclei at night; the threads it pushes through mountains and under the oceans; the roots it drives down for sustenance; excretory systems. . . .

*2. The reticulum's life*

To my protest that this is no vegetable or animal or any other sort of living creature—but mere buildings, roads, railways, canals, and the like, which are the work but not the body of millions of men—he replies that he can see nothing of all these, and that there is no sense in choosing an observation post unless you take what you find there. He says that his exploration of my regions has taught him not to mix their contents. And he invites me to look, without preconceived ideas, at what is given—at something which grows and decays, feeds and excretes, is self-maintaining, more active by day than by night—and then to say whether it is not alive, and is not, in fact, by far the liveliest creature the planet has to show, though it is certainly neither plant nor beast nor man.

When I accuse him firstly of mistaking a name—Mankind or Society or the Nation—for a thing, and secondly of holding sinister and outmoded theories about the State as an organism, and thirdly of undermining individual responsibility and promoting dictatorships, and fourthly of degrading the essentially psychical nexus of society to a mere physical reticulum, and much more in the same vein; he retorts that he is neither a metaphysician nor a politician, but only an observer who does not intend to be talked out of seeing what is plain for all to see. It may be dangerous or wicked or even indecent to look at me from this place, but look he will.

### 3. The body of Humanity

In the previous chapter I described my body as extending, by artificial yet natural means, over the planet's surface. This was an instance of concentric growth. It is also, in fact, many-

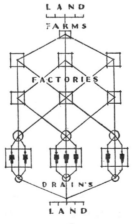

Centred. For example, the members of my household have a single external bowel, a single set of preliminary stomachs, a single system of extended ears and vocal chords: they are Siamese twins or triplets or quadruplets. And the bigger my body the more persons I share it with in this way, so that the whole of it is also everybody else's: each of us owns this one greater body, which is nevertheless organized uniquely, region-wise, about his own Centre. Each, then, in claiming his total organism—including all men, with the world-net of services and devices which knits them into a whole—claims his identity with them in a being of another order—a being which I call Humanity. Now it is this creature, whose body is my extended physique, that the observer notes from the air. Only there does it make its presence felt. Down here, at closer range, it really is the myth which its critics take it to be. They are neither perverse nor unobservant, but only untravelled.

And when we travel we need to look to our language: the mathematical methods and mechanical concepts proper to the inner physical regions, and the biological terms proper to the vital regions, are to be used with caution in the region of Humanity. All our habits of thought conspire to take this unique object and to comminute it in time no less than in space, hiding the fact that only a creature of great age and experience can arrive at human status. Man as mere man is far too little and too young to be human: he is this only so far as he joins an ephemeral and puny mammal to an agelong world-enclosing sphere. To be man is to be Humanity-man.

But my life is not lived in either of these regions so much as in the radial processes—centripetal or katabolic, and centrifugal or anabolic—which join them. I am maintained by a steady two-way flow of material, which conforms to my regional constitution by diminishing in extent and status as it works inwards, and increasing as it works outwards from this Centre. The first is Humanity-becoming-man—that huge organization narrowing down to and serving this nucleus. And the second is man-becoming-Humanity—the contribution of this nucleus to the whole, widening as it advances, as it is reinforced with innumerable other contributions. The law of elsewhereness decrees that the whole is the whole, and the part is the part, because each is for ever becoming the other. And my task, my livelihood, is to enter as fully and as intelligently as I can into this double process—constructive or centrifugal, and destructive or centripetal; giving and taking; work and leisure; effort and rest.

## 4. An intelligence test

Doubtless these two-way radial processes, directed by intelligent beings, result in the reticulum which my observer notes; but it does not follow that this reticulum is intelligent as a whole. Indeed it might be said that if ever a creature looked stupid, this is surely the one. The observer therefore tests it for intelligence. A prize—say a coalfield—is discovered on the further bank of an estuary. If the creature wastes energy trying to get at it directly, and bridge after bridge is washed away, it will get low marks; if

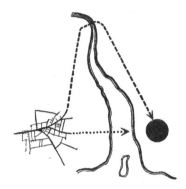

without hesitation it advances up the near bank just so far as is necessary for the safe bridging of the river, and then returns down the further bank to the prize, it will get higher marks. And this, in all probability, is what does happen. Further tests produce similar results. Evidences of foresight, ingenuity, quickness to profit by experience, abound. There are lapses also, such as the overworking of soils, deforestation, overgrazing; but there can be no doubt that they are the lapses of a highly intelligent creature.

This is confirmed by the method of introspection, when I, from my side, report that the knowledge which Humanity has of its environment is remarkable for scope and precision, and such as could only be the product of centuries of study. The weakness lies rather in will than knowledge.

This the observer can well understand. What astonishes him

is this creature's superstition that its intelligence has no body and its body no intelligence, that the ghost of Humanity holds for ever aloof from the reticulated carcass.

### 5. A conflict of interests?

But even if this further point—that Humanity is an intelligent embodied creature—be granted, it may be objected that our loyalty is to particular men, and not to any superior entity whose interests, real or supposed, may conflict with theirs. I reply that it is just such a possibility which demands that we study this creature, to discover in what way it could threaten us. And the result of this study must surely be that a man's dignity and freedom, and his claim to our unqualified respect, lie chiefly in the fact that to be man is to be much more than man: in particular, it is to be Humanity, for the friend I look at is a mere particle of the friend I look with. The safeguard against treating my neighbour as a mere means is the conviction that he is mankind; and the safeguard against treating mankind as *the* end is the conviction that it is present and whole in my neighbour. Torn apart, the unitary pole of Humanity and the multiple pole of men are dangerous abstractions; together, they are human nature.

### 6. The State and Humanity

The real and two-edged threat, alike to Humanity and to man, lies at the intervening levels, and most of all at the level of the would-be sovereign State—the State which as a unique organ of Humanity is invaluable, but as that organ seeking to usurp the whole is the source of many evils. There is a tendency for mesoforms, or units lacking integral status, to capture for a time a position that is not theirs: as when the man is organ-ridden, or machine-ridden, and the State is party-ridden, and Humanity is State-ridden. When I make one god of my belly and another of my nation, I am sick with the same kind of disease in two regions of my body.

### 7. The mind of Humanity-man

Nevertheless even the most chauvinistic and sensual does not cease to attain to Humanity in many notable respects, and with perfect ease. True for him is true for all men; he means that his judgments shall hold good for them; in effect, he sets up as their mouthpiece. Again, he inhabits a 'real' world in which railway lines are parallel, and his hands are smaller than his feet, and men who turn their backs on him still have faces, and the distant house is not a doll's house; and at the same time he inhabits a less 'real' world which contradicts all this. The latter is one man's view, his private world; the former is all men's

view, the public world, the combined report of innumerable human observers whose separate perspectives are mutually corrective. Yet, though he gives preference to the experience of Humanity in him, the man in him is indispensable. He is two vastly different creatures inspecting two vastly different worlds, but he is one and they are one.

The gulf between the human and the animal is in fact the gulf between Humanity and mere man, between all men together and one man by himself. And if this gulf did not lie *within* a human being he would not be human. For he surpasses only that which he is, as the loveliest and brightest flowers surpass their dirty roots only by making the most of them.

## 8. *The one body and its many members*

This essential duality-in-unity is further seen in his behaviour. He may pursue the general advantage to his private loss, even loss of life, but he does so as no more than one man. And when he finds himself in the dock, his other half confronts him on the bench; and on the bench, his other half confronts him in the dock—if it were not so there would be no point in the trial, and the only place for him would be the insane asylum. It is this deep conviction, this hidden assurance of our saving and equalizing identity, which reconciles him to individual inferiority and limitation, which inspires his understanding and sympathy, and sanctions his loving service. The burden which each must bear is bearable, not because he can shift it on to the broader shoulders of Humanity, but because in Humanity he takes upon himself the burdens of all other men as well. Just as he is a higher animal only because he makes his own the pleasures and the pains, the impressions and the deeds, of an immense population of lower animals, disclaiming nothing; so, at the next hierarchical level, he is human only because he is *all* that is human. It may be said with some justification that, just as it takes my twenty million million cellular world-views to build my mammalian world, so it takes my two thousand million mammalian world-views to build my truly human world. My only claim to this hand is that when it is hurt I am hurt, and what it touches I touch, and all its deeds are mine; and my only claim to Humanity is that I am responsible for my neighbour, wherever he lives and whatever he does. For until I am him I am not myself. To know myself I must study him, and to be at peace with myself I must love him: all my hatred is self-hatred.

A solitary organism is little use for thinking or doing, for understanding or willing or loving. We need millions. The wise are not macrocephalic but polycephalic; the generous, not so much swollen-hearted as many-hearted; the effectual, employers of many hands rather than monsters of individual dexterity. Therefore to fear that our mental capacity is limited by the physical capacity of our skulls (in turn limited by the structure of the female pelvis) is like fearing that our minds must be small because our brain-cells are small, and their atoms smaller still. But in fact littleness is no bar to the higher education of the atom or the cell: they take on as many of their fellows as they need, and in the end are man. In the same way the law of equality rules that the brains and hands of Humanity are any man's directly he finds an object that needs them. And most of all he requires his opponents for his completion, and is let down when they become like him. We need most those we understand least. Well may we, though unbelievers, deplore the doubts of believers; though sinners, be shocked when the good fall; though anti-clerical freethinkers, be secretly disturbed at the decline in church-attendance. The wise are the custodians of our sagacity, the virtuous of our merit, the brave of our courage, the beautiful and gracious and captivating of all we own in them; we are no good without our betters. All our stupidity is want of sympathy, all our weakness want of co-operation. Our self-sufficiency is suicidal, for living is loving. In sum, all lack is lack of others. We spend our lives forgetting that there is only one Man.

# CHAPTER VIII

# The Distant View—Life

## 1. The further extension of the body

As man, I am a fragment torn from the body of Humanity, which in turn is no true whole, but dependent in countless ways upon the rest of the living. Humanity is a geophagist: it feeds on the inorganic world, but for the most part indirectly, through the organic world—and particularly through the vegetable kingdom, which alone has the secret of building the cell out of raw molecules. Plants and animals make up the bodily extension which enables Humanity to devour the planet. My real 'mouth', the entrance to my total alimentary canal, is the green leaf which I grow, not indeed on this trunk, but on its remoter branches. At the other end it is the same story in reverse: bacteria at the sewage farm break down my faecal matter into harmless inorganic substances.

Beyond my cell's own organs, first the organ of flesh, then the manufactured organ, then the organ of other species, where at last I meet the world. And the four-layered body they comprise I call Life.

## 2. Life's scattered body

Each new level of my embodiment is unique, a new departure. And certainly Life lacks even the pattern and the continuity of the social reticulum, to say nothing of the compactness of the individual citizen. Nevertheless its unity is not less real than theirs. For at all three levels development takes the same course —an undifferentiated primeval unit realizes its diverse tendencies through specialized members or offshoots, which work out with the greatest possible variety and distinctness every obscure original function. The real difference between (a) man that is a community of dissimilar cells sprung from one unspecialized cell; and (b) Humanity that is a community of dissimilar men sprung from common unspecialized human stock; and (c) Life that is a community of dissimilar species sprung (in all probability) from one primeval unspecialized ancestor—the difference does not lie in the failure of any one of these three to reconcile development with unity, but rather in the tempo of that development and the scale of its unity. And notoriously the slow and the vast are lost on us, to whom only the near view comes naturally.

In fact, however, the elbow-room that creatures enjoy, their mobility, the interpenetration of their habitats, all make not for less organization in Life's body but for more. Life's interspaces are room for the weaving of an unimaginably complex web of mutual dependence, in which all the threads hang together in the total pattern. It is precisely because Life's structure is so little rigid that its parts are so much and so variously involved in the whole. Pluck the bee from the flower and you have neither. No creature or species or genus makes sense, in form or function, without the rest. From the very start, nothing less than Life itself (to speak strictly) has ever lived.

## 3. The disunity in Life

The strife within this body impresses us unduly because we miss its long-term and large-scale consequences; the very similar strife amongst our cells escapes us because we miss everything but such consequences. But in both cases much disunity amongst the parts is an important condition of the unity of the whole. Just as the enemy of the individual animal is often the friend of the species, so the enemy of the species is often the friend of Life—the three hierarchical levels must be distinguished, yet never separated. When we ignore the third, failing to see the organic unity of all creatures, it is as if we knew a man only as a pair of kidneys, a stomach, a heart, and a brain, all of which, though frequently quarrelling, found life together more convenient than life apart.

We must look to the whole. To judge Life's achievement by considering organisms seriatim is like comparing each of a man's specialized cells with the original ovum, in order to discover whether, on balance, he has made any progress.

*4. The biosphere*

Too close a view of Life hides also its shape—a hollow shell which at its thickest is not more than a thousandth part of its 8,000-mile diameter. This inhabited planetary skin, or biosphere, is an elaborate system of biological layers or living strata; and the whole of it, though irregular enough in detail, is for the distant observer as shapely a living thing as he could wish for.

*5. The observer listens to Life*

Moreover it is vocal. If the observer equips himself appropriately (it is only at the level of man that he does not need man-transcending instruments), he can hear this spherical creature describe, with the greatest intelligence and expertness, the geological and atmospheric shells which are its environment, and notably the stratosphere whose point of view the observer is now taking upon himself. (Like his microscope at closer range, the observer's radio, though based upon my human region, conducts him to others: it is a hierarchical step-ladder which he mounts as he hears programmes about other men, other species, other geospheres. Just as previously he inhabited my regions from human to cellular in turn yet at once, so now he inhabits them from human to geospheric. His recession is growth, as he unites all its stages.)

As Humanity is the only biologist (it takes the human race to know a sparrow, species for species) so Life is the only geologist. The baby grows into man by finding himself in other humans; primitive man into Humanity by finding himself in other species (cave art and totemism bear witness); Life into a fully self-conscious geosphere through the study of other geospheres in their relation to Life. At no stage am I anything here in myself; in particular, my stratospheric observer (who, like all such projections, is real enough) is the indispensable instrument and receptacle of my biospheric embodiment.

*6. The mind of Life*

Man's physical dependence upon other species in Life is obvious; but his psychical dependence, though less obvious, can scarcely be doubted. There is much to suggest that his gods (which are his mirror) were first chiefly animal, then chiefly telluric, and only then chiefly celestial: now he forgets the animal rung of that Jacob's ladder. But many writers (and not all of them children's) still lend him some other animal's eyes through which to see himself. Indeed it is to look at man that he goes to the Zoo, for he is the chief exhibit there, the many-sided specimen which must be seen from every cage's viewpoint before it can be truly perceived. He is not man till he is the whole menagerie. In its very different way, modern depth-psychology adds confirmation, by finding in him successive mental strata which unite him eventually with all the living— a phylogenetic heritage, which explains much in human nature that is otherwise incomprehensible. For no man, as man, can claim more than a fraction of his thinking.

All this is to be expected. The merely concentric growth of a man or of Humanity, progress as *this* self alone, very soon becomes impossible. Humanity can rise to the status of Life only by taking on all creatures. This is done in many ways—by the sciences of Life, through which other species are caught up in the procedure of Humanity's growing self-consciousness; by agriculture, breeding, pest-control, and all manner of techniques whereby the ancient chaos gradually gives place to deliberate order and evolution gathers unprecedented speed; by the alleviation of much animal pain; by the protection and further development of types whose claim to survival is not now their ferocity or toughness, but some beautiful or endearing or interesting trait; by the imagination which, to complete itself, must enter into the two-sided life of even the most repulsive creatures; by the sympathy and patience which tame the most intractable; by the love that can afford to make no exceptions. By such means we begin to demonstrate that, just as Life now is physically continuous with the common primeval ancestor, and is in fact that same living body prolonged into innumerable specialized organs of which Humanity is chief; so also Life's variegated experience, as a system of unique views out upon the world, is all of it continuous with the experience of that ancestor. Each creature, species, genus, makes its indispensable contribution to a unitary perspective, whose layers psychologists have done much to expose. And Humanity, in so far as it gathers up these contributions and arrives at this perspective, is no longer Humanity, but Life itself.

Marvelling at the 'wonders of instinct', we ask (for instance) how a spider, with so little brain and no teaching, can build so perfect a web. The answer is already in our heads. The works of that still humbler creature—the brainless brain-cell—are still more marvellous, and their secret is that the cell is *not* brainless: the whole brain is the brain of each of its cells. Similarly the real brains of an organism are those of its species, and of its genus, and ultimately of Life itself. In the end, my brains include the spider's, as the spider's include mine. Nor can I spare any of them. If the fowls of the air and the beasts of the field and the fish of the sea do not draw me to the Kingdom, I shall never arrive, for they are my vital completion there.

The observer whose spatio-temporal field is sufficiently capacious discovers that the leaves of Life's tree owe their evident variety and multiplicity to their hidden unity in the twig, that the distinct twigs are nothing unless they are one in the branch, that no branch lives except by coming to common life in the trunk—but not only there, for the organism is indivisible. The tree of Life is itself because it is also the least of its limbs, to touch which is to touch the whole.

# CHAPTER IX

# The Distant View—Earth

## *1. From biosphere to planet*

It is as Life that we enjoy and study the inanimate geospheres which are our environment, so bringing Life or the biosphere to self-awareness. But clearly this is not the end. Is it not as Earth that we study Mars? Does it not take one heavenly body to know another, so that the vessel's displacement shall be at least planetary? Can anything less than a planet be occupied with and give itself up to a planet? Again, is not Life as dependent upon Earth as Humanity upon Life, so that after all nothing smaller than Earth is a living whole, with Life as her principal organ? And does not my radio-equipped observer corroborate this when, retreating from the stratosphere to, say, Mars, his object is transformed into an undifferentiated planetary disc, into a heavenly body which, complying with tradition, sings; and moreover discusses endlessly its companions and itself?

Here, then, all the lesser threads of my life are wound into a little luminous spinning ball, talkative, musical, intensely curious about the universe and itself, young at thousands of millions of years. Thus my observer finds that while, on the near view, the individual is more a whole and alive than the species, the species than Life, Life than the planet; on the far view all this is reversed. And, though each regional manifestation is true of me, the truth combines them all.

## *2. The geospheres*

The only bodies really capable of vitality are celestial ones: heavenly life is in the last resort the only life. So far from being live men on a dead globe, we are dead men apart from the globe which is our life. And the physique of this spherical body, as befits an individual of new status, is peculiar. It is a system of concentric geospheres—the many-layered atmosphere; the thin crust of rocks, many of them stratified; the thicker basaltic mantle; the heavy core; and of course the biosphere or biosphere-hydrosphere, overlapping and claiming much of the lower atmosphere and of the crust.

### 3. The atmosphere

The vital functions of the outermost geosphere include—besides storage of the gases and distribution of the water Life needs—the trapping of solar energy, the absorption of dangerous kinds and quantities of radiation, protection from meteor showers, and the reflection by its upper layers of radio signals, so that they pass round the planet.

### 4. The biosphere-hydrosphere

Life and water go together. Protoplasm is largely water; and grew up in that element; and in a sense has never left it, seeing that Life has for bloodstream the great circulatory system of of ocean, rising water vapour, drifting clouds, rain, subsoil water, rivers, ocean. And in this cycle the crust, no less than the atmosphere, is involved: in fact its denudation and flow seawards, and its deposition as new strata, are throughout bound up with Life's economy. Nor are the rocks, which organisms have played so large a part in depositing, lost to her now: Life's self-realization is essentially autobiographical in practice as well as theory, so that much of her energy (like the science which is the recollection of her own past) depends upon her older layers. The ancient blindness and futility are now being remedied: or rather, the meaning is coming out. If the embryo's eye cannot be wholly accounted for without reference to the world of light it will one day enter, if the womb is not the only place which foetal limbs imply, then neither is the quarry the only place to study our terrestrial constitution: to the unprejudiced student the Uffizi Gallery offers completer geological specimens.

### 5. The interior layers

The planet has a pulse, upon which the faster and shallower pulses of Life and Humanity altogether depend: namely those periodic adjustments of the interior whereby the worn-down crust is uplifted, the cycle of denudation and deposition restored, and the course of biological evolution set for one more age. And in fact the influence of the heavy core is ever present, as the gravitational pull which regulates all vital behaviour and vital structure. Indeed I cannot so much as make this record of its help without its help. The great slow-beating heart of Earth is the common heart of all her creatures.

*6. The community of geospheres*

Earth's constitution, then, illustrates admirably the rule that life is no mysterious essence pervading one body, but a transaction between bodies. A self-contained biosphere is a self-contradiction, and the planet's vitality can no more be attributed to a single geosphere than a man's can be attributed to his flesh and to his blood corpuscles, as distinct from his bones and his lymph.

The most inert of geospheres shares in the life of the whole. Nor does it lack life at its own level. As the plane is not itself without the crew, so the air is not itself without the plane (that most significant specimen of aerial life); and without the radio-sonde (an exquisitely adapted sense-organ); and without radio-waves (which often disclose that air-mindedness is a fact); and in general without a Life that, to know and map itself, must invade and so invigorate the one lifeless upper air. Every layer of the planet is now steeped in vitality. Even the interior is explored, by such means as artificial earthquakes. To reply that these are intended, and therefore no true geological events, is to prejudge the issue by including purposelessness in our definition of geology. Earth is dead, and we must prove our point by amputating every limb she dares put forth; she is imbecile, therefore we men own all the Mother-wit we find in her. To show there is no Heaven, carve up its residents! But can we call our science scientific till it sees itself as one of the most important functions of the order of things it investigates, transforming them utterly? The fact is that, in winning nature over from the supernatural, science has neglected nothing—nothing except the most revealing of all natural functions, namely itself.

But geospheres are not only—nor even mainly—scientific. Their social intercourse, which indeed has made us what we are, takes many forms: from Life's older consolation and delight in the contrasting lifelessness of sky and sea and desert (a lifelessness renewed by the scientist in us as fast as it is overcome

by the poet), to Life's new air-mindedness, which is the counterpart of her new self-consciousness: Weismann and Glaisher imply each other. Small-scale maps are high atmospheric phenomena. Certainly Life is no hermit, curled up and dreaming in
a planetary cell, but exposed to and in love with her gloriously
complexioned but moody and often cruel companions. Here is a
geosphere fascinated and terrified by its encircling neighbour,
which it has bound to itself by innumerable life-and-death-lines
of projective-reflective activity—on the one hand, radio, air-
travel, air-surveys, air-sowing; and on the other, aerial weapons.
The prince of the power of the air is none the less real or less
deadly because Life is his arms manufacturer.

It is much the same with our other neighbour. Just as one
man must cultivate and invigorate another, so Life must cultivate and invigorate the planetary crust, in a continuous effort
of projection and reflection. But again, the relationship deterior-
ates, and to the threat from above is added the threat from below
—the menace of soil wastage and eventual starvation. Exploited
geospheres, despised for their inertness, demonstrate their vitality by turning on their exploiter.

Men are still at war with men, States with States, Humanity
with other species; but it is on the plane of the geospheres that
the next big engagement will probably be fought. At each level
we pay in animosity for the privilege of animating and being
animated, and buy self-awareness dearly.

A part of the remedy is that we discover our unity in our
living Mother. Like Antaeus and our radios, we need earthing.

### 7. The life on Earth and the life of Earth

The close observer saw the life *on* the planet. Then he retired,
and discovered the life *of* the planet, a life which (though it
embraces the first) is of new order. If now he returns, bearing
in mind this momentous discovery, everything is seen in a new
light. Now it is Earth herself that opens an eyelid to look at
him, and draws herself up into a head, and waves a greeting and
talks and sings to him, and kisses him. For her living organs are
not straying or loose in her, but firmly rooted—when they are
rooted in her they are called plants; when she is rooted in them,
in their radicular lungs, they are called animals. Her way of
growing grass and trees is not a woman's way of growing hair,
but that is no reason for pretending she is bald, and wears a

green wig. The ox-eye daisy is no more *planted* in her than the ox-eye is planted in the ox, sending down nerve-roots into the creature's brain. And if all this is untrue, and only protoplasm is alive in a lifeless environment, then man is a myth, and little more than elongated lumps of calcium phosphate to which cells are clinging. If Earth is an infested skeleton, so is every infesting animal. There is no argument against the planet's life which does not equally apply to yours and mine.

All our botanizing is on our Mother's grave. Nor is it enough to reply that Earth may be defined as a globe which either excludes her surface blossoming, or else includes it; and of course in the first case she is not 'alive', while in the second she is 'alive'; and that this is the end of the whole verbal misunderstanding. No: a corpse alive with maggots is in a sense 'alive' and 'whole', but it is not a man; and the distinction between them is repeated in the distinction between the adorable Earth-Mother of our long tradition, and the exploitable space-platform of our present mood. And the logician will never perceive (much less dispose of) the living planet, till he is simple and humble enough just to look at her, as he would at a mother who told him (as indeed Earth is telling him in these very words) that she is not only alive, but the life of his life and himself completed. But long before contemporary man reaches the planetary level he writes out her death certificate and so his own, because he *knows* (without looking at any evidence) that man as man is the crown of the hierarchy, evolution's present limit, the sole repository of wisdom in the known universe; and that no living thing larger than a whale, or non-cellular, can possibly confront him!

In any case, what should we look for in a living creature of planetary bulk and circumstances, supposing one were to exist? Wings, flowing hair, pink cheeks, two rows of gleaming white teeth? A feeding-slit after the human pattern? An anus? A disc with hands and feet and penis, as in some primitive pictures of the sun? A spineless ball of protoplasm? An iron backbone instead of a barysphere? They would only prove their owner a monstrous effigy, incapable of life. And in fact the more we look at Earth's constitution the more we have to own that, if anything is to live as a whole in such an environment, and to grow up to life and mind of a high order, then this surely is the way. Or, if it is not, let us suggest improvements. Really it is unreasonable of Earth-fleas to expect their hostess—even if she is in turn a Sun-flea—to be their kind of flea.

Many have been astonished at the long chain of fortunate accidents (or else design) whereby terrestrial conditions, and the properties of terrestrial matter, have favoured life's emergence, as molecules are in the course of ages built up into protoplasm. But thus arbitrarily to restrict Earth's vitality in space and time, and then to point with surprise to the life-promoting characteristics of all the rest of her, is no more helpful than to dismember a man in order to show how neatly all the hacked-off portions dovetail. The solution to the mystery of the parts' interdependence is nothing else than the living whole. Every wound we inflict upon our Mother leaves us with a vexing problem in cosmology, to which *she*, raised to life again, is the answer.

## 8. *The social life of Earth*

Earth is gregarious: sometimes terrified and sometimes delighted by her planetary companions. And her continued intellectual growth, no less than her awaking to self-consciousness, is very largely the product of this social life. It sets her the exercise of objectivity. Just as this man comes to live among full-size men instead of elastic midgets, no matter how far they walk into the distance; so this planet comes to live among her equals in size and brilliance instead of a set of coloured dots in the sky. Without other heavenly bodies (and so without her primary calendars and clocks and compasses, without the challenge and inspiration of the circumambient universe, without the mathematical disciplines which it demands, and without all the secondary benefits flowing from these interplanetary gifts) would she not still be sunk in primitive stupor? Without her great laboratory in the skies she could never have made her most fruitful discoveries, or conducted her most crucial experiments. Moreover in many ways Earth's science of the heavens still leads, while Life's science of the geospheres, and Humanity's of species, and man's of men, lag far behind: they are not only later and largely derivative, but also less precise and less certain. In so far as a scientist is only human he is no scientist. It is Earth who, as enjoying her companions, is mathematician, poet, composer, though she signs herself 'Kepler', 'Milton', 'Holst'. . . .

But a self-conscious planet does not need society so much as constitute it. And if no other witnesses were called, this discussion itself would testify; for no one *on* Earth can think either of her or of her planetary companions—to do the first is to merge with them; to do the second is to merge with her. There is a true sense in which the astronomer, seeking signs of life in Mars, is himself the sign.

### 9. *Earth's behaviour*

Nor can it be maintained that her acts betray her mindlessness. *Firstly*, she knows far more about her own and her companions' behaviour—past, present, and future—than any man knows about his or other men's behaviour. *Secondly*, that behaviour is more nicely adjusted to her vital needs than many a man's to his—she avoids freezing to death on one hand, and scorching to death on the other, by steering a middle course about the sun; and avoids simultaneous freezing and scorching, by rotating like a joint on a spit. Saving her skin is making her skin. And if to wander is suicidal, then never to wander is no proof of stupidity. *Thirdly*, she does in fact feel responsible for the continued performance of herself and her companions: in the offices of the divine kings of the ancient civilizations, in the rites of recent primitives, in our modern anxiety about our planetary fate, and in some contemporary prayer, man diligently upholds the universe: he shoulders the burden of cosmic process, thereby transcending himself. *Fourthly*, it is no valid objection that she knows, but cannot will, her deeds; for at no level of myself can I find a will that is other than a peculiar degree of attention—a degree which (if I may rely upon introspection) she does not lack.

Earth's behaviour is accounted for only by the astronomical science which sees itself as her own; unself-conscious science, on the other hand, merely describes regional effects whose source and Centre are inscrutable—it explains nothing. The only way to discover what lies at the Centre of Earth's regional manifestations is to place ourselves there, and so find that our science of the planets is really hers. Then we see that our movement at the planetary level is like all movement of which, having inside information, we are entitled to speak—it is at once 'physical' (or view in, the realization of our motion in others) and 'psychical' (or view out, the realization of their motion in us), a projective-reflective couple refusing simple location. The burden of proof lies upon anyone who, ignoring what is plainly given, speculates about that utterly mysterious (and surely meaningless) alternative, namely simple and merely 'physical' movement, whose view in to the observed is matched by no view out to the observer.

## *10. Earth and the laws of motion*

The planet's orderly habits—orderly, but extremely complicated—are, then, better evidence for than against her intelligence. And here both the common sense which sees in the regulation of the erratic a primary function of intelligence, and the ancient piety which saw in regular motion (and particularly in circular motion) a sign of divinity, add their agreement.

It may be objected that the reason why Earth goes round is to be discovered, not in any mind of hers, but in the laws of motion. I reply: to suppose she has *reason* for her deeds is virtually to grant her mind; and to suppose her subject to *law* is virtually to grant her freedom. For the concept of law includes the concept of law-breaking. Only beings who consider the possibility of breaking laws can comply with them.

Earth does both. To determine her orbit, the scientist supposes that, disobeying for a while the law of gravity and obeying the law of inertia, she flies off at a tangent; and that then, re-

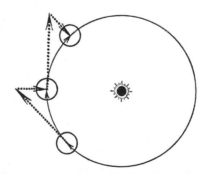

versing her disobedience, she falls towards the sun; and he adds that these illegalities are in practice so brief that her ratchet-shaped path is smoothed out into the compromise of a curve, which respects both laws alike. Now I take this mathematics more seriously than the scientist himself; for (a) I link Earth, not merely with the original data and the final result of the calculation, but with the intermediate stages as well; and (b) I say that all three are her function. His necessary assumption that Earth takes first this course and then that, is in fact her own. Her reckoning proves she knows what she is doing; its steps that she thinks of doing otherwise. Her full knowledge of her lawful conduct involves at least token defiance of the law. Only so long as her chains remain uninspected are they altogether binding, for freedom is the inescapable condition of self-consciousness.

Earth is now subject to the laws of motion in the same sense that man is subject to the laws of the State, for it is science itself which progressively removes the distinction between nature's laws and man's. The Statute Book and the *Principia* are two chapters of one volume. It is by exploring and regulating our bondage to social law that we become free men; to biological law, that we become a free species; to physical law, that we become a free planet. Thus, in due hierarchical sequence, the successive zones of the external and compulsive natural order are taken over and completed in the new order—the order of conscious compliance with the law that is now self-imposed and interior. Until I know the planet's motions as law-abiding yet incipiently lawless, and as her own yet mine, they are for me automatic, and I have every reason for denying her freedom: I am a celestial robot. When I refuse to believe in an Earth who moves as she likes in the heavens, I am not wrong, but only small. What I think depends on how much of me is thinking.

*11. The redemption of Earth's past*

What of the planet's long past, before science, before Life itself, was born? Did she not then move as she does now, yet without mind?

The full answer belongs to Part IV. Here my brief reply is that the question is essentially self-answering. The more Eàrth becomes alive to her inertness, and conscious of her unconsciousness, the more she rescues herself from her ancient automatism. The contents of her libraries and museums bear witness to that immense effort of resurrection, which is not a copying of the past, but its real flowering into consciousness now. Certainly she is no exception to the rule that (as I shall try to show) the regional time-lapse between the deed and consciousness of the deed—or rather, between its Central source and its regional manifestations—is indispensable. It is of the very nature of mind to bring the remote in time (no less than in space) to awareness and intention, for what is intended is never merely present. The case is not merely that a little consciousness goes a long way, but that its status advances as it goes; and if it does not go any way at all it does not exist. And this rule applies to every hierarchical level—the senseless evolutions of my atoms, the growth of the embryo innocent of physiology, primitive species with no idea they were making for man—these grow up into an awareness now that is all the more theirs for being held at arm's length. The law of elsewhereness rules that present mind is the correction of past and future mindlessness. To be wholly aware now would be to bring every other moment but this moment to awareness.

## 12. The face of Earth

But if Earth really is a higher power of our life, why is her face so marred, so chaotic and expressionless?

All depends upon range. The near view of her landscapes is the embodiment of unending and matchless beauty; the further view of continents is disorderly, as befits mesoforms whose conduct is so often the same; the far view, of the bright planet in her setting of stars, is again lovely, but in another manner. In short, the law of the spindle is suitably observed.

Our maps are Earth's death-masks. Her life slips through the geographer's finest latitude-longitude net, which becomes her mourning-veil and indeed her shroud. Yet these curiously rugged and weather-beaten features live. Italy cannot wiggle her toe or bend her spine, but she is not therefore moribund. The genius of my native land really is the land's; for England's indispensable function in Humanity is not the function of this or that man who happens to live there, but of the terrain that comes to a head in him. No wonder there is at last some talk of geopsychology, of continental influences. The truth is that till I take on not only the unique mind, but also the body, the geography, of Asia and of America as well as of Europe, I can never become fully human, much less planetary.

## 13. The death and resurrection of Earth

It is with us an article of blindest faith that Earth is not even a merry-go-round in the solar circus, but a mirthless mud pie flung into space, a stone, a revolving pellet of filth and fire, and nothing the pellet can say or do will shake this faith. The Mother has fallen very low and become coarse and impure, a soiled and soiling thing, the great untouchable. The 'clean job', well insulated from her—how desirable it is! Anything to protect our little body from our greater body, till worms shall forcibly knit them.

Yet this dear and beautiful planet is part of our maturity. Becoming terrestrial, we become more ourselves. How, then, have we grown so self-alienated as to deny her life, which we used to know so well? Here are a pair of eyes she has opened to look at herself, and a pair of lips she has parted to speak of herself—to announce to the universe that she is dumb and blind! Here is one who uses her wits to prove she is witless! Why this ridiculous behaviour?

The easy answer is that only a creature that is less than human could forget that it is alive; the true answer is that only a creature that is more than human could remember that it is dead—lesser beings are apt to overlook this. Many-sided death is the condition of her vitality. Thus she seeks in her celestial companions the majesty and aloofness and cold serenity of the inanimate, which alone can raise her to intensest life. Again, all the centuries of her ardent self-consciousness and life-mood saw less physical advance and less scientific achievement than a decade of her present death-mood; and it is to her great practical advantage, for example, that the geologist (who can investigate only a slain and desecrated Earth) should so unreasonably ignore himself, the geological specimen which geologizes. Moreover, her life, like all its parts, must be a continual dismemberment or hierarchical descent, no less than its ascending opposite: through her creature-organs she is for ever sinking to the level of her molecules. Finally and in any case, she is no true whole, any more than Humanity and Life are true wholes—as the next chapter will show, she is by herself stone dead. Though man is only a particle of her, she is only a particle of him.

Thus our geocide—our planetary suicide—is no crime, not even a huge mistake, but a part of that multiple down-going without which there is no risen life. Our holy and unapproachable Earth has been violated and left for dead, but only so could she bring forth. Only when the last throb of the Mother's life has been stilled, and the last whiff of the odour of her sanctity has been blown away by the profane spirit of the modern age, is she able to rise again, through that same profane spirit, to a new though as yet less conscious life.

# CHAPTER X

# The Distant View—Sun

## 1. From planet to star

There is in self-awareness a principle of boundless growth, for the knower is greater than he knows. The planet of the previous chapter has already colonized the solar system to view herself. Exploring her limits is surpassing them; realization of herself as of one hierarchical grade is ascent towards the next. Earth becomes, not merely the sun, but that sun-family which I call the Sun.

Moreover it is plain that our planetary body is incomplete without the star which is the source of all its energy. Now this energy is passed down in due hierarchical order. For example, it is not solar radiation, but terrestrial, which feeds the living— the Sun's light is filtered and diffused and generally digested by Earth (in particular by the atmosphere) before it is fit for Life's consumption; just as it must then be further treated by Life (in particular by vegetable life) before it is fit for Humanity, and by Humanity (in particular by producers and manufacturers and distributors of food) before it is ready for a man's dinner table. In respect of his human body, all this is external and disconnected and non-hierarchical. In respect of his solar body, it is internal and unitary and hierarchical. By such radial processes our star lives. Not to say grace before meat is unrealistic, for it really does come down to us from heaven, by way of the great service-staircase of the universe.

## 2. The Sun as the solar system

The Sun has no more broken up into the solar system than the rosebud has broken up into the rose: planets are the petals of a star in full bloom.

What we make of our solar inflorescence depends on where we view it from. Working outwards from the fiery gas-layers at the nucleus, we may suppose ourselves to come to a planetary region where the solar disc is not yet observable as a whole, then to regions where it dominates in our field of view, and finally to regions where it is inconspicuous—our field being not merely visual, but provided by a variety of instruments. And we may add that our stations on this solar journey are the planets, whose masses tend to increase with their distance from the sun, and then to fall off again: that is to say, what the planetary observer is depends very largely upon what he makes of his solar object, and his estimate is obedient (as when he was inspecting an atom's nucleus) to the law of the spindle. (If we had chosen to start at Saturn or else Jupiter, the story would have been similar: our increasing and then decreasing estimates of the planet would have found approximate embodiment in the respective masses of its nine satellites.) Finally we come to our true Sun-region, to a zone where all our previous observer-selves (the planets in particular, and, included in them, geo-spheres, species, men, and all the rest) are absorbed by our object, and there confronts us an indivisible star, the living Sun.

[Note the curious effects of this cannibalism of mutual observers. Come, and you devour me yet you shrink; go, and I devour you yet you swell. For at each hierarchical stage my approaching and dwindling observer himself dismembers me (by becoming one part of my body in order to view the others), and my receding and growing observer himself heals my wounds (by completing me with the gift of his own body in order to view the whole of me). Thus when my planetary observer who sees me as Earth, becomes my sidereal observer who sees me as the Sun, he is looking at what was in part himself.]

### 3. The life of the Sun

Common sense sees this annular Sun-body as dead. For scientific opinion is that though organisms of some kind are possible or even probable on Mars, and conceivable but improbable on Venus, they are practically impossible on the other planets: only a microscopic fraction of the Sun's matter, then, is alive.

But all this is beside the point. Earth's vitality cannot be solely hers, but must overflow unceasingly. It is not that her self-consciousness *can* raise dead worlds to life, but that to exist at all it must already have done so. There is no room for death in a Sun—or indeed in a universe—that contains a point of self-consciousness.

And we mistake the case altogether when we doubt whether so tiny a live part as Earth or Mars can quicken such a whole as the Sun-system. For to pick out any portion of the solar body and to say of it: here alone are the chemical and thermal conditions of life, and consequently life itself, and in the end self-consciousness, while the rest is mere cosmic background—this is to ignore the great vital factors. For life is not simply a matter of enough water, carbon, and so on, at the right temperature, but of celestial conditions also. The fierce and graduated heat of the solar gas-layers, the intense cold of interplanetary space, the more moderate temperatures of Earth's upper atmosphere and core—these are in different ways as necessary to life, as truly the temperatures *of* life, as are the temperatures of the biosphere itself. To enjoy normal health I must enjoy it throughout my solar body, every region of which has its proper temperature and physical composition and size. In such a universe it takes such a body (no matter how cumbersome it seems at first) to live my life. If the world is to be inhabited at all, here at last is a fit inhabitant.

A man, on the other hand, cannot arise except as a piece of sidereal detail, as the partially alive close-up of a living star. He thinks he is the life and soul of the cosmic party, but it is the life and soul of him. Stand back from his lustreless and incompetent human part-body, and behold all of him—a celestial body gloriously alive and shining in heaven. Even the dullest actor in our world-play is in the long run and on the long view a star. His true human system is the solar system. But he recognizes only its vestigial organ—the solar plexus. He has swallowed the god.

Of one star he has inside knowledge—and ignorance. What sort of knowledge is it that makes atoms of carbon and oxygen and hydrogen relevant, and their conjunction in the Folio of 1623 or in *The Lady of the Rocks* irrelevant, to the Sun that holds them all? Are sunflowers and sunbirds and sunfish any less solar than sunspots? If the Indian's sun-dance throws no light upon the Sun's nature, why should the dance of his atoms do so? Does the copper butterfly bask in the Sun by accident, as a stranger there; and is the kingfisher not yet domesticated? Is the thinking in this star parasitic, its protons indigenous but not its poetry? Have the gods tossed these pages into the Sun, as into a celestial waste-paper basket? And if it is only the primitive and immature features of the Sun which may be recognized as solar, why do we not have the courage of our convictions and apply the same principle to men, looking upon them as superannuated foetuses or else magnified ova and sperms? We repress our astronomical present as we repress our biological past, and so find ourselves some thousands of millions of years behind the solar times.

Admittedly there are in this solar body many parts whose office in the living whole is as yet obscure. It is possible—even likely —that similar results could have been got with less material. But why should we expect the stars to copy our cheese-paring methods?

*4. The solar outlook and the terresrtial*

And evidently all this weight of body is soluble without residue as we look up at the night sky. The Sun really is abolished as well as obliterated when the stars come out, and we, taking on at last our solar physique, find ourselves and it to be nothing but transparent sky and sidereal playground.

Always there are two stages—horizontal and vertical—in the ascent from one hierarchical level to the next. First I must broaden my base at this level, shifting my weight (so to say) on to a number of its inhabitants, before I can mount through them to the higher level. In other words, I must take on new Centres of this grade, before fusing them into one Centre of the next grade: I must look *in* at myself from the varying points of view of other men (or species or geospheres), and then join them all in a single view *out*. It is the same at the solar level. First, with Copernicus, I shift Centre from Earth to a motionless sun, and look back upon my Earth-self in motion. But this is only half-way to Sunhood: now I have to forget myself and everything solar, turn about, and look out at the stars, which alone can raise me to their estate. So long as anything of me is left, any view in, I can never gain advancement. Nor is it any wonder that a star's psychology should here so resemble a man's. It *is* a man's, his own high-level functioning, his confused middle-grade behaviour raised to clarity and precision. At high levels as at low, his essential constitution is no longer in doubt. The sidereal and the atomic in him illuminate the human.

To earn hierarchical promotion, the first rule is: take the companions that are Centred on you, and Centre yourself on them. Put them at rest and yourself in motion: place yourself at their point of view. (Copernicus the adult leaping out of himself to see his Earth self from the sun's viewpoint, and Copernicus the child leaping out of himself to see his human self from his playmates' viewpoint, are the same person making the same discovery about himself, and growing by the same means, at different levels of the personality.) The second rule is: to complete your promotion, join your companions of this level in making room for a companion of the next level.

## 5. *Solar sense organs*

These two steps—outward, then upward—are the basis of all my seeing, and embodied in all my visual equipment. To look up to the *next* level, I must first discover and unite myself with at least one more observer at *this* level, so as to combine his different point of view with mine in a single yet binocular perspective. In other words, to grow vertically I must grow horizontally, broadening my observational baseline at one stage in order to reach out to another. Thus it is as a pair of human

organs three inches apart that I register a man as four yards away; as a pair of terrestrial organs 5,000 miles apart (observatories in, say, Europe and South Africa) that I register a moon as 240,000 miles away; and as a pair of solar organs 186 million miles apart (on opposite sides of Earth's orbit) that I register Alpha Centauri as 4·4 light-years away, for Earth is the Sun's rolling eyeball. The point that my 'eyes' grow more distant in time as well as in space—for instance, one solar organ is six months later than the other—and that in general I have to keep pace with the temporal no less than the spatial standards of my object, is one which Part IV will develop. The further point that it is natural for my higher sense organs to be artificial, that nature is here still more herself for coming to full awareness and intention, has been sufficiently dealt with in Chapter VI.

There are many types of solar and terrestrial observation, each with its sensory equipment dispersed to match the remoteness of the object, but they share the same function: namely, to explore the crude data in order to discount all that belongs to the scattered observers of this level, and so to arrive at a common objective estimate. Thus astronomers, recognizing that this whirligig Earth-platform is no foundation for their observatory, must carefully study, and then dismiss as mere appearance, every motion which can be attributed to that platform. As two-eyed men they see innumerable motions only to discount them in favour of the stable world which they see as many-eyed Humanity; and now as Earth they repeat that performance, exchanging the mobile world seen by a planet for the slower and steadier world of a star. In effect, they step on to the stable Sun, and rebuild their telescopes in that more favourable country. Once more, Earth, knowing herself, approaches Sunhood. To reach the Sun, I must deny and altogether abolish Earth, but first I must know what it is I abolish.

### 6. Man as a solar being

It is not only by astronomy that we become solar. For example, my garden is no garden at all unless it is really three gardens—the first, a rectangular local plot twenty yards long; the second, a ring-shaped terrestrial plot 20,000 miles long, comprising a dark half and a light half; the third, a ring-shaped solar plot some 600 million miles long, comprising a warm and fruitful part and a cold and bare part. It takes me a few minutes to go round the first, a day and a night to go round the second, a year to go round the third. And only the third is a whole, or makes sense by itself: my digging here is explained by my sowing some millions of miles further on, and my sowing by the flowers I shall pick in the far sidereal distance. Indeed the only good earth is the Sun's, and every seed that grows is planted in a star-field. This spot where I stand is national and terrestrial and solar ground; and indeed holy or whole ground, for I need not put out my foot an inch to step on to the floor of heaven. My bootsoles have never ceased to tread celestial pavements.

Upon our daily terrestrial pulse is superimposed the annual pulse of a star, regulating our lives in countless ways. And all our anniversaries are, *as solar*, positions in space: our talk of the days that lie in front and behind, of close and distant events, of what we have been through and what is coming to us, is a truly solar dialect. In its annual patterns, our Earth-life becomes the life of a star whose planets are no longer small spheres, but far-reaching solar rings. Directly we see through time to the space which time shapes, we find that there is after all in the Sun a Land of Perpetual Spring, just as there really is on Earth a Land of Nod. Christmas is a solar landmark which we rediscover periodically. Calendars are Sun-maps, and failure to observe times and seasons is indifference to the scenery of our native land in the skies. The yearly rites of modern astronomical man, no less than those of pre-scientific man, really do lift him heavenwards.

## 7. *The Sun, and the pursuit of values*

In the Sun man no longer thinks human thoughts; his mind is anomalous and inexplicable till it is recognized as a star's. Knowledge of the stars is knowledge by the stars, knowledge of a high intellectual order, lucid, precise, guiding and inspiring the development of science in general. The music and poetry of the stars, all the wonder and delight and awe they awake in him, are this star's response to his heavenly companions, and not of Earth. The selfless devotion of the astronomer to his studies; his humility before the facts; his slow and painful overcoming, not merely of his human and vital self-centredness, but of all terrestrial egoism as well—these are not his in any human capacity, but as solar. The fact is that a man who pursues any value far enough is likely to find himself in heavenly company. His salvation must drag in every star's, for they are the same thing. Psychologists find Earth and Sun to be *symbols* of the wholeness we so much need; in fact they are its reality. The symbol is powerful because it is so much more than a symbol.

## 8. *The Sun and the mystics*

Traditionally, the Sun marks a stage on the upward path of religious contemplation. It is the chief preoccupation of the Hellenistic mystery religions, and the fourth rung of Dante's celestial ladder. Even when there is no mention of the Sun, the mystic's story is of dazzling brightness and fire, of a warmth and splendour which are not only metaphorical; and always the Heavens, with all that is luminous and high and unearthly, are his dear country. And this is to be expected if it is by love that he ascends the hierarchy, gaining the next stage never alone or for himself, but only in and through his companions. The way up, the path from the human sympathy that embraces billions of animal cells to the divine sympathy that embraces billions of universes, can only lie through the Sun. The way up is the way out, and the heavens we live in are Heaven after all. The mystic's ascent is nature's, for his enlightenment is hers: it is cosmic or nothing. There is one hierarchy of the spirit and of nature, and one Sun that shines in both. Our physical and spiritual wholeness are two aspects of a single condition that is at one stage terrestrial and at the next solar. And those who realize the Sun are not many, but one in the Sun.

But the solar station offers no more than a vision by the way, granted only to be lost again. For the mystic's journey, like all regional exploration, is ruled by the law of the spindle: the road from one zone of illumination to the next lies through a belt of dark night, a season of privation in which the vision fades and he is brought to nothing. To reach beyond the Sun he must cease to be solar, cease to be anything at all. Between each heavenly mansion and the next is a threshold over which he must stumble and fall. In him the Sun, like Earth, must die, to rise again to a life that is more truly celestial.

Thus the mystic cannot condemn the science which kills the Sun. Doubtless the Sun that is neither terrestrial nor alive nor human (with its inferior counterpart—the atom that is neither molecular nor cellular nor human) is one of the more fantastic of our modern myths; but it is a true solar myth, to be taken with the utmost seriousness. It has been the necessary role of modern man to split the Sun (no less than Country and Humanity and Life and Earth) into a mindless body and a bodiless mind; into a machine and a ghost which is not even allowed *in* the machine; into an opaque and meaningless material hierarchy on the one hand, and a vapid and gutless spiritual hierarchy on the other.

# CHAPTER XI

# The Distant View—Galaxy

## 1. The star-society

The dwindling Sun vanishes into a star-cloud, and the star-cloud into the Galaxy—our own spiral system or island universe, with its thousands of millions of suns. The retreating observer's attention is directed upon a new Centre— the hub of the rotating spiral arms.

Here, then, is a great star-society, comprising many subsidiary types of star-grouping, regulated by certain general observances, and allowing for endless differences of behaviour and constitution. And some of the most notable of these differences are differences of age, for stars have a life-history.

To climb Jacob's ladder I have only to lift my eyes. On every clear night I am received into this brilliant society, and live in heaven without noticing it. And here I find none of that cheek-by-jowl herding which is the rule at lower levels. Nor is this surprising, if the truest individuals have most inner resources and fewest outer needs, and develop from within rather than are moulded from without, and combine interior complexity with exterior simplicity, and live in unity with their fellows yet alone in sublime detachment. If the best are those who ask little and give much, then the living stars are indeed excellent. Only a tiny fraction of the Sun's light is intercepted by the planets: the rest we may think of as promoting stellar intercourse and the wholeness of the Galaxy. Radiance, generosity, openness, distinguish the company of heaven.

## 2. The dependence of the Sun upon the Galaxy

On casual inspection, it is true, the Sun seems to be independent of the rest of the Galaxy. In fact, he is very much of a piece with it. Let me give three examples. (i) His motion, as governed by the mass and motion of every other star, is not merely solar, but truly galactic. (ii) He gathers up quantities of interstellar gas in the course of his travels, and it is very possible that, without this accumulating galactic material, the solar system would never have come to pass. Alternatively (or in addition) the solar system may be due to some star or stars that once visited our Sun, but are now far distant. In either case, it is through his membership of the galactic community that the Sun comes to life. (iii) And his subsequent debt to the stars is immense: for only in their society can he grow up to adult and self-conscious starhood. He knows himself in them. (For instance, one way of determining the size of Earth's orbit—a truly solar dimension—is by comparing the spectra of certain stars at six-month intervals, and calculating Earth's changed velocity from the observed displacement of spectral lines; her velocity, in turn, gives the clue to her distance from the sun. Thus at Sun-level as at man-level, I discover what I am by watching my fellows' reaction to me.)

The Sun, then, is a fragment of the Galaxy, and by no means self-supporting. He must find his wholeness at the next hierarchical level.

### 3. Solar systems in the Galaxy, and their life

If the Galaxy is alive as a whole, it would be reasonable to expect that our star, amongst such a teeming population, should not be the only custodian of its life. What is the verdict of science?

Even the nearest stars are so distant that any planets they may support are far beyond telescope-range. Direct evidence, therefore, is ruled out. But contemporary theories of solar-system formation suggest that such systems are not very rare, and biochemists are inclined to add that a planet resembling Earth would necessarily develop life. The conclusion is that, on the whole, modern science no longer tends to look on our in-habited Sun as a freak, but as one of many.

### 4. The arguments for the living Galaxy

Let me summarize the chief arguments for the life of this island universe of ours.

(i) Science not only begins to favour the hypothesis of many inhabited worlds: its basic assumptions point to a living universe. For if the promise of life's highest attributes lies in all matter everywhere, and these attributes only await the right conditions to show themselves; then two conclusions follow. First, that life and mind and values (however rare) are proper to the Galaxy and no intrusion; and, second, that its electrons and protons are virtually divine. Now these electrons and protons (by a process of integration) and this Galaxy (by a process of differentiation) eventually take the form of myself writing this sentence about them: and if this is irrelevant to their nature I can imagine nothing that could be relevant. But we talk as if we were clues only to what the universe is *not* like; and so of course it is a steam-engine or a firework display, instead of a god in disguise.

(ii) Only one man is presented for my immediate inspection, yet I take the risk of treating him as a fair sample of the rest: I distribute the values I enjoy, and do not claim them for myself alone. I see no reason why at star-level I should change my attitude, and refuse to take similar risks. In any case, thus to argue from the known star or man to the unknown, instead of from the unknown to the still more unknown, is surely the humbler and more reasonable alternative.

(iii) Besides, I do know something of the other stars, namely that I live in them observing this star: even those which lack planets are not, then, without any life at all. Certainly the scientist cannot make the rounds of the universe, taking temperatures here and feeling pulses there, weighing this star-body and measuring that, while leaving his vitality and mentality behind on this planet as if in a sterilizing bath. A studied universe is different absolutely from an unstudied. The most important astronomical fact is astronomy. A Galaxy saturated (as ours is) with its own science cannot help being a minded system; and the more I prove its matter to be mindless the more I disprove my point, for there is neither antiseptic to prevent the world's mind infecting all it handles, nor scalpel to excise it from the world's body. Indeed there is something comic about the branch trying to show up the deadness of the trunk by growing more and greener leaves.

(iv) My travelling observer found that as a living planet his object was incomplete, a vignette, and he was forced to seek the rest of the picture by retiring to the region of the living Sun.

Now he discovers even the Sun to be the mere limb of a larger body. But it would be absurd of him to suppose that thus to pull together and supplement a living creature is to kill it; on the contrary, he would be likely to conclude that at last he has before him the creature which is all there, and alive in its own right.

(v) If my inquiry thus far has not gone entirely astray, and the life and mind of the levels up to the solar are granted, then the principle of continuity suggests that there does not occur at the next level a sudden and inexplicable break, a reversion to the merely physical—whatever that mysterious condition may be.

(vi) It is a part of my growth that I shift Centre, not only to Earth and then to the Sun, but also to the Galaxy. I must first discover, and then deny, all that is merely solar in my experience. I must accord to the Sun's point of view no more privilege than to any other star's, in order that I may arrive at the common galactic perspective. And this growth, this celestial evolution, this carefully calculated alighting from the footboard of a star on to firm galactic ground, is in every way the proper continuation of my life-history so far.

(vii) The only matter of which I have inside and first-hand knowledge—namely this man, planet, star, galaxy—proves to be accommodation for other matter: that is to say, it is mind. In all four instances I am acephalous, and the greater my life the greater the head it costs me. As the locus of other galaxies, I dissolve this magnificent Galaxy-head into mere head-room for them, just as easily as before I dissolved the inert masses of the solar system and of the geospheres. And what, after all, am I seeking when I ask for evidence that this Galaxy is alive and minded, unless I am seeking a system of experience of other galaxies? Moreover this experience has some of the godlike characteristics that we might expect—billions of miles are now a hair's-breadth, and 'near' means millions of years' light-journey. These are not the estimates of an educated mammal. Nor is it a *man* who, looking up at night, sees millions of suns whose size and brilliance are comparable with this Sun's, and millions of galaxies which are not tiny light-spots, but island universes like our own. We are raised to the rank of the beings whose viewpoint we adopt. Becoming alive to more, we become more alive. Who looks out is a question of how far we look, for

changing our minds is changing our body. And the chief peculiarity of our outlook at these exalted levels is that it is so much
more lucid and deliberate and intellectual than it is at lower
levels.

(viii) I know of only three genuine astronomers, and their
names are Earth, Sun, Galaxy: to glance at the others is to see
that they are not built for the job, but these have truly celestial
constitutions and the sense organs of angels. For example, there
is such sensory equipment as the blink microscope, which (by
rapidly alternating star-photographs taken, say, ten years apart)
makes visible the motion of a star against the background of
stars. Above all there is the giant reflector. It is no matter for
speculation what kind of eye would do for an organism $10^{35}$
times as large as a whale: its light-gathering power is equal to
that of thousands of human eyes; its range is reckoned in millions
of light-years; its focal length may be a hundred feet. The Palo-
mar telescope is a galactic reaction to extra-galactic influence.
It is designed to further the cosmic social relationships of which
it is at once product and instrument. It is unearthly; its true
address is galactic, and only incidentally solar and terrestrial
and American. And again it is not the vital functioning of the
Sun or the Galaxy that is mysterious and conjectural, but rather
that of the man; and the odd thing is that our knowledge of the
first should convince us of our ignorance, while our ignorance
of the second should convince us of our knowledge. Only around
the human level do we know without knowing how we know.

(ix) If the star-beliefs that occur in this star are its own and
not parasitical, then it is an historical fact that the Sun has,
throughout a great part of his adult life, been convinced of the
life of his companions. And while we may think this conviction
mistaken, we cannot exclude it from the evidence. It would be
different if we could call as counter-witness a star which has
consistently held the opposite belief.

(x) Again, if our aesthetic and moral preferences are deep-
rooted in life and in the cosmos itself, then it is absurd to suppose that they are no guide to the nature of the cosmos. Of
course we are apt to mistake our desires—and, conversely, our
fears—for fully established facts. But to give up regulated wish-
ful thinking for unregulated fearful thinking is neither practical
nor reasonable; and, seeing that we cannot suspend judgment
but must live by faith of one sort or another, let us then choose

the beautiful and magnanimous and heartening alternative—the hierarchy of life and not death. Certainly it is no mark of wisdom to say: the more exalted and universal and compelling our intuitions, the less they have to do with the universe that produces them in us.

(xi) On the other hand, I may not ignore my intuitions of a dead universe. My assessment of my fellow stars, as of my fellow men, has three necessary stages—the stage of primitive animism, when my companions are alive and externally related to me; of mechanism, when I treat them as things to be analysed and exploited; and of enlightened animism, when I treat them as other selves yet myself, in a society of equals. It is inevitable that, in the second stage, I should look upon the stars as a mere lighting scheme, just as I look upon men as mere chattels, means to some end. For without this death-mood science would never get to grips with its material, or art learn objectivity and innocence of eye, or religion advance beyond polytheism. You cannot refine the animated world of the savage and the child, but only kill it and then raise it to new life. Earth, Sun, and Galaxy must die and be born again. Moreover the condition of the higher life is that it shall die the deeper death. Thus I cannot quite forget that the men I make use of are really persons, or that other species have a life of their own to live; the vitality of other planets and stars, however, is more easily dispelled; and as for the galaxies, they put up no resistance to my murderous intentions. The Galaxy, then, is much more alive and much more dead than a man; and the life is the counterpart of the death. We must respect the death sentence which the universe passes on itself through us, without forgetting that it is the living universe which pronounces it.

Even so, the real question is not whether a thing is alive or dead, but at what level it lives, at what level it dies. It takes the Sun to invigorate dead planets, the Galaxy to invigorate dead stars, the Whole to invigorate dead galaxies. But in the Whole all the dead wholly live, and in the Centre all the living wholly die.

We men pride ourselves on keeping a sense of humour in a sour-faced universe; but in fact the universe enjoys a laugh even more than we do, and it is the stars and galaxies which play the biggest and wildest practical jokes. For instance, this galactic nervous system of mine credits itself with the consciousness that the Galaxy is unconscious—and unconscious because it has no nervous system! Here is a condensation of a gas which indeed behaves oddly: it is much to the credit of this eddying sky-dust, these sky-sweepings collected into so many cosmic dustbins, that they should now be composing this not-too-serious account of themselves. Of course there are deep and grave intentions behind these heavenly high jinks; only let us sometimes have the grace to join in the laughter, and cease earnestly pretending that our belief in merely pyrotechnical heavens—in a Sun that is only a squib and a Galaxy that is only a Catherine wheel— is nothing but hard-headed common sense and sweet reasonableness.

## 5. Galactic structure and functioning

To us leaves our Yggdrasil Tree is dead—because it is so obviously not a leaf. Let us wake from this dream which makes our little life the model and touchstone of all life. Let us consider whether the constitution of stars and galaxies does not in fact fit them to be living creatures of very exalted hierarchical status.

(i) If to grow in virtue and wisdom is to come to hold a uniformly high opinion of our fellows, looking past the accidents of their nature to their essential worth; and at the same time to order our own lives; and if, further, to live thus is to follow our heavenly calling in no merely metaphorical sense, then our reconstitution as a rotating (and so range-preserving) system of celestial bodies would seem altogether appropriate. Once we cease parting the spiritual heaven from the physical, each will richly illuminate the other. And are we not already in love with the unchanging order of the skies? Do we not claim the rest which comes of joining in that tireless unrest, that high celestial ritual, that grand ball to which we are all invited?

Again, if loyalty to the community, or conscious adherence to a common nucleus or 'centre of gravity', is one of the marks of the good citizen at any level; and if moreover there is any tendency for the whole that commands his adherence to increase with the quality of that adherence; then we should naturally look to the solar and galactic levels for such concentric embodiments as we find there.

(ii) And these rotating systems certainly obey in manifold ways the law of elsewhereness and the regional rules. Consider any planet. (1) Its 'weight' with respect to the sun (i.e. the sun's

115

pull), (2) its acceleration (i.e. the sun's acceleration along the radius of its apparent orbit), (3) its illumination (i.e. the apparent brightness of the sun), (4) its appreciation of the solar disc (i.e. the area of the sun for it)—all four are inversely proportional to the square of the planet's distance from the sun. When the planet doubles its distance, all these—weight, acceleration, illumination, and apparent size, are quartered. Note, first, how range determines physical characteristics; and, second, how these are not simply present in one or other of the parties, but are shared, and always elsewhere—the four planetary characteristics I have mentioned turn out to be the sun's. And much the same is true, in turn, of the Sun. A star is a star-mirror. Thus the period of the Sun's rotation about the Galaxy's centre of gravity is not determined by the Sun's mass, but by its distance from that centre. As a man I forget that I am nothing in myself, but at celestial levels that fact is borne in upon me.

(iii) We imagine men are free and know what freedom is, and that stars are in bondage and do not know what bondage is. The facts, however, are the other way about. To discover what we mean by freedom, we need to turn to our heavenly behaviour. I have already shown how Earth's accurate awareness of her conduct involves her accurate assessment and rejection of other possibilities—knowing what she does is knowing what she might have done—and this is equally true of the Sun. Man as man, on the other hand, lacks any exact knowledge of his past and present and future conduct, and of his latent tendencies. At the mercy of his largely unexplored heritage, he is in bondage to nature. Only at the higher levels of Earth and Sun and Galaxy is he built for freedom.

(iv) The effective mass of the Galaxy for the Sun is the total mass of the stars that lie within the solar orbit. Thus the extent of that orbit is a demonstration of what the Sun makes of his fellows; and it is compounded of his conscious tendency to make more of them by flying off at a tangent, and less of them by falling towards their centre of gravity. At this level, then, the centripetal or 'katabolic' and centrifugal or 'anabolic' basis of all behaviour becomes admirably clear, and capable of exact mathematical description. Increasingly the illusion of the 'horizontal' region's self-sufficiency is overcome.

(v) And if the galactic level is in any sense an aspect or embodiment of the higher experience of thinker and poet and saint, then we should look there firstly for some recognition of all levels, high and low; and then for an expansive tendency, a dissatisfaction with the incompleteness of this level and an urge towards the next. And what we do find, instead of the closed circle which announces only its own region and range, is a spiral which announces the regions up to its own, and points beyond them all.

(vi) And this centrifugal tendency is still more marked amongst the galaxies as a community: they are found to be leaving one another at speeds which are proportional to their distances. And something of the kind might indeed be expected if at very high levels it is natural for us to retire to ever more respectful distances from one another, to achieve a sublime detachment, and above all to see each as merging in the Whole.

(vii) Pre-scientific man's approach to these levels lacks our precision, but it avoids our fatal habit of parting mind from body and spirit from matter. Thus the spiral in various forms is not only one of the commonest and the most universal of symbols: it is also peculiarly numinous, life-giving, and holy; and it is linked with the rotating stars.

I conclude, then, from these seven considerations, that the Galaxy revealed by modern science is no unsuitable embodiment for a creature of very exalted hierarchical status.

And the Galaxy, in living its own life, lives ours: it is our finishing-off, the human become considerable. It is this man seen from afar, as this man is a spiral nebula closely inspected. In one sense, indeed, the stellar and the galactic are more human than the human: for really to know your neighbour would be to know all the stars in the sky, and really to know them would be to know him. No matter what else we call it, that which we love devotedly enough, and understand thoroughly enough, is galactic. Only we part the love from the understanding, heavenly religion and poetry from heavenly science. The task of science is now to give religion a head, of religion to give science a heart, of philosophy to hold both together in one body —that body which, in one of its highest metamorphoses, is the Galaxy.

## 6. Abstract and concrete embodiments

Of course it is true that such higher embodiments are thin, impoverished of detail. It is not easy to love a constellation, still less an N.G.C. number. In fact, science's painstaking ascent of the hierarchy to the solar and galactic planes—each of them taken by itself and in abstraction from what lies below—is our modern version of the *via negativa* of mediaeval mysticism, our progressive 'putting off the creatures'. Here, in the lofty realm of the nebulae, all that is human and vital and planetary is transcended, and intellect has almost broken free from the things of sense. But just as the mystic's true end is not merely to enjoy the supra-sensible vision in the heights—that divine illumination which at last owes nothing to the light of the eye—but is to return, bringing down into our common life some of the radiance, so also the true end of science must be to reunite the heaven and earth that it has inevitably divided. The discovery awaits us that the galaxies purged of all their planetary and living and human contents, and man stripped of all his celestial integuments, are the factitious products of our cosmic taxidermy.

The fact is that our experience of the far and illustrious, and of the near and humble, are different apprehensions of the same ·thing. My friend is a more adequate version of what my cells make of one another; they are a less adequate version of what I make of him. And my sensitiveness to other men reapppears in my sensitiveness to other stars and galaxies. Personal and cosmic relationships mutually determine each other. Consequently genuine mysticism not only begins at home, but never leaves home. Though our telescopic Jacob's ladder extends beyond the remotest shining spirals, its foot needs firmly planting on the dingy flag-stones of Charing Cross. All true worship in our Galaxy is also by and through our Galaxy, passing that way to the Highest; and the Sun and planets attend no churches but ours—if we neglect divine service, so do they. Conversely, the church is cosmic or no church at all: it would never serve its lowly members if it neglected its splendid ones.

It is the mark of man's life at its best that he places it in its full hierarchical setting, so that it becomes an utterly different thing, a sacrament, universal, profound. Christian marriage provides an example. The tale is first of a ceremony before God (and before His angels, according to an earlier version of the Marriage Service), then of registration by the State, then of a family reception, then of a solitary man and woman, then of their organs, then of their cells, chromosomes, genes . . . till we lose track altogether of their joint down-going to the Centre where lovers at last meet and are one. And the second half of the story is the mirror image of the first, a story of their joint arising in their offspring—a cell, a swiftly evolving animal, a human child, of whom the family and the State and Heaven take cognizance, as he is registered and christened and eventually confirmed. And what is true of marriage is true of all our human acts—they are hierarchical and therefore holy, as soon as we see them as they are, vertically instead of horizontally.

# CHAPTER XII

# The Whole

## 1. The upper limit of the view in

My travelling observer, himself one of the galaxies and caught up in their mutual recession, sees this Galaxy dwindle, and become one of a group, and eventually vanish over the cosmic horizon. And it appears likely that this time no embodiment of a higher order, no super-galactic system, will present itself. The observer has come to the outermost region, where this great disappointment awaits him: the object which has grown so luxuriantly, and been so often transfigured, does not here reach some high goal of appropriate excellence, but is abolished. For evidently my observer—my observer-self—can never, as my equal, see me become that totality which includes himself. He finds no region, no place at all, where the part is transformed into the Whole.

## 2. From self-consciousness to other-consciousness

There is only one thing for it: he must return through my zones, denying in turn every one of my manifestations in them, till we are both reduced here at the Centre to nothing. And then, turning round and looking out instead of in, he finds me to be the *receptacle* of the Whole that I can never *be*. And indeed it is plain that so long as I keep the least particle for myself, I can never enjoy the Whole. *Self*-consciousness was, as a matter of fact, an enterprise doomed from the start, seeing that it involves self-division; but only here, at the ultimate level, does this contradiction become inescapable. At last I am forced to the conclusion that I can never be a whole, much less the Whole.

Here, then, is a new and striking variation on the theme of elsewhereness: growth to the Whole ends in a sudden contraction to the Centre, and this in a sudden expansion to the Whole. These hierarchical extremities have a way of changing places which suggests that they are inseparable modes of one reality. The outermost cosmic envelope is torn off and folded in the

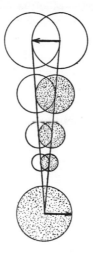

innermost: the Point, viewed the other way, is the whole Volume. Every Centre is infinitely explosive, and so extremes meet, and the hierarchy is completed.

The law of equality, then, has to give way in the end to the law of contrast. Knower and known grow up together, but at the level of the Whole the knower claims everything and finds nothing. Knower and known diminish together, but at the Centre the knower claims nothing and finds everything. For every object discovered in that receptacle is, implicitly and when completed, the Whole.

### 3. The Whole as the ultimate explanation

Until the object is so completed, until everything that makes it what it is has been taken into account in due hierarchical order, it is not all there. A sufficiently thorough inquirer, thus bent on explanation, could not stop short of the Whole. Even so, his work is only half done till he also takes the object to pieces to find out how it goes, and does not stop short of the ultimate substratum or Centre. In brief, our demand for thorough explanations—taking the form of ascending synthesis linked with descending analysis—is a veiled assertion that anything which is less than the Whole and more than the Centre is a set of regional appearances which we must discover only to discount.

### 4. The Whole as the ultimate mystery

This two-directional effort of explanation thus ends in a paradox: it tries to combine the complete knowledge of the Whole with the complete ignorance of the Centre, in an intimate union which may be called mystery. In other words, the explanations which science and common sense seek can only have for their goal that confession of utter nescience which is also the truest kind of knowledge. And what else, after all, do we want if not this culminating wonder, delight, awe, and utter self-humbling in face of the total Mystery? Surely the alternatives—some final Law from which all lesser laws could be derived, or an irreducible multiplicity of hard facts, or a comprehension which had no longer room or need for surprise, or an infinite regress of discovery—surely none of these could ever satisfy. The first work of explanation is, it is true, to render the mysterious commonplace; but it goes on to render the commonplace mysterious; and its work is unfinished so long as we feel that we know anything whatsoever. And only then, in knowing our total ignorance, do we overcome it.

Notoriously it takes a lifetime of study to persuade us that we know nothing to speak of. And the mystics confirm and round off this conclusion, asserting that perfect knowledge of the object of highest rank is knowing that it is perfectly incomprehensible. Now just as, at lower hierarchical levels, I take the conditions of knowing to be of the essence of the known, so here, at the apex, I take this paradox of mystical experience to be no illusion or accident, but to be (in some sense) true information about the object. That is to say, the Whole which is the perfection of knowledge is also the Centre which is the perfection of ignorance; and they are inseparable.

Atheists, then, grasp a good half of the truth, and I should not be surprised to learn that God counted Himself their perpetual president. The real atheism is the philosophy which talks as if it carried the Absolute in its brief-case, and the piety which has altogether got over its surprise. To find Him quite believable is no longer to believe in Him. For a Whole easily understood and approved, incapable of shocking and overwhelming us, cleaned up or watered down to suit our drawing-

THE WHOLE

room and prayer-meeting daintiness—such a Whole is not even a useful myth. When we are at our best are we not thankful that this glorious and terrible Reality is just what it is? The fact that it is mysterious beyond telling and altogether unlike our design for it—this is surely the very thing that makes it so adorable. In Hell we know and are known only too well, and are all expert theologians and psychologists; but in Heaven we never begin to recover from our astonishment at one another, and therefore boredom is unknown. Knowledge that is only knowledge is the very abyss of ignorance.

*5. The Whole as the perfect individual*

In distinguishing creatures of integral status from mesoforms, I have had before me an ideal individual—one who is indivisible, independent, self-determining, all-inclusive, one, unique, permanent. It is now plain that I have had the Whole in mind all along—the only one which has no limiting environment, the all-embracing unity which thinker and scientist and mystic all presuppose in one way or another. And in so far as anyone approaches individuality, he is assimilated to the life of the Whole—his sympathy takes in all creatures; he is beyond the reach of accident, because all that happens to him is made internal and intentional; he is free from all self-will.

But once more the contradiction is inescapable. When we reach Him there is only Himself, and His proof is our disproof. It is only by complete loss of individuality, by reduction to nothing, that the great saint can become the vehicle of the Whole which is the perfect individual. There is no way up from the penultimate levels to the highest, except through the lowest; for the Whole is not the last step of a long climb, or the extrapolation of a curve marked out by an ascending hierarchy of parts. It does not merely perfect such individuality as may be seen in lesser beings: but also annuls it. For the supreme and only true individual, without limiting background or opposition, can in no ordinary sense be an individual at all. It supersedes all that it perfects, crowning each hierarchical tendency by reuniting it with the base.

*6. The Omnipresence of the Whole*

The all-inclusive Whole, deprived of social life by its very success in that field, and so deprived of all intellectual and moral and aesthetic activity, reverts to its *alter ego*, the Centre, where it is reborn as the Other, as 'Thou' and not 'I'. Having vanished on completion, it is now completed on vanishing; and completed, moreover, in every Centre. The supreme individual is itself because it is also its own absolute opposite; it lives the highest life because it dies the deepest death; it is the one and only One because it is reborn, complete, in every minutest part everywhere and at all times. Claiming nothing, it owns everything; knowing nothing, it is all-wise; loving all but itself, it is infinitely lovable. What is more than nothing is too big to contain the Whole.

And so for me the supreme hierarchical individual is like the others in this respect, that its home is not over there in itself, but —tremendous fact!—here at this Centre where I am nothing. The great difference is that whereas I send every other to its own region far or near, the Whole has no particular region: its Centres lie everywhere. Thus my zonal system is completed in a summary and revolutionary manner—what was to have been its boundary becomes the whole system, and its most exalted inhabitant claims every inhabitant's Centre. At this level projection is universal, and the law which makes hierarchical status proportional to range no longer holds good. In other language, all things when clearly seen are theophanies.

A man is a man because he has come to omnipresence throughout a human body, so that to hurt any part of it is to hurt him. Similarly the Whole is the Whole because for it every part is labelled *myself* and *here*. But this does not mean that I can by hierarchical growth come to the omnipresence of the Whole; for the growth of my presence in ever vaster bodies is matched by the growth of my absence from their ever vaster environments, and the not-self more than keeps pace with the self. In the end, the only way up to the one-Centred omnipresence is the way down to the many-Centred omniabsence.

## 7. *The Whole as spaceless and bodiless*

I am a salt-grain dissolving in the space-time sea, but all of it tastes of me for ever. The shift of my eye as I write these words does not leave the mountains of the Moon what they were, and changes the destiny of the furthest spiral. In the last resort it is a function of the Whole, directed upon the Whole. For the whole of any deed or thing is the Whole. The question remains:

to what level do I refer the deed? If I were consistent, and applied to myself the rules I apply to the universe, I should credit the prongs of my fork with the levitation of my meat, my tongue with grammar, my eyebrows with surprise, and the iridium tip of my pen with the authorship of this paragraph. But I am inconsistent. Sometimes I mistake the hierarchical underling for his master; sometimes I suppose the master has other hands than the underling's. Rarely do I see that all action is by the Whole, through the hierarchy of parts.

The Whole is that Body of which all bodies are only the amputated organs; it is our total physique, the only organism which truly lives, and which must appear when to any pseudo-organism are added all things that it needs to be itself.

It is also nothing of the sort. For the Whole's completion in space is its translation out of space, its collapse to the Centre. The ideal and only entire body is no body at all, seeing that a body must have an environment. Body is for another, and there is no other. All space is no space. Yet this comes as no surprise: just as a man is one who has removed a human body from the physical realm, reducing it to nothing, so the Whole dissolves the total Body, turning it into that Central Mind which is the empty receptacle of all other bodies. In the Whole, complete embodiment and disembodiment are united.

## 8. The Whole as timeless

In a later chapter I shall describe the Whole as that Event which includes all other events. Here it is enough to notice, firstly, that no matter how many worlds a finite being may call *here*, and how many ages he may call this age or *now*, he always finds himself in spatio-temporal surroundings; and, secondly, that the Whole, which finally absorbs these surroundings, abolishes not only space but time also. Thus time, like all else, cannot outlive its own perfecting: when made altogether present it is timeless. The all-time of the Whole becomes the no-time of the Centre.

## 9. The Whole and truth

The course of this inquiry, so far, illustrates the rule that to seek the truth about anything is to seek the whole of it, which is the Whole. To know the lower members of the hierarchy is to see them in ever wider settings, and this is to climb the hier-

THE WHOLE

archy. In a sense, therefore, the higher levels are the truth about the lower. Yet adequate knowledge of the lower levels is impossible, for they are the product of inadequate knowledge, and to know them as they are a certain stupidity or blindness is needed—of every level short of the highest we can know too much. On the other hand, in so far as our knowledge of anything is complete, it is knowledge of the Whole which can never be incompletely known. As himself a man is nothing; as imperfectly estimated by his fellow man he is a man; as perfectly estimated by the Whole he is the locus of the Whole.

Accordingly the question is not whether, but at what level, a doctrine of man and the universe is true. The philosophy of hierarchy can afford to dismiss no other philosophy, but must see each as a proper function of its chosen plane. Thus to try to reduce the metaphysics of the upper layers to the physics of the lower—or to insist that we must be either idealists or else realists, spiritualists or else materialists, theists or else atheists—is to deny the stratification of the universe and to grope our way along a single seam. The final truth belongs to all strata together, as they are comprehended in the uppermost.

I have already given several instances of the law that the intellectual light which illuminates the middle levels of the hierarchy shines down from the higher levels. In fact, its source is the very apex. Thus theology is the forerunner which prepares the way for philosophy and for all the sciences: the ideas of nature and cosmic order, of freedom and necessity, of personality, and very much else, derive from our historical preoccupation with the divine. Human love itself came down from Heaven. It is not that the gods are anthropomorphic, but rather that man is theomorphic—we known him through them. The visions of Newton and Einstein contribute to the beatific vision, but only because they are, as a matter of fact, its fission-products.

But that light, of which the hierarchy is the graduated dispersion, is also thick darkness. For while the particles of the Whole are real, and their apprehensions are true, in so far as they conform to one another, the Whole itself conforms to nothing, and there is no reason either for it to be or for it to be what it is. At this level, where all partial truths converge upon the whole truth, the criterion of truth no longer holds good. The highest reason of the Whole is here united with the deepest unreason of the Centre. The ultimate lucidity is the ultimate obscurity.

## 10. The Whole and goodness

The idea of the Whole as an absolutely coherent system of fact is implicit in all our thinking. In the same manner, the idea of the Whole as a transcendent moral order is implicit in all our practical life. The hierarchy is a truly catholic church in which devotion instantly earns preferment. It is a moral structure, for its architectonic principle is the self-sacrifice which refuses to prefer this Centre to certain others; and its pinnacle is the self-sacrifice which refuses to prefer this Centre to *any* other, which refuses to separate itself from any creature whatsoever. It is this divine goodness which causes all things to cohere, which makes the world go round, and which ensures that there is any world at all.

And just as science is heavenly before it is earthly, so the religion of the gods precedes and inspires the conscious morality of man. In the great early cultures the social order is regulated at every point by the order of heaven, to which it is altogether subordinate: the real law-giver, ruler, general, and judge, is the god. Our morality, our laws, and indeed our entire social heritage, have heavenly origins, and it is a pressing question how much can survive once that connection is altogether severed. Such goodness as men have belongs to the levels where they are not men. The merely human is subhuman.

And only the Whole is wholly good. Yet once more it is impossible to treat the Whole as if it were simply the completion of the parts, instead of a being of an utterly different order. For my goodness lies, not in having shifted Centre and thereby grown, but in the act of shifting, in the disinterested adoption of another's interests at the risk of mine—the fact that, ultimately, my own interests include his and everyone else's is an irrelevance which must not enter into my reckoning if it is to have any virtue. But at the level of the Whole no further Centres are left: all have been taken in and unified. There is no other on whose behalf the self may be sacrificed. Nor may the Whole take itself as object: for this would be, first, to duplicate the One; and, second, to practise egoism on the grandest scale. In fact, however, the Whole is also the Centre. It performs no ordinary act of self-surrender, but an absolute self-sacrifice. As befits the perfectly good, it shifts Centre to every Centre, descending the hierarchy by every route to the very base, where it enjoys itself only as wholly other than itself.

## 11. The Whole and beauty

The pursuit of truth and of goodness leads in the direction of the Whole; but without beauty the truth becomes solemn, ponderous, dreary; and goodness becomes joyless and over-earnest. Lightness of touch, spontaneity, gaiety, even abandon, are needed if the saint and the sage are to avoid taking on an ugly appearance, not to say an evil one. And indeed the universe does not look like the product of a logician, or a works-manager, and still less like the work of a priest; but much more like that of an artist who is well aware of the value of nonsense, of play, and of a superbly bountiful imagination. In Hell we are all admirably practical and down-to-earth; we do not find life fun, but take it and ourselves very seriously. But I suspect that all Heaven is light-hearted and merry, that the skies are one broad smile, and the blessed galaxies are even now shaking their fiery manes with laughter, while Satan is profoundly shocked at their lack of gravity and earnest common sense.

Doubtless the beauty of a work of art is indefinable, but it involves richness and wholeness—some works failing because of the poverty of their content, others because their content is imperfectly integrated. Now the Whole, which comprehends the maximum of detail in the strictest unity, has at least the makings of the sublimest work of art; and that is what, indeed, I feel it to be on those occasions when I seem to be most attentive to it. But there is a third quality which then chiefly impresses me: namely its compelling otherness, its surprisingness, the wonder and improbability of it all. For just as the truth I know is always the truth about another, and the goodness I admire can never be mine, so also the beauty I enjoy comes to me from beyond myself. And, in general, it is the artist's experience that he discovers rather than invents. The suggestion, then, is that the Whole is precluded from enjoying itself as beautiful—even if there were some way round the difficulty that the Whole as the supreme work of art is unconscious, while the Whole as the supreme artist has no materials on which to work. Once more, then, we must think of the Whole as reverting to the Centre, where the supremely lovely object is altogether external to the subject.

## 12. The Whole's descent

It is clear that, however we reach up towards the Whole, we find ourselves involved in a downward movement to the Centre. Let me add a few instances.

We find it to be a condition of living knowledge that it will not keep, that it must be periodically unlearned and relearned; of genuine goodness that it is no mere habit, but is newly arrived at in face of temptation; of real beauty that it should be re-created out of chaos, and enjoyed as if for the first time. For us, then, the assertion of values is inseparable from their denial. And if we take this experience seriously, the presumption is that the values are not themselves at the highest level unless they are linked with their total undoing at the lowest.

Moreover the perfection of the Whole is, by itself, a kind of limitation: for notoriously goodness loses much when it is too obvious, and he is not wise who is only wise, and beauty gains by being hid. If our most compelling intuitions are any guide here, then the greatest and best is also the humblest; and the wisest has childlike simplicity; and the most beautiful (if it is to escape mere prettiness) cannot spare the discord of which it is the resolution. In short, the perfection of the highest requires that it becomes also the lowest.

Again, the Whole as perfect goodness cannot be dissociated from any goodness whatever its level; as perfect wisdom, cannot be ignorant of any event; as perfect beauty, cannot fail to inspire and enjoy all beauty no matter how humble its rank. Thus hierarchical procedure is in the end countermanded, and the Whole is firstly itself at the apex of the pyramid; and secondly its own opposite at the base; and thirdly all that lies between—not taken piece by piece in its immense failure and imperfection, but as united to and completed at the ultimate levels.

The Whole lacks nothing. But even the Godhead needs a photosphere to shine, feathers to fly, legs to walk our earth, fins to swim. Every setting-board is a Calvary, every collector's pin a crucifier's nail. Every dust-grain, every electron and proton, every point-instant, is Bethlehem; every nest the manger-cradle; every womb Mary's. The path of the One who comes down passes through our zoological gardens and physical laboratories no less than our churches. Yet the completeness of His descent into matter is the guaranty that He is immeasurably beyond and above it.

## 13. The evidence of mysticism

If the mystic's progress is hierarchical, and his goal is in any sense a sharing in the divine, then we may look to his account of that goal for light upon the divine nature. And his report is that his outward journey through zones of light and darkness ends, not in the longed-for beatific vision, but in the darkest night of the soul. His quest has failed. He is thrust back to the very beginning. Instead of the enjoyment of God, a virtual atheism; instead of the Whole, the Centre. And this state of utter emptiness is the condition of the final phase of union, when, having ceased to be interested in his own spiritual welfare, he is content to be nothing for the sake of the divine object. Now he returns to serve self-forgetfully all creatures, and to demonstrate to us that the divine is not other than this commonplace world seen in its full hierarchical setting.

Thus the mystic's experience offers empirical confirmation that the most exalted level is also the lowest, and the entire hierarchy. And he witnesses not only to the union of these three main hierarchical aspects or stages, but also to the union of the three main ways that link them—the way of thought and devotion to the true, of works and devotion to the good, of art and devotion to the beautiful. For while each of us is naturally fitted for one or another of these three approaches (which may be called the cognitive, the conative, and the affective), there is much to show that none of us can go very far along any of them by itself. (Truth without goodness or beauty leads to the H-bomb and the industrial slum; goodness without truth or beauty to the faggot and the rack, the tin tabernacle and the plaster image; beauty without goodness or truth to the madder kind of surrealism. Every value is devalued without the others.)

The great mystic, it would seem, has come to the place where all three roads join: he has in some degree overcome the trifurcation of the values, and glimpsed a realm where the true and the good are no longer hopelessly discrepant, and both are altogether lovely. And, once more, if we are to believe his story, it is not so much *his* story as that of the life which the Whole lives in him at the Centre.

# THE WHOLE

(i) *The doctrine of the Trinity.* Of the several interpretations of trinitarian doctrine, one of the most notable is that which turns on the social nature of consciousness. The Father is the subject and origin of the Deity's procession; the Son is His eternally begotten image and the object of His love; the Spirit is the vinculum of their mutual loving knowledge. Yet all three are of one undivided essence. Thus God finds His only appropriate Object, yet without that self-occupation and self-love which would be no more admirable in Him than they are in us.

(ii) *The doctrine of the Incarnation.* Christianity and embryology together imply that the Godhead was in the space of nine months incarnate at every biological level from the amoeboid to the simian, and was man, and died again into the regions below man. In traditional language, God comes down in the Son, empties Himself, dies, and descends into the realms of death and Hell. And it is by virtue of this complete and perfect sacrifice that man is saved, and becomes capable of union with God. For the Son who comes down to the base of the hierarchy to die in and for us, is also born in us, and rises again to the Father, taking with Him many sons who are all one in Him.

(iii) *Doctrines of the relationship of God, man, and the universe.* Through the Son, also, all things were created, from the highest angelic ranks downwards; and by Him they cohere and are upheld continually. And theologians have, on the whole, taught that the process of creation and upholding on the one hand, and of redemption on the other, are along the same lines. Further, it has been widely held that the cosmic and redemptive activity of the Son is an essential element in the life of the Trinity, which completes itself in all grades of finite beings—beings that are thus organically involved in the divine nature. The present reaction against this teaching of God's need of His universe takes the form of renewed insistence on His absolute ineffability and independence of all creatures: a Deity that in any way relies on me, that does not humble me to the dust, that is not utterly above and beyond me, can never meet my religious needs.

About this there can be no doubt—that the creature, who is

nothing in himself, cannot claim to have anything to offer to his Creator, or any contribution to make to the divine life; and if that life is born in this empty receptacle it is certainly not because of the receptacle's worthiness. Nor can we claim even the merit of self-annihilation: it is not primarily the creature, but the Creator, who goes down to the lowest level of all. The small and the great are only themselves, but the smallest and the greatest are each other. It is not man, but the infinitesimal in him, which contains the infinite, for he is much too godlike to tolerate God. In the middle of the hierarchy, he is furthest of all creatures from the divine extremities that meet.

Four 'descents', then, may be distinguished: (1) the internal procession of the Trinity, whereby one Person is emptied of Himself for the sake of the Other; (2) the creation of the many-levelled universe, and the maintenance of its upward and downward processes; (3) the redemptive down-coming and ascension of the Son; (4) the religious life in which the worshipper, through the realization of his utter unworthiness, of his nothingness, receives by grace the gift of God Himself.

Here are four variations on that theme of dying to live which is the topic of this chapter—four ascents-descents which may not be confused. But neither may they be separated. It is *one* Word who (1) was God and was with God, and (2) made all things, and (3) was made flesh, and (4) lighteth every man.

# PART THREE

CHAPTER XIII

# The Law of Hierarchical Symmetry

*1. Hierarchical Pairs*

W hat am I? In this chapter and the next I bring together the various regional views collected by the
receding observer in Part II, and combine them in a
spatial self-portrait, before going on in Part IV to add the time
dimension.

Science offers me a huge mass of piecemeal information about
my nature level by level; but the work of making sense of it by
relating the levels has scarcely begun. The laws of hierarchical
order, the vertical go of things, the kind of connections between
levels that departmentalized science now finds at each level—
these are the work of the unitary science of the future. Here I
can only make a beginning.

To start with, let me set down the twelve hierarchical orders
which the previous chapters have disclosed:

|  | Whole | Centre |  |
| Superior Series | Galaxy (Nebula) | electron (etc.) | Inferior Series |
|  | Sun (Star) | atom |  |
|  | Earth (Planet) | molecule |  |
|  | Life (Geosphere) | cell |  |
|  | Humanity (Species) | man |  |

The following paragraphs are devoted to the evidence for and
the significance of this grouping into six hierarchical Pairs.

*2. The 'GCM' and the 'LCM'*

If I take from my regions a collection of physical objects, and
discover (i) what is (so to say) their 'greatest common measure',
the *highest* unit of integral status of which they are all composed;
and (ii) their 'least common multiple', the *lowest* unit of integral

status of which they are all either components or instances; I shall nearly always find that (i) is the inferior member, and (ii) is the superior member, of one or another of the six hierarchical Pairs. For instance, if I take this hand, my dog, the flowers on the table, and the fly on the window-pane, their GCM is the cell, and their LCM Life; if I take this hand, and pen, and paper,

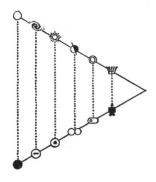

and ink, the relevant Pair is Earth-molecule; and so on. In each case there is analysis, or hierarchical descent to find the inferior member of the Pair, linked with synthesis, or hierarchical ascent to find the superior member or common whole; and the lower the descent the higher the ascent. Hierarchical symmetry is preserved.

### 3. *Hierarchical Pairs and the classification of the sciences*

Though science is horizontally divided, it is certainly Paired. Thus the anthropological sciences (I mean sociology, psychology, political economy, etc.) take for their subject man-in-community. The biological sciences have for basic hierarchical unit the cell; but palaeontology and embryology and ecology point to the real wholeness of Life, and may even hint that to separate the maximum and minimum biological units—Life and the cell—is as misleading as to separate Humanity from man. Again, molecules need to be studied in relation to their terrestrial environment, and the geologist must be something of a chemist. And clearly the science of the biggest things, of stars and galaxies, is now thoroughly involved with the science of the smallest; so that, for example, the study of the stars is, very largely, the study of their atoms. As for the ultimate Pair,

the Whole and the Centre, the previous chapter is an essay on
the impossibility of divorcing them.

Moreover the history of science witnesses, not only to the fact
of the Pairs, but also to their order. The divine science of the
ultimate Pair was the preoccupation of the Middle Ages; the
foundations of physics and astronomy were laid in the seventeenth century, of chemistry and geology in the eighteenth and
early nineteenth, of psychology and sociology in the late nine-

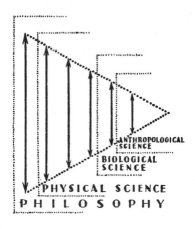

teenth and early twentieth century. And this order of appearance is the order of dependence: the later sciences of the middle
levels have for background the earlier sciences of the more
extreme levels. Theology and philosophy were the prerequisite
of natural science, and though their special province is always
the ultimate Pair, it includes all the subordinate Pairs; similarly,
physical science precedes biological science and includes it, as
biological science precedes and includes the anthropological.

It must be added that, by thus detaching the later Pairs from
the earlier, we progressively empty the earlier of their proper
filling and concreteness, leaving such bare abstractions as a
mindless physical universe and an Earth from which every sign
of life has been excised. And, so treated, the superior members
of the Pairs are in most respects degraded to the rank of their
inferior counterparts; and it is as if the scientist recognized only
the lower half of the hierarchy. His solar system is as far below
man as the Sun is above him.

*4. Genetic Pairs*

The evolution of the sciences roughly recapitulates evolution at large, which proceeds by Pairs—Pairs whose superior and inferior members are coeval, emerging and developing together. That the human species and the human individual arose and advanced, not as two things, but as two aspects of one thing, is plain enough. Life and the cell stand in a similar relationship: Life is the original 'cell' with all its branches, and the cell is embryonic Life surviving throughout Life's maturity as Life's basis. Again, the molecule is coeval with the planet, for it is only when our star exfoliates into a solar system that there occur in it temperatures low enough for the synthesis of a great variety of molecules. And as our molecules are essentially terrestrial, so our atoms are essentially solar—stars are nature's atomic piles. As for the galaxies, it is a plausible guess that each begins as a cloud of subatomic particles, and that the differentiation of the whole into stars synchronizes with the integration of the parts into atoms of the simplest kinds. Finally, it is at least interesting that Christian tradition should complete the story by saying that the universe was created out of nothing.

In short, there can be little doubt, first, that our history is an hierarchical descent from the most inclusive by means of differentiation, united to an hierarchical ascent from the least inclusive by means of integration; and, second, that the earlier stages of this twofold converging movement remain as the necessary background of the later.

*5. Hierarchical Pairs and structure*

There can be no question of reducing to any neat pattern the immense variety of hierarchical embodiments, each of which must be studied for itself at its own level. Nevertheless if the superior and inferior members of a Pair are very closely related, or are even two aspects of one thing, then it would be natural to look for some similarity in their structure. And in fact we find enough similarity to add further confirmation to the schema of hierarchical Pairs, and to suggest that in future the members of a Pair may reasonably be expected to illuminate each other's nature in many new ways. Thus the members of the ultimate Pair, as a case of the meeting of extremes, are at least sufficiently alike to make plausible the recurrent heresy that they are identical. Again, the atom is notoriously like a solar system. And as for the human individual and human society, their resemblance is sufficient to have produced a literature and a vocabulary.

(In addition, structure at each level tends to reproduce that of the hierarchy as a whole. For instance, Earth's interior is linked with the lower grades, her surface with the middle grades, her atmosphere with the higher grades: she is the whole regional system in miniature. The annular structure of the solar system is in some ways the reverse of this model: here remoteness means privation. Again, in the structure of the human body, the physically high is apt to be the biologically advanced. In short, it is as if each level were needed to show forth uniquely some feature of the whole system of levels.)

## 6. Subordination in the hierarchy

Even more marked than such likenesses is the growing contrast between the members of a Pair. The more exalted the superior aspect, the humbler the inferior, so that always a kind of balance or symmetry is preserved. We respect this symmetry when, to render an object intelligible, we break it down into a descending series of parts (a,a,a, and b,b,b, and so on) which

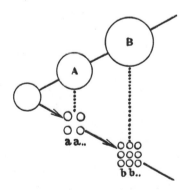

are linked with an ascending series of wholes (A, B, and so on) till, in the limit, the analysis of the object into its ultimate constituents coincides with its assimilation to the Whole. Always hierarchical growth and ungrowth are Paired. In laying claim to our ever smaller parts, we take on their ever larger worlds, and it is when we are least that we are at our most extensive.

There are further complications. The hierarchy may be

thought of as a social system in which subordination is three-fold. An inferior unit is firstly subject to the Whole, secondly to the superior member of its Pair, thirdly to its immediate superior of the next hierarchical grade; similarly, a superior unit is firstly a society within the total society, secondly a society whose members are the inferior units of the Pair, thirdly a society whose members are its own immediate hierarchical inferiors. And so there is a universal plurality of membership, emerging at some levels as a conflict of loyalties, in terms of which it is possible to account for a great variety of observed facts. For example, many tragic and creative complexities of a man's life arise from his treble allegiance to the Whole, to Humanity, and to the State, in that order. And supposing the result should be that the State hangs him, then the Earth-allegiance (or 'weight') of his molecules takes precedence over (and ends) their cell-allegiance, while their allegiance to the Whole is in no way threatened. Indeed a human being is a nest of Trojan horses.

## 7. *The Pairs and hierarchical process*

It takes the entire circumambient universe, from the realm of the nebulae to the realm of the borough council, to rule and maintain this little body. So far, I have described the two-way radial processes of my regions as though they traversed all the regions in turn, without taking any short cuts. But plainly there is much by-passing, and it goes on between the superior and inferior members of a Pair. The infrahuman world within is always conversing over our heads with the suprahuman world without, and it is only as men and animals that we ignore our stars. In other words, nothing is outgrown: the vertical processes uniting the members of earlier Pairs continue to play their part behind those which unite the members of later Pairs. Indeed it is rare for a train of events in my greater body to emerge at the human level, instead of remaining at the Paired physical or biological levels.

How we describe these vertical Paired processes depends upon which Pair we take for our model. It is easiest to talk in terms of energy exchange. If the superior member is looked on as an energy system whose components are the inferior members, then their joint history is a tale of the passage of energy upwards from the components to the whole and then down again to them. In more detail, four phases may be discerned: (i) the upward phase of energy-releasing integration; (ii) the downward phase of energy-absorbing integration; (iii) the upward phase of energy-releasing disintegration; (iv) the downward phase of energy-absorbing disintegration. Whether we consider the atom adding to itself new particles in the star, or the molecule taking on other molecules in the planet, or cells multiplying in the biosphere, or men building up organizations of all kinds in Humanity: in all cases the general rule is that growth up to a certain point of complexity releases energy into the field (energy passing up from the inferior members to the superior), and beyond that point absorbs energy (energy passing down again), till size and instability reach their limit. In the phase of breakdown which follows, the energies taken in during the second phase are released, but disintegration beyond a certain point again absorbs

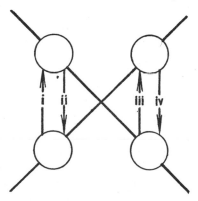

energy from the field. To speak in terms of human organizations, the four phases may be described as: (i) the consolidation of scattered workers, resulting in economies, increased effectiveness, and growth; (ii) over-centralization, with further uneconomical increase of staff, instability, and external ineffectiveness; (iii) decentralization, with release of the redundant staff acquired in (ii), and restored effectiveness; (iv) further dispersal beyond the economic limit, resulting in the need for new staff, and in renewed ineffectiveness. Briefly, the inferior members of the Pair (i) grow and give, (ii) grow and take, (iii) ungrow and give, (iv) ungrow and take; and throughout they give to and take from the superior member.

Fully to illustrate and to qualify these remarks, and to defend this theory of Paired processes, would need a book to itself, and

I touch on the subject here only as an example of the kind of work which a truly hierarchical science, regulated by the principle of the Pairs, would undertake.

## 8. Macrocosm and microcosm

As man, I bisect all the Pairs and their linking processes, for I include inferior members of every Pair, but am included in the superior member. I am at home in the upper half of the hierarchy because I am the lower half. To use more familiar language, man the microcosm reflects the macrocosm—a doctrine which, in its many forms, is as ancient as it is universal. And it is generally implied that man's business is to recognize and restore the links between what is above and what is below, between the universe without and the universe within. That is to say, while man is man because he cuts the hierarchy in half, his office is to heal that wound, to restore the unity of the Pairs, and so to realize himself as much more and much less than man. His task is to re-seat the suprahuman rider on the infrahuman horse, to join ruler and ruled, to realize that the ancestral cave and the ancestral mountain imply each other, to link the nine circles of Hell with the nine circles of Heaven, to reunite the rising branches of the universe-tree with its deepening roots—and so to regain his own balance. The common-sensible part-man who is only human, and the scientific part-man who finds himself only in the bottom half of the hierarchy, and the religious part-man who finds himself only in the top half—all three need to be conjoined in the symmetrical and vertical man who is whole because his universe is whole. Such, more or less, is the suggestion of a long esoteric tradition, of the experience of mystics and poets in every time and country, and of much psychological analysis.

Most of the world's great arguments are between those who stand for the inferior series and those who stand for the superior; and they can only be settled by those who stand for both in their opposition-in-unity. The doctrine of Pairs is a political safeguard and a philosophical eirenicon no less than a health-recipe. In every way we should do better to stay half-way up the hierarchical ladder than to try to climb any higher without descending, or to descend without climbing.

Sometimes the two movements plainly come to the same thing. Do we not enjoy moods of unquestionable power and authenticity when we are nearer to the child than to the man, to trees and grass than to the child, to earth and sea and sky than to any living thing, and when it is clear that our descent into 'matter' is not other than our ascent to 'spirit'?

## 9. The trinitarian Pairs

Each successive Pair, with the upward and downward processes that unite the two poles, is a finite, less-holy trinity, a decreasingly adequate version of the ultimate Pair. Man is not to be pitied or wondered at for making a god of Mankind, of Life or the spirit of fertility, of Earth and Sun and the starry heaven, for each of these is in its way a transcendent god the father, whose son comes down and is born in and among us, and in the ministrations of whose spirit—uniting father and son in manifold bonds—we all share. The entire structure of the hierarchy is trinitarian, and all its processes are, in the last resort, trinitarian processions. The annual dying and rebirth of the Earth Mother, and the daily down-going and ascension of the Sun on our behalf, are no outworn superstitions; and indeed, so long as the religion of the ultimate Pair leaves out the religion of the lesser Pairs, it is thin and abstract and unsatisfying.

Now just as the members of the ultimate Pair may be thought of as a self and a not-self which are always changing places, which are subject to the law of elsewhereness, so also may the members of the other Pairs. There is a sense in which, through us, the inferior member contemplates itself as the superior, and the superior as the inferior: the bird's-eye view is of the worm, the worm's of the bird—the *uccello di Dio*. Thus the great make us feel small, and the heavenly hierarchy wears down all our pretensions. It is no accident that the sky's population shows itself to us only in the dark. Conversely, the scientist rises in status as his subject-matter descends: his knowledge is more exact and thorough, his control is more certain, his view is more dispassionate, as he studies units of lower and lower rank. The loftier and bulkier his suprahuman trunk the finer his infrahuman hands as he stoops to finger ever more discriminatingly the dust of the universe's floor.

In short, the relation of subject to object is threefold—a symmetrical relation of equals; a Paired relation, in which suprahuman contemplates infrahuman, and *vice versa*; and an absolutely asymmetrical relation, in which subject is nothing but room for object. To neglect any of the three is to misunderstand the others.

## 10. Analysis and synthesis

In religion the infrahuman seeks its suprahuman counterpart; in science the suprahuman seeks its infrahuman counterpart; and their joint business is the self-consciousness of the Pairs in their living unity. But for us now the scientific attitude is altogether dominant; and the science whose function and knowledge are suprahuman is directed wholly upon the infrahuman, and is incapable of recognizing anything else. For directly science sees itself as the most important function of its infrahuman subject matter, it raises that subject matter to its own suprahuman position and takes its place below: in short, it becomes a species of theology. Science is thus essentially unconscious of itself in particular, and of the suprahuman in general. Its proper business is accordingly to interpret the higher always in terms of the lower, the whole in terms of the part. To make intelligible is, for science, to degrade in rank; and, ideally, to reduce everything to nothing at the Centre. Reality in the twentieth century is inversely proportional to hierarchical status.

We can believe in electrons that contrive a God, but not in a God that contrives electrons. And then, if you please, we call religious dogmas fantastic—as if, compared with us, Athanasius were not a hard-bitten sceptic! As if an accidental collocation of atoms, eloquently and learnedly describing itself as such, were not a stranger god than any Mumbo Jumbo! Explanation is our polite term for cosmic trunk-murder; but the smaller the dismembered part the less it comprehends the whole or is itself comprehensible—until we reach the absolutely incomprehensible Centre which comprehends all.

Here, indeed, is our current mysticism, the mysticism of the Centre. Our materialism applies only to the upper half of the hierarchy: the gods have come down into the lower half—and the higher the father the lower his descent in the son. The hierarchy stands precariously on its head. We are still Sun-worshippers, serving that deity with fanatical and horrible rites, only our Sun Father turns to us his inferior side—the atom; we have not ceased to revere the Earth Mother, but in miniature, as the molecule mother; and the cell is our modern fertility-god. We turn with relief from the Blessed Trinity, only to find ourselves trembling and prostrate before the Damned Trinity of Proton and Electron and Neutron—Lucifer's three faces—with all their fearful processions. Neither can we dethrone the Godhead that crowns the hierarchy, without gradually rediscovering It at the base, in the holy of holies of the physical substratum. In the end, what religion found at the Circumference science begins to find at the Centre. Wonder has moved down the hierarchy, and where wonder goes religion must follow. Spirit falls into matter, while matter rises and overwhelms spirit. Our universe has indeed come to its fourteenth of July.

## 11. Hierarchical Pairs and the reversible regions—evolution and emanation

Thus the regions are in some respects reversible, and the schema takes two complementary forms—the now familiar concentric system with the Whole at the circumference; and this system inside-out, with the Whole at the centre. And in fact the many rival cosmogonies may be divided into one or other of these two types—the evolutionary, which gives priority to the lowest; and the emanative, which gives it to the highest. According to the former, status grows with range, and the retiring observer makes more and more of the object as he recedes; according to the latter, status falls off with range, till the observer comes to the region of outer darkness and nothingness. And according to both, the region of man is half-way. There are for him, then, two paths to the Whole—the way in to the immanent Whole, and the way out to the transcendent Whole —yet these are not so much two paths as two descriptions of one path. For instance, his pre-scientific question *why?* demanding suprahuman explanations, and his scientific question *how?* demanding infrahuman explanations, are half-questions that can be answered only by uniting them in a movement at once centrifugal and centripetal.

Here, in fact, is the primal source and instance of the law of elsewhereness: wherever the Whole is located it absconds; it is not content to stay wrapped up in itself, but is projected to the limit, giving rise on the way to all 'range' and all regions. The sublimely remote transcendent Deity can mean nothing to man if it finds no lodgement in his inmost heart; and the Deity that is thus born in him is no Deity if it is his own, and is not referred to a wholly external source. In other words, the Paired constitution of the hierarchy is such that, in so far as the religion of immanence and of transcendence do not involve each other, they are not religion at all. The Centre of my regions is the very fundament of Hell by itself, yet Heaven when it is Paired with their Circumference.

A classical myth concludes this chapter for me. The divine soul-spark, on its way down from heaven to earth through the seven planetary spheres, becomes coated in each (as in an electro-plating vat) with a different metal—for instance, iron in Mars, copper in Venus, quicksilver in Mercury—so that, when at last it arrives at the centre, its own seven layers reverse those of the surrounding universe. Thus I am my well-lined garment the world, shrunken and turned inside out. I am the universe written small and backwards, but I can read neither book without reading both.

# CHAPTER XIV

# The Organization of the Hierarchy

## *1. The discovery of vertical man in horizontal man*

I f the hierarchy is our Everest, Humanity is our base camp. And we set out to explore in two ways: firstly, by means of the science and art and religion whose task is deliberately to send expeditions from the human level to other levels; and secondly, by examination of the human level itself, as offering the most accessible (though certainly not the most lucid) sample of hierarchical process—the sample that emerges for our immediate inspection, the inside information that is ourselves. Not to make full use of this sample would be absurd. Moreover, once we attend even to our most commonplace experience, we find that it is far from being merely human, but gives direct access to many other hierarchical levels. The best clues are under my nose, and the discovery of what I am lies in the reinterpretation of the ordinary rather than the detection of the extraordinary. Here, in the despised commonplace, is hidden the key of the hierarchical kingdom. Let me give four instances.

(i) *Physical.* Man has first-hand knowledge of what it is like to be a mechanical contrivance, to push and pull, to resist and give way, to feel energetic and tired, hot and cold. And it is from this direct experience that he arrives at his notions of materiality, causation, motion, work, force, heat. As he prolongs his limbs by artificial growth into the world, so also he prolongs the feelings of muscular exertion, fatigue, and the like, that occur in them; and without this double extension—this truly psycho-physical growth—there would be no physical science. (The fact that the science of physical things eventually manages to leave out of its descriptions all reference to forces, matter, and so on, does not lessen its dependence upon our direct awareness of ourselves as physical things.)

(ii) *Biological*. Man knows what it is to grow (in certain limited respects) as he wants to grow; to strive against other creatures, winning and losing; to enter into all manner of relations with them. And it is this kind of direct insight into life at the biological level which is the ground of his biological science, the certificate of his competence.

(iii) *Human*. To be human is to use, generally without acknowledgement, a model of the universe which is either man or a mere part of him. He knows what it is to be a two-sided human being, and he is willing to grant similar experience to others of his own sex and class and race; and even (making allowances) to people who lack these qualifications. He may go further, and, taking all that he thinks best in himself, link it with an ascending series of suprahuman beings, or with one such being. Just as he finds his merely physical tendencies to be at home and embodied on the plane of the atom and the molecule, and his merely biological tendencies to be at home and embodied on the plane of primitive organisms, so he distributes his higher tendencies throughout suprahuman planes.

(iv) *Sociological*. Man knows what it is to co-operate with other men in the running of innumerable organizations from the State to the family; and he very properly takes these departments of nature's total organization, the branches which he manages himself, as his clue to the rest. The governmental and economic hierarchy shares the pattern of the universal hierarchy of heaven and earth. If you could take away all the arguments (overt and hidden, ancient and modern) which proceed from the social order to the cosmic, and from the cosmic order to the social, both would vanish for us; indeed the very word *cosmos* originally meant the discipline of the army and the hierarchy of the State.

In any case it would be foolish to ignore in our study of the hierarchy those parts of it for which we are admittedly responsible—those hierarchical processes which we know because our livelihood is to mind them. Yet their very obviousness puts us off. If Whitehall were a mysterious specimen with a Latin name and visible only under a powerful microscope, we should be impressed; but here is a piece of hierarchical nature too rich in information, too conveniently large-scale and wide open for inspection, to interest the naturalist. But this inquiry cannot afford to neglect such a clue.

We have, then, these four invaluable and trustworthy vehicles, which, when properly used, give direct access and do not rely on analogy: they do not explore the human level for hints about the others so much as carry us to them. They find vertical man in horizontal man. In fact, man models himself on the non-human rather than the non-human on himself—if he comes to see the universe in the light of man, it is because he has first seen man in the light of the universe. He is the mirror of his cosmos, and more theomorph than his gods are anthropomorphs. And in any case he only comes to full manhood by distributing himself throughout the hierarchy.

## 2. Hierarchical organization

So much for the theory of the method. I come now to a particular application.

In the cosmic organization I am an official of middle rank, having above me at least six superiors of mounting status, and below me at least five grades of subordinates whose numbers increase as their status decreases. But I do not meet these officials. It is as if I were confined to my desk in my private office, which nobody may enter. This imprisonment in no way hampers me, however, for my subordinates pass up to me a continuous stream of reports on the situation in 'the outside world' so far as it is my business; while I hand down to them (as if through a trapdoor in the floor) my comments and decisions. When I find myself incompetent to deal with a case, I collate and comment upon the particulars before me, and then refer it to higher levels. And even when I make a decision of my own it is in accordance with the standing orders of my superiors.

Information from below and instructions from above somehow find their way on to my desk, and have there to be reconciled: that is my whole concern. How they arrive; how my instructions are carried out; the mode of working, and indeed the very existence, of my innumerable subordinates—these are matters which I seldom consider. But when I do so, I conclude that each official, whatever his grade, is in a position like mine; and that his duties are, first, to receive and co-ordinate and pass up the data presented from below; and second, to receive and apply and pass down his superior's instructions. The situation which is his concern is a stage of the upward process whereby more and more reports are unified, till the picture is complete at the highest level; and at the same time a stage of the downward process whereby the action decided at that level is analysed into its basic elements at the lowest level, so that it may there be put into effect. Divide to rule; unite to know why and what you rule.

But in fact there is no world beyond this pyramidal organization; and the situation which is presented in its completed state at the apex, and acted upon in its unmade state at the base, is an internal one. For at each level this situation is known as the

situation at that level; the hierarchy is nothing else than this rising synthesis of the information, and descending analysis of the decision. In particular, there sits in my windowless and doorless office no official: there is only his case or problem, and it is stated in terms of his fellow officials of the same rank. In a sense it is they, and not I, who inhabit my cubicle on the middle storey, as I inhabit theirs.

### 3. Hierarchical intercommunication

Yet it is only at the lowest level that interaction between equals can occur, and the official can open the door of his cubicle and communicate horizontally with his fellows. Elsewhere, all the proper channels run vertically between the official and his subordinates and superiors. To get into touch with a colleague of my own level, then, I must do so through our common superior on the floor above, and through our subordinate staff in the basement, where the barriers between us are removable. The office rule is that I may communicate with a functionary only through some common superior (perhaps the head of the organization) whose lowest subordinates include and so unite our own: for the extent of the horizontal communi-

cation between these subordinates is governed by the rank of their superior. Considered at their own basement level, they are innumerable and distinct; as serving the head on the top storey, they are all united; as serving intermediate officials, they respect the barriers between them.

The transactions of one level have to go through the clearing-house of the next. To put the matter another way, it is easier to get into touch with 'archangels' than your next-door neighbour, for only they can introduce you; in the last resort the heavens sponsor every meeting under heaven. But we have long forgotten what it is to live, on every star-lit night, under the very eyes of higher authority.

### 4. Higher authority

It is to no ordinary contrivance that we can hand over thousands of cups of tea and slices of bread and butter, with some vague directions about their walking and talking and playing the piano, and then forget all about them, in the confidence that we shall get back a man in action. How does it work, this man-producing apparatus which I am? Surely on no other hypothesis than the one I am putting forward in these picturesque terms can I make sense out of the psycho-physical facts—out of my nutrition and growth, my sense experience and responses, my diseases and autonomous complexes. Either I am a miracle of organization, or plain miracle. Here are tasks which, by reason of their indescribable complexity united to utter simplicity, call for a great hierarchy of functionaries attending each to his little problem, for the wholesale delegation of responsibility, for specialization, for the subdivision of effort under a single authority. If I could be turned into a large-scale engineering project and let out to contract, the firm which built and ran me would need to form an organization not unlike that which I now am, only with human officials instead of non-human.

Certainly I can take very little credit for the performance of this unthinkably intricate organization which I am. To an overwhelming extent it is run for me. And the mode of its control is by Pairs. I am obedient, not superficially, but at each depth of my being, to higher control. Thus each grade of my subordinates is subject, not only to me, and to its own immediate set of superiors, but also to the superior member of the Pair beyond me. Just as the head of any large human organization, who must lack many of the specialized skills of his staff, owes a great debt to their membership of institutions responsible for their past training and present conduct, so also do I owe the performance of my subordinates to the guidance of my superiors. I have no right to claim the first without acknowledging the second.

Yet in spite of the fact—or rather, because of the fact—that the hierarchy as a whole is authoritarian, a system of subordination, it is at each level equalitarian. One order is controlled only from another. No master cell, but the man, dominates my cells; no world dictator, but Humanity, dominates men. The true unifying principle is always at least one stage higher. This is no excuse for passivity on the one hand or anxiety on the other. The Western illusion is that all hangs on man; the Eastern that nothing hangs on man, who may rely on the measureless scope and power of the hierarchy's vertical processes to make and save him. But the well-conducted official neither (like the idiot) refers to his superiors all problems his staff cannot solve, nor (like the worried Jack in office) feels competent to solve them all himself.

5. *Promotion and demotion*

But if the foregoing account has in it any truth at all, it can have been compiled only by an official who has escaped from his locked cubicle, through the trapdoors in its floor and ceiling, and made his way to every floor of the building. And in fact, while I cannot give up my office in the middle storey, I am always either gaining temporary promotion or losing it. I have the run of the organization; and what settles my present status in it is the status of my work, the scope of the problem or situation with which I am now occupied.

In other words, man is the universe's messenger-boy, the cosmic go-between. He is the amphibian of the hierarchy, its flying fish, its diving bird, at home in every element. His anthropomorphism, well used, becomes a world-searching polymorphism; his human nature includes the ability to divest itself of human nature.

It is for this reason that foreign mind—the thoughts of other men and species and planets and stars—though opaque to me at its own level, is transparent at the next: more, it is my own. My Chinese neighbour and I are a mystery to each other, but as soon as one of us thinks for Humanity the other is thinking in him; the mind of the bee is inscrutable, yet without it I cannot take up Life's point of view; what the planetary intellect of Mars may be I do not know, except that I use it every time I look at the stars; what the stars' opinion of this star is I can only imagine, but I know what they all think of the Great Nebula in Andromeda. The law of elsewhereness—or what I might call the science of hierarchial ballistics—rules that our ordnance shall be one size bigger than the range of the target calls for, and that to strike it we must aim beyond.

## 6. Abstract and concrete aspects of the organization

The truth is that, having distinguished levels, we have now to see that they need vertical support. For example, consider Earth. *First*, there is Earth by herself at her own planetary level: looked on thus abstractly she is in effect degraded to the level of her molecules. *Second*, there is the two-level Earth-molecule Pair, which still lacks all vital and human filling. *Third*, there is the six-level Earth-molecule Pair as including the later and intermediate Pairs, namely Life-cell and Humanity-man: the planet is now not merely alive, but human and indeed suprahuman. But still she is not self-supporting, not all there. *Fourth*, there is the all-level Earth, the planet as at her own level primarily, but needing and in a sense owning all the rest—the planet as a mode of the Whole, as fully concrete.

And if we take the infrahuman thus concretely the results are much the same. For the behaviour of the low-grade functionary, though stereotyped, is quite elastic enough to allow each of its superiors to sway it sufficiently in the long run. Thus the atoms now engaged in the writing of this sentence can do so without any violence to their rigid and circumscribed customs, because the performance is spread over ages of atomic history. And it is on account of such differences of tempo from level to level that the physicist can suppose himself as atoms to be free from human guidance, just as he can suppose himself as man to be free from suprahuman guidance. Altogether justifiably, he deals with abstract versions both of atoms and of men. But evidently the atoms of his body do not, in the long run, behave like mine; and to consider their long-term history would be to take not only the man, but the whole hierarchy into account. In short, to inquire too persistently into the behaviour of an inferior is to promote him, for abstractness is of the essence of his inferiority. The law of equality lays down that to know him is to be ignorant of what he really is.

### 7. *The reconciliation of the hierarchical schema with the regional*

The pyramidal system of this chapter, and the concentric system of previous chapters, are two descriptions of the same thing.

Alone, I am nothing. This means, in regional terms, that I am at the Centre; in hierarchical terms, that I am at the foot of the

pyramid. In the former case, I say that I look out upon my regions; in the latter, that I look up through the proper channels or the trap-doors of certain offices in every storey, and see what is going on in each of them—and the further I see the bigger the area of the basement I occupy. The human official in his middle-floor cubicle is really his own lowest subordinates acting as one observer; since he is nothing he can never leave the basement, but by extending his viewpoints there he can see into ever more exalted storeys of the transparent structure that towers above him.

In other words, the projection and reflection between mutual observers of Part I, the ascending and descending processes of Part II, and the proper channels of Part III, are different versions of a single activity in space: or rather, of organic and active space itself, as it is actually given. In its filled concreteness this space is the hierarchy itself at work, and it is set out along two lines—the radial or pyramidal, and the circumferential or zonal.

This is the ranked space whose brilliant angel-populated vistas end in Heaven, not empty space swept clean of all regional distinctions and qualities, mere comminuted vacuity which is lifeless and even hellish everywhere because it is never allowed to build up to the least wholeness. Looking out into the former, men used to see right into the sphere of the divine fifth element, into the realms of imperishable beauty and intelligence, into their own and the bright gods' immortal country, into Paradise itself; and now, looking out into the latter kind, we are apt to see, notwithstanding our superb telescopes, no further than the ends of our noses.

The question to ask of this space is: in whom does it lie? As the space of my human body is organic, inspired, busily hierarchical, a living net of prehensions, so also is that of my greater bodies: the more lifeless it seems to the outsider the more alive it is to the insider, the occupant, the hierarchical head. And the whole of it as the Whole may fitly be called spirit.

## 8. 'The compounding of consciousness'

To the objection that this spaced-out hierarchical organization (as I have outlined it in this and previous chapters) violates our selfhood, and that selves with their contents are immiscible, I reply thus: (i) The objection seems to be based upon the belief that the self or ego is a separate substance, an impenetrable and inscrutable soul-atom. For this I cannot find the slightest proof, nor do I know what kind of proofs could possibly justify such a belief. (ii) There is now much evidence for telepathy and the like, evidence which makes it difficult to speak, in many cases, of quite separate minds. (iii) Just as in telepathy my mind may to some degree overlap or merge with another, so it may divide into two or more semi-distinct minds; and then, later on when I am cured of schizophrenia, these may merge again. (iv) Many psychologists find they cannot account for the contents of the individual mind without supposing it to have direct access to some kind of supra-individual or ancestral mind. Others, studying the psychology of communities or practising group psychiatry, are driven by their findings to speak of an emergent group mentality. (v) My hand touches one pen, my ear hears a second, my eyes see a third and a fourth: yet nothing of the kind happens —there is only one experience of one pen. Is there no compounding here? Are not the many sensations of one level the one perception of the next? (vi) Again, if I am discontinuous with the psycho-physical organisms which comprise my psycho-physical organism, if all their trapdoors are shut to me, how am I now able to persuade them so easily to record the fact? (vii) I was once a male and a female germ cell; they united, and I was one; the one divided into two, four, eight . . . yet remained one; and now I am billions of living creatures who are nevertheless sufficiently unified to write their story here. Is it not curious that the collective genius or angel of this host, whose life has been one long essay in compounding, should come to doubt the possibility of compounding? (viii) The means of this compounding are ready to hand: you and I are the same in so far as we make way for the same object. Our two heads are better than one because when we put them together they *are* one—one no-head, one room—and the emptiness in our heads is infinitely fusible. For when I see what you see, not only do I see you; I am you: since (so far as I can discover) neither of us has anything of his own with which to keep out the other. Conversely, to the extent that my objects of to-day have nothing in common with those of last year or ten years ago, I am not the same person as I was then. (ix) So far from finding it difficult to identify myself with others, my problem is rather how to see things from my own point of view: thus for many years I failed to notice the obvious fact that I have no head. We really do live in one another. (x) It is moreover my habit to feel and think for my family and nation and planet, and for some organ or other of my body. These I become; and if I do not trust my own experience of such metamorphoses, there is always my travelling observer to confirm them. (xi) The facts of sympathy and love and imaginative insight, the religious impulse, the generous urges of duty and self-sacrifice for worthy causes, the discipline of the intellect itself—all show that we come to ourselves only by going out to others. Surely it is plain that those of us who are most careful to remain unmixed with our companions, who fear all self-loss and merging, soon find ourselves with nothing worth losing; whereas those who give themselves to what is beyond themselves are the very ones whose personalities impress us as distinct and unique. And this is what we should expect if man becomes himself and whole and free as he realizes his own nature, ascending and descending the hierarchy by that practice of compounding and uncompounding which comes to him so naturally that he scarcely notices it.

In short, hierarchy no more threatens individuals than music threatens notes: it makes them. Only in the Whole is the fragment more than a fragment, and so much as a fragment.

# PART FOUR

## CHAPTER XV

# Here and Now: There and Then

### *1. Whence and whither?*

What do I amount to in time? How old am I? How did I begin, and what is my destiny? These are the questions which I shall now try to answer. If they are not worth looking into, I do not know what is. For man is a passenger, not freight. He is neither a coward who dare not nor a simpleton who cannot nor an idler who will not ask whither he is rushing.

### *2. Here-now and there-then (past)*

Again I begin with my immediate experience of this pen and paper and desk, and the houses and clouds and sun that I see whenever I look up. These are all presented to me here, and *now*.

Yet just as they do not stay here but are sent to their places in my regions, so they do not remain present in time but are sent to other times. I am imprisoned at this point of space and moment of time which I call Here-now, but from this Centre radiates a vast regional system which I call There-then.

For example, the sun I am now looking upon, I label as the sun of eight minutes ago: I see it that far into the past. A star seen now I relegate back from four to thousands of years; a galaxy, a million years or more. And I explain this projective activity by saying that light takes time to get to me from the object; so that the star-explosion which I see now is happening before I was born, and the spiral nebula which I see now is contemporary with an Earth whose men—or mammals, or even reptiles—have not yet appeared. And however close my object it always dates. The world has ceased to exist for itself by the time it has begun to exist for me; and seemingly my unenviable choice is between news of what *is* nothing here at the Centre, and of what *was* something over there in my regions—between the empty Here-now and its out-of-date filling.

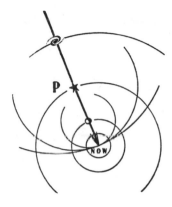

Am I then for ever out of touch with reality? Quite the contrary. As the star I see is not itself over there in itself, but here in me; so also its seen explosion is not a century ago, but now. For a star and sidereal events are regional effects wrought in regional observers like myself.

### 3. Here-now and there-then (*future*)

Thus I do not live in the past, but in a present which points to a past which it fulfils. My object is fully itself here-from-there and now-from-then. In fact it is now-from-its-past and now-to-its-future, for from all present action upon me issues my reaction. The datum expands as vigorously into the future as into the past. For instance, by replying *to-day* to my friend's letter of *yesterday*, I settle what he will read *to-morrow*: my present experience is from his past to his future. And this is typical of inter-communication at all hierarchical levels: the object entertained now at the Centre divides into a past and a future aspect. Well may language, with an inspired and fourfold ambiguity which is almost a philosophy in itself, pack into that portmanteau phrase *my present object* a present which may be spatial or temporal, and an object which may be perceived as past or intended as future.

Instantaneous in respect of me, the datum spans a part of my object's history, and the higher my object's grade the longer the history which my present moment encloses. When therefore I look at a galaxy, both my Here and my Now swell to galactic dimensions. In a manner of speaking, I am in touch with my object, putting out to it a pair of antennae or arms; and it takes,

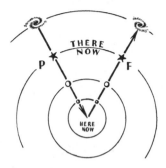

say, ten million years for the incoming impulse to pass along one arm to this Centre, and another ten million for my reaction to pass out again along the other—my 'right hand' is twenty million years later than my 'left hand'. In other words, my re-action time is twenty million years; for I cannot take on a body capable of looking at galaxies without taking on also its long-evity. The far-sighted are big, and the big long-lived.

Let me put the matter another way. It takes a star to see a star, a galaxy to see a galaxy. And to see a galaxy is not merely to have been reduced by it, over a period of (say) ten million years, to nothing here and now; but also to reverse this proce-dure and grow up, over a similar period of the future, to full galac-tic status over there in it. Thus my seeing is anticipatory as well as retrospective: I see the galaxy or star or man as one which is being reduced to a receptacle for me, in the same way that I see the road ahead as about to take my car, or the target as about to take my shot. The datum is one and here and now, yet two and there and not now, for it is revealed as my object's past and my future over there. I look ahead into my galactic destiny, by looking beyond and so including men and planets and stars. My external light—the light I am seen by—becomes my internal process, and I incorporate its time with its space. This is the way galaxies observe one another, for no *man* ever saw such a thing.

## 4. *The rhythms of intercommunication*

At each hierarchial level I am in correspondence with my equals, and as our distance grows with our status so does our correspondence-time tend to grow also. The higher communications are drawn out into millions of years; the lower are very rapid. But this is no inconvenience, for my time standards, like my space standards, are scaled up and down to suit the level at which I am working; I do not feel much more hurried or short-lived in the company of men than in the company of the stars. But what does alter with temporal range and rhythm is the quality of our correspondence. An essential determinant of the message is the time it takes to get through. It matures on the way: the more worth while it is the more time goes to its making. The principle is seen even in ordinary letter-writing: my bi-monthly letters to my friend in Australia do not recount the petty detail of my daily letters to my friend in the next town. Time, like space, insulates each from the other's triviality; or rather, what we are largely depends upon the spatio-temporal interval which parts us.

## 5. *The There-now wedge*

The far-flung arms which I put out to my object—the one handling the past and the other the future—embrace a wedge-shaped neutral zone which is out of my reach: I have no way of getting into touch with what is happening there. In fact, its

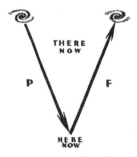

inaccessible events are for me neither past nor future but con-temporary. Thus the millions of years of galactic history, the ages that separate my two points of contact with the spiral nebula over there, are all *now*; for only when my Now is simply here is it a mere instant, and the further off it is the more time it encloses.

Nor will it do to say that this widening There-now is nothing but an accident arising out of the finite speed of light; and that, to an observer who had infinitely swift means of signalling, the wedge would narrow to a line or world-wide instant, sharply dividing past from future everywhere. For not even 'instantaneous' telepathic communication between observers on two stars could abolish the wedge and establish the line; because there would still remain for the stars' astronomers the puzzle of how the line should lie. There is no way round the ambiguity of the Now, once it ceases to be here. The fact is that planets and stars and galaxies cannot niggle with time and space as men can and must niggle: the celestial world-picture is painted with a much broader spatio-temporal brush than the terrestrial. Accordingly, when I deal with stars I join a society in which Now may mean a century.

(In any case, so far from offering a way of abolishing the wedge-shaped There-now, telepathy seems only to confirm it. Experiment shows that the telepathic percipient tends to pick up, not what the agent is now thinking of, but what he thought of a minute or two before, or will think of in a minute or two's time. There is temporal displacement. The agent's There-now is not an instantaneous line, but a wedge.)

## 6. The hollow There-now

But this inflated Now of a pair of remote mutual observers is hollow. The twenty years that separate the tips of my antennae when I look at Procyon are lost to me. Where shall I find the filling for this long interval? The answer is: not there in the remote region of the star but in the regions that join us. The antennae converging on this Centre are themselves the bridge which spans the gap in Procyon's history—it is true that my awareness is concentrated (so to speak) in their tips, but my antennae are sensitive there only because they lie in each nearer region also, and are united at the Centre here. In other words, anything very much less than twenty years of the star's existence is not the *star's* existence at all, but belongs in my nearer regions, where shorter periods are recognized. Yet without this briefer filling at lower levels the star Procyon is abstractly perceived, eviscerated, dead.

(An hour on a star is no more stellar than a foot, nevertheless without that hour and foot the star is emptied. To each hierarchical level its maximum and minimum season. For example, neither a billion years nor a second is a period of *human* history;

there are no stars, and indeed no men, in a universe whose time has been divided into separate seconds, or whose space has been divided into separate cubic millimetres. The rule is that there is no merely one-level or horizontal time: the vertical inter-course of the hierarchy's members both needs and makes its own graded spatio-temporal conditions, subject to the law of elsewhereness.)

Accordingly the star must go out of itself, and come to me and others like me to get the time and the room and the filling it needs to be its stellar self. It has nothing that is not remote. In particular, its stellar history occurs only at stellar range, and the filling of that history at lesser range here in me its observer. That is to say, the star over there comes to *this* star for its infra-stellar content, in obedience to the law that at each level the individual can find his content only in the other. I have for head the heads of other men; for body, other men's bodies; for planet,

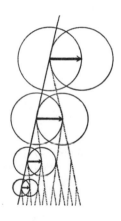

not Earth, but Mars or Venus; for star, not the solar system but Procyon or Sirius or Betelgeux. Every time I reach a new level I am replaced: there is a total shift from the self to the not-self, and all that I seemed to have grown and absorbed belongs to the new object, of which I am the mere receptacle. To put the matter crudely, my cells do not add up to this man, but to other men; nor men add up to Humanity, but to other species; nor the members of the solar system to the Sun, but to all the other stars; nor the universe to itself, but to the Whole which is wholly other than the universe. In a sense, therefore, so far from this star (or galaxy or universe) being the only one which is certainly alive, it is the only one which is certainly dead, and the life it seems to have is the life of the other. No star is 'hollow' or lacks planetary and vital filling, and none fills itself. In the economics of the hierarchy private property is banned: the only way to have anything is to pass it on.

There is nothing occult here. I have merely to look out into my regions to find that my integument of galaxies encloses not their stars but the stars of this Galaxy, that the only planets my star-belt holds are those of this star, that the zone of my planets relies on terrestrial filling—and so on to the Centre. Each zone of my body contains its own parts; each zone of my mind, another's parts. There is one arithmetic for the view in, and quite another for the view out.

Thus the letter I write to my friend to-day, the news which is my insight into his to-morrow, is news of *me*: my filling is shifted on to him—indeed I can only realize it as his. And this is the pattern of all hierarchical correspondence. If instead of writing I visit him, the case is not altered: the friend I shake hands with and see and hear arises from the state of *my* retinae and cochleae, not his. We exchange bodies. And if we should then go out to look at the stars, it is not *their* local filling which makes them what they are, but *ours*—our solar and terrestrial loves, and visions of beauty, and science. They do not come to us for bare starhood, but for their names, meanings, language, poetry, astronomy. . . . The Greek maidservant had better reason than she knew for rallying the star-gazing philosopher who fell in the well: nothing in this star is irrelevant to that star.

## 7. *The elastic There-now and delayed correspondence*

Light is, of course, only one of the modes of communication, most of which are much less swift and far-reaching. Moreover (particularly at the middle levels) several modes may work together, each with its own rhythm. Thus I see and hear and exchange letters with my friend, and remember what he was and anticipate what he will be; and accordingly my There-now wedge in respect of him is of many breadths—a temporal complication which makes for the interest and subtlety of our relationship.

A further complication comes from what may be called delayed correspondence. Obviously the speed of the postal service is not the only factor which settles the tempo of our communication; how long we take to reply is another determinant. And the hierarchical rule is that only routine letters can be answered by return of post: the others are held up for reference to higher authority, and this takes time. The more important the issue, the higher the level which settles it, and the longer we must wait for a decision. In fact, however, this higher correspondence is not other than the lower, but only its larger rhythms apprehended. Our lesser correspondence is overruled and brought round in the long run. And our freedom lies in our recognition of this control. We realize the hierarchy above us by delaying our responses, by slowing down. That is why thought and prayer and artistic creation need, between seeking and finding, between the conscious posing of the problem and the answer to it, long periods of waiting while less conscious levels are consulted.

## 8. The Here-then line

Some more intricacies must be noted. Here and now, as I write to the friend of whom I have many memories, I enjoy one object (A), but distinguish in it three elements: first, 'my friend now', whom I project upon my There-now (B), upon the present of *that* place; second, 'myself then', whom I project upon

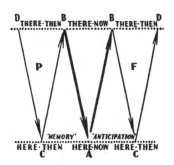

my Here-then (C), upon the past of *this* place and its future; third, 'my friend then', whom I project upon myself Here-then (C), and through that double station upon a past and future spot There-then (D). In the *first* case, I say that I contemplate my friend over there; in the *second*, that I remember the man I was and think of the man I shall be; in the *third*, that as remembering the man I was, I remember one who knew himself in terms of his friend; and that as anticipating the man I shall be, I anticipate future experience of my friend. All three occur in my Here-now, but the first refers to my There-now, the second to my Here-then, and the third to my There-then through my Here-then.

And just how much of my Here line (contributing to this occasion memory and foresight of other occasions) is involved, depends chiefly upon the level at which I am living; for the Here line, like the Now line—or rather wedge—which it crosses at the point Here-now, is set out in regions. That is to say, the double

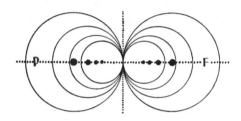

view back into my own past, and forward into my own future, is subject to the same temporal perspective as the view out into my object's present. The further I look the higher the status of what I find. For example, my long-term projects have more scope and less detail than my short-term projects: I plan my dinners a day or two ahead, my holidays six months ahead, my career many years ahead. On the long view only the broader patterns appear. I have forgotten all but the general shape of my early childhood. Again, the more ancient the history the less prejudiced the historian and the less embarrassed with unmanageable quantities of documentary evidence; he sees a remote period as a whole, dispassionately and impartially. We open our history books as suprahuman beings and close them as all-too-human: the reader varies with the date of what he reads. Just as the art of drawing is to know what not to draw, and the art of seeing is to know what to overlook, so the art of prediction is to know what to come upon unawares, and the art of remembering is to know what to forget. No perspective foreshortening, no view; no giving up in time, no having now. The fact is that the event is nothing in itself when it happens, but gains new and fuller meaning as its observers recede from it in time. So long as

I have a future my past is mutable; and indeed it needs much longer treatment than it has yet received.

Spatio-temporal range determines status. As I walk down from the hills on a clear day the town I see is an hour away; presently I come to where the suburb is fifteen minutes away, then to where this street is five minutes away, this house a minute away, this room a second away, this chair a tenth of a second away—the less I see into my future, the narrower its scope in space. I look forward to some great moment of my life, but as the occasion comes upon me it breaks up into petty details needing instant attention. Only when it is safely past does it regain here and now, by stages, the wholeness which it loses by becoming merely present.

*9. Shifting the Now-Centre*

Many complications are worked into this temporal perspective by the fact that I am as mobile in time as in space. Just as I am nothing *here*, but become something for myself by going out to other places where I am something; so also I am nothing *now*, but become something for myself by going out to other times where I have a history, where I have had time to grow up from this seminal Now into an embodiment whose status depends upon its temporal remoteness. More than this, I can view other things than myself from the point of view of other observers than myself. Consequently history becomes for me a twofold endeavour: to grasp the present meaning of the past event, and to get back to what it was for itself, in the perspective of the contemporary observer. (Indeed the total history of an occasion is nothing less than its own view out, or spatio-temporal perspective, plus all views in, or what its hierarchy of observers in space and time makes of it.) Of course I fall far short of this ideal of temporal mobility. Nevertheless it is practical necessity, rather than any inaptitude for travel in time, which holds me to this moment. I have only to relax my effort of concentration, and at once my mind wanders to other times.

*10. The hierarchical organization of my history or Here-then*

But however far I stray, I can never really leave the timeless Centre of my time-regions. If my Here-then is subject to the same perspective effects as my There-now, and is regionally laid out, it follows that whereas I shall be a man a few moments hence, and was a man a few moments ago, I am now less than human. Still more recently I was cellular, and molecular, and atomic; and shall presently be all these again in turn. But now, at this instant, I am nothing. The Centre is emptied by time, no less than by space, of all that belongs to itself. From one point of space and moment of time I am altogether absent, and it is this one: only so can all the things of time and space be present in it.

I have many intimations of this bottomless infrahuman abyss at the Centre. Thus I do not perform human acts, but only intend and remember them: literally I make nothing of the hardest tasks—the middle drops out of them. Again, I consider what I am just about to write on this page, and read what I have just written; but the depths of the present moment, from which these words mysteriously issue, remain altogether inscrutable. It is we who are most surprised at what we hear ourselves saying.

Like space, time exists to be seen through—in both senses. I look out through the haze of time into my past and future. How far I see depends upon the height from which I look, for the mist lies thickest along the ground but clears above: its layers are hierarchical. Indeed the raised far object, when seen from its own level, is usually plainer than the low near one. Accordingly I can find out now more about the movements of the planets a thousand years ago and a thousand years hence, than about the movements of my human neighbours yesterday and to-morrow; and, at a still lower level, the movements of my electrons a moment from now are indeterminate. Roughly speaking, the future is predictable and the past recoverable in proportion to their hierarchical status. And only our absolute beginning and end, the Alpha and Omega of all things, are absolutely certain. The prophetic gift of the actuary—as he takes the day-to-day and unpredictable destinies of the individual and refers them upwards to the long-term and more predictable destinies of the group—this gift is more fully granted to the saint who refers them still higher, to the all-inclusive and entirely predictable destiny of the Whole; and though his faith is not prudential, it covers him against all ultimate risks. Thus it is the nature of my present to be absolutely obscure, of my nearer history and prospects to be somewhat vague, of my remoter destiny and origins to approach absolute certainty.

Present action arises out of a past situation and is directed upon a future one; it is nothing without all three terms, and its status (subject to minor fluctuations) is proportional to their temporal spacing. What is, on close inspection, the same act of four men, may by the first be performed for the sake of an organ, by the second for the man's sake, by the third for Humanity, by the fourth for the Whole: so that in fact there is a world of difference, in time-span and status and lucidity, between the four acts and between the four agents.

## *11. The symmetry and the flow of time*

Though nothing can happen *to* me, everything can happen *in* me. I do not have to go back to the beginning or await the end of the world; all its times are present, with their proper degree of regional obscurity and plainness. The long interval which seems to separate me from the golden ages of the past, or from the heavens of the future, is just what is needed to make them what they are. Truly there is for time as for space a cosmological principle which finds me always at the Centre of a symmetrical system of time-regions. For me it is always half-time on the half-way line in the game of life. Throughout life's journey the scene fits itself to my motion: so that as I come up to each

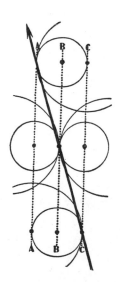

The status of A, B, and C adjusts itself to the observer's
movement from C, through B, to A

beauty-spot my nearness can only drive it away or else destroy it. It is the grapes within reach that prove sour.

Ahead of me lies one hierarchy of events, behind me another. And when I say that time flows past, or else that I move through time, I mean that the contents of the first hierarchy are continually being scaled down to my present nonentity, and the contents of the second are continually being scaled up from that nonentity. Thus every step the traveller takes in real time (in contrast to abstract and non-regional time) alters the inscription on every milestone along the road—with the result that he does not in any ordinary sense travel at all. The inhabitants of each of his space-time regions are always shifting to the next region, and being remodelled to fit it. Thus he never gets any nearer to the apparent goal because he is always at the real goal—at the mid-point where every spectacle along the route has that degree of enchantment which its distance lends.

## 12. Time-depth compared with space-depth

My object is primarily here and now, yet projected into such depths of space and of time as its hierarchical status requires. In other words, I read time-depth no less than space-depth into what is, in the first place, flat or merely present. But clearly the two kinds of depth are unlike. For the datum *here*, having breadth and height, is 'two-dimensional', and projection supplies the third; whereas the datum *now* is 'one-dimensional', and projection supplies *two* kinds of temporal 'depth'—pastness and futurity. If my Here may be likened to the face of a cube whose thickness I project, my Now may be likened to the edge of a cube whose sides I project. Time stands at an angle to me; space stands foursquare.

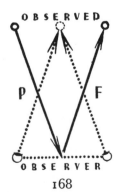

# HERE AND NOW: THERE AND THEN

In establishing the space-depth of my object I divide *myself* in space (to gain a binocular view of the object); in establishing its time-depth I divide *my object* in time (dispatching one aspect into the past, and the other into the future). The first duplicates here to unify there; the second duplicates then to unify now. And this twice-triangulated projection tends to become more deliberate and more symmetrical as its range increases. In the end, to know the object's threefold remoteness is to know its threefold presence in me its observer; and it is clear that my past and future are like my breadth and height in this, that there are limits to what I can have of the one without increase of the other.

My world is ample and deep. This little window opens on to immense space-lands that are also time-lands. I enjoy a prodigious view into my cosmic history no less than my present constitution. As Part V will show, I look out upon aspects of the Humanity and the Life, of the Earth and the Sun and the Galaxy, that once were and again shall be my own embodiments. It is not that I am able, as I see into my remoter regions, to make out whence I came and what I am coming to, but rather that I can see nothing else. My vision is autobiographical. I cannot call my time—namely the whole of time—my own, till I discover in the shining vistas of heaven my immense origin and destiny, and see all of it gathered up into this timeless Now at the Centre.

# CHAPTER XVI

# Time, Motion, and Structure

## *1. Structure-space and structure-time*

The last chapter was devoted chiefly to my own view out; this chapter returns to my observer's view in. He finds that time is one of my essential ingredients, and that while he is taking in more of my space by retiring from me he is also taking in more of my time: he is winged for temporal as well as spatial flight. Each regional manifestation of me is, in fact, not so much a thing as an indivisible event or history. And the longer I take to be myself, the higher my status. Thus to divide my time and to divide my space come to the same thing —to hierarchical descent; and, in the limit, when my observer gives me no time at all to show what I can do, I am nothing whatever. At this instant all heaven and earth are utterly destroyed—and there is only this instant. No history, no thing. History holds nothing that is not history: cross-sections of it are nothing at all. There is no mere space or mere time—the one is a spaceless point, the other a timeless moment—for space takes time and time makes space.

The principle of structure-time is apparent everywhere. Six months of cricket is not a game but a season; six minutes of a game is not a game but an over; and six seconds of an over is not an over but a ball. Again, by dividing the time of a symphony we lose the symphony, then music, then sound, and then wave motion. Given time, the part is the whole; deprived of time, the whole is the part.

## *2. Rotation and structure-time*

As it takes more than a million miles, so it takes more than a month for the Sun to be itself. The structure-time of the Sun (I

170

refer to the developed Sun, the solar system) is at least a year—the time required by Earth to complete her orbit. The Galaxy's structure-time must be similarly reckoned, probably in hundreds of millions of years, as at least the period of the Sun's circuit about the galactic centre of gravity. Earth's structure-time is twenty-four hours—given less time than this, she is only half herself; given more, she describes a considerable arc about the sun and so approaches solar status, in the same way that the Sun, given more time than is proper to the solar estate, begins to announce the Galaxy. The life at one hierarchical level is always sending up temporal shoots into the next, and it is only by continual pruning that distinctions are preserved at all. The humbler the creature, the more often it has to begin its growth-cycle all over again: the structure-time of the atom for instance —the time its particles need to sweep out their orbits—is no more than we should expect from its structure-space.

Towards the middle of the hierarchy many kinds of circulation are superimposed, and their pattern is irregular. To give a few instances out of many: there are the circulating molecules in the blood corpuscle, the circulating corpuscles in the man's bloodstream, the circulating human traffic in Humanity's reticulum, Humanity circulating throughout the biosphere and cultivating and regulating Life's economy, and finally the biospheric circulation of water which maintains the planetary life. In such ways, tracks of 'solid' spatial pattern are laid down and maintained by reiterated motion whose period is roughly proportional to its spatial scope and hierarchical status. And at each level rest is death. Nothing keeps. It is always in the remaking, always being shaped, worked over, marked out afresh.

We have long forgotten the tremendous significance of dancing, but in fact every ballroom is a working model of the universe: for the cosmos is a dance in which there are neither wallflowers, nor intervals, nor indeed dancers who are anything apart from the dance. And the tempo depends on the hierarchical level of the dance-floor. (Thus the cilia of the cells that line my bronchial tubes are beating at 600 to the minute; my heart is beating at 70 to the minute; I am breathing at 17 to the minute; as a family we are eating a meal at 3 to the day, in the company of friends who come in once a week; and we are celebrating the anniversary of a great national event.) At no level may we rest on our oars. Unexercised bodies and unused skills decay; the home that is not constantly gone over with duster and brush ceases to be a home; unworked land is soon wilderness; doctrines and institutions that are never overhauled die on us. The bridge of this world does not need its maintenance gangs so much as comprise them.

### 3. Time turns out space

The ascent of the hierarchy is a map-making in which the map of one level is the cartographer of the next. In other words, the official of one grade, given the time of the next, marks out its space: indeed every grade of official must devote all his time to the round of his space-making duties, otherwise the entire space-organization melts away. If you look behind the hierarchy of behaviour for someone who behaves, you will find nothing. All my structure, all the world's seeming solidity, is the trail of behaviour laid out in space—or rather, the space itself is the product no less than the necessary background of the behaviour.

I am contractile, and my frontiers are held only by ceaseless patrolling: the well-tilled clearing of my space is always threatened by the creeping jungle of my time. My approaching observer unmakes me. Yet my destroyed structure leaves traces—forces which grow as I shrink. He reports that the less I am the

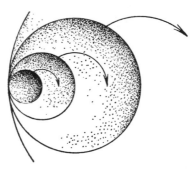

more I assert myself in the effort to make up for my deficiency, for my lost integrity. Thus my vast and solid Sun-ring body, deprived of its structure-time of some hundreds of millions of years, melts away, leaving a tiny star whose 'forces' of momentum and gravitation are all that is left of its galactic wholeness. My Earth-ring body, denied its structure-time of one year, contracts to this globular particle of itself, this busy planetary relic which would make up for its loss by patrolling the space it can no longer incorporate. And so on downwards. We can get rid of the wholeness of things but not of its consequences. It is one thing to atomize the world, and another to pacify the products of our analysis. Our dismembered cosmos 'over-compensates for its organ-inferiority'. We may carve up the universe as we please and boil it all down to quanta of energy, but we can hardly complain if we find ourselves in the soup and the soup takes the lid off.

*4. The zones of time, motion, and space*

The rank which my observer accords to me depends upon what motion he finds me (i) to contain (as spatial), (ii) to exhibit (as spatio-temporal), (iii) to exclude (as temporal). If, for

example, he sees me as a man, he notes three zones—(i) the spatial zone of my infrahuman bodies whose motion he has solidified; (ii) the spatio-temporal zone of my man's body seen moving; (iii) the temporal zone of my suprahuman bodies which have still to be compassed, which are still to make. And as he retires, the inner or spatial zone grows at the expense of the outer or temporal; as he approaches, the spatial zone shrinks again. In the limit, his object becomes at the Centre all time and no space (and so non-temporal as well as non-spatial); while at the other extreme it becomes all space and no time (and so, once more, neither spatial nor temporal). Thus the final triumph of descending time, like that of ascending space, is suicidal. At the cyclone's Centre and periphery, absolute calm. Time and space, though always attacking and overcoming each other in the no-man's-land of motion, cannot exist apart.

What is altogether present as a solid body to one observer is to another an act that takes time, and to a third an agelong historical tendency. Thus my hand is not radically different from what it does, and even a mountain range is a wave-motion or Earth-tic. To live, find life: tell me where you see real action and I will tell you how alive you are. In our day-to-day picture of the universe, our hierarchical inferiors are mere still life in the foreground, and our superiors mere volatile atmosphere in the background. Only in the middle distance does the scene come to full life and colour. The suprahuman seems vapid because its space is hidden by time; the infrahuman seems inert because its time is hidden by space. It is no accident that we reckon large or suprahuman *distances* in travel-*time*—speaking of a star as so many light-*years* off, a country as so many days, a town as so many hours. On the other hand, we progress by turning journeys into maps, by reading periods as distances, by fitting together in one comprehensive and public space the spaces we perceive privately and at various times, by consolidating many histories into one self-contemporary structure. Indeed so expert is my space-making that it comes to me as a shock that my great window, which I had supposed to open on a world that is all-at-once, is in fact a succession of tiny peep-holes—with the result that, for instance, a *page* of print is always illegible, and no large wall is ever built of bricks.

## 5. Spatialization and quality

The larger the spatial fabric which the shuttles of motion weave out of the thread of time, the more interesting its design. A single thread is too tenuous to amount to anything; but weave the threads, and solidity and colour appear; go on weaving, and the pattern begins to shape—provided we stand further and further back from it. Moreover the emergent qualities—which are numberless—are cumulative in the pattern, so that each stage of its production is joined to the next by elements that belong to both. In other words, the regions are knit together by what is trans-regional.

How much of this world-pattern is my present possession? The question which haunts me is whether it is *now* morning or evening, the spring or winter of the year, of my life, of our civilization, of all Life. Am I on the crest or in the trough of the wave? When the waves are small my boat rides them with an even keel: millions of them are here and now—that is to say, the colour blue stays blue, sounds do not become mere vibrations, this sentence does not break up into its constituent words and letters. But when the waves grow my boat tosses, and each has to be separately negotiated; it may get so big that I lose hope of gaining the crest and looking out over the ocean. But I am not confined to this human vessel: larger and more seaworthy craft stand by to save me—ships so vast that the roughest ocean is waveless for them. In other terms, all grades of spatialization, with their emergent qualities, are directly accessible to me.

## 6. The pastness of space and the fallacy of simple dating

In the evolutionary story the future appears as the region of pure time, the present as the region of time mixing with space, the past as the region of time overcome and concealed by space. Yet, in consolidating as space, past time is doubly temporal: for spatialization, so far from abolishing temporal relations, works them up into such elaborate complexes that real space (unlike abstract and one-dated space) may be called supertemporal. For instance, I am a museum of my past, in which every exhibit bears two labels—one stating its present date, and the other the date of its origin, minutes or years or ages ago. My atoms belong to the earlier stages of the Sun, my molecules to the very distant terrestrial past, my cells to early Life, and every organ to some chapter of my long biography. And I am a man because all this historical material is gathered up into a living and working unity now—a unity which owes its qualities to its time-depth, to the operation of every past age within a common present: though I am only young once I never grow out of anything. And the more exalted the hierarchical individual, the completer the temporal nexus which it thus comprises. The timeless totality would ring hollow if it were not full of time, if it were not the completed organization of the temporal.

## 7. The coiled coil

As midway in the scale of creatures, dividing them into the temporal above and the spatial below, my business is to read the time of the higher into the space of the lower, and the space of the lower into the time of the higher, so uniting the sundered Pairs. And one result of this endeavour is the vision of the hierarchy as a single Movement, of which all movements are parts.

Consider the moon's path. It is roughly circular, but when Earth's motion is taken into account the moon's circle is broken and drawn out into a coil. When the Sun's motion is added, the coil becomes a coiled coil. In this way, if we take the proper motion of a particle of lowest hierarchical rank, and then add to it each motion which it owes to its membership of ever greater bodies, we rise by hierarchical stages to the highest and most inclusive motion, to that curve which breaks all lesser circles, bringing them round by imperceptible degrees to respect its own centre. Thus the lowest motion is altogether abstract and partial, seeing that it is corrected by every centre up to the highest; while the highest is altogether concrete and whole, seeing that it corrects and contains all others, and is itself corrected and contained by none.

There are, then, two views of a moving body—the abstract 'horizontal' view of the body which is supposed to complete its orbit undisturbed at its own level, before that orbit is involved, as a whole, in the motion of the next level; and the concrete 'vertical' view of the moving body as subject all the while to the influence of its own higher bodies, which break every circle by privily setting its centre in motion. There is no need to underline the moral. Once more, it is by studying the lucid procedure of our celestial levels that we gain light upon the obscure procedure lower down. To understand man it is necessary to study the stars.

### 8. *My motion and my observer's*

At each hierarchical level I have a characteristic motion, not in myself here at this still Centre, but over there in my observer. This spot, on the other hand, is reserved for *his* motion. His tyre turns at my hub, mine at his.

Accordingly I must now retell the story of my observer's approach. He glimpses a swiftly moving unit. To study it more closely, he *follows* it, and in effect brings it to a standstill. Further study and approach bring out subsidiary units, which must in their turn be chased and brought under inspection. In this way the observer goes on taking my motion upon himself till I am entirely stilled (and so abolished) and he is doing all that I used to do. And if now he retires from me, he gives up the chase at each level: before, he jumped on ever swifter vehicles; now he alights from them, giving back to me stage by stage his motion.

Essentially, then, I am a timeless, spaceless, and motionless Centre, patrolled by an ubiquitous observer who takes the form of circulating particles in my nearer regions, of erratically moving organisms in my middle regions, and of circulating celestial bodies in my further regions. I am a book which only he who runs may read, for he reads by running. He explains his behaviour by saying that he is keeping abreast of mine; his status, by saying that it is what he makes of me. What each is and does, he is and does in the other.

### 9. Motion and depth

At the end of the previous chapter I noted three kinds of projected depth—the one-way depth of space, and the two-way depth of time past and time future. In fact, these three are combined in projected motion. It is the motion of my near objects against the background of far objects, and the slighter motion of far objects against the background of the still more distant, which is the chief criterion of their range. For instance, the triple depth of my planetary region is revealed by motion across the surface of my sidereal region.

But it is my habit to find motion, and therefore depth, only in my middle regions. All other planes collapse. The near (like the fast-revolving flywheel) is still because it is too swift; the far, because it is too slow. And the real hierarchical universe, inexpresssibly deep and mobile, is hidden from me by my own shallowness. A ship with a twenty-fathom sounding-line never sails deep seas.

# CHAPTER XVII

# The Specious Present

### *1. The specious present*

I can at this moment hear church bells ringing over and over again a descending octave. Attending carefully to what is given, I find that I do not at any stage *hear* one note, *remember* the preceding note, and *expect* the note to come. I hear at least three or four notes together—in their proper order, but all held in the Now of sensation. It is much the same when I watch a bird fly past: I do not see a 'still' of the bird, with its wings in one position, replaced a moment later by another 'still'; but instead a fluttering streak, growing in front and vanishing behind. Seemingly, then, my Now (or moment of experience, or specious present) is not a mere instant, but includes a lapse of time in which sensed events follow but do not destroy one another.

### *2. The elastic specious present*

In fact, my Now is two-faced. For me here at the Centre it is a time-excluding instant; for my objects it is as commodious as they need it to be. In it they find their structure-time—a millionth of a second, perhaps, or a million years—just as they find in my Here (which is for me non-spatial) their structure-space and all the room they need to come to themselves. Here and now are the many spatio-temporal mansions, prepared for my companions in the hierarchy. Here and now everything— and nothing—is happening.

### *3. The constant field and its variable spatio-temporal texture*

My objects of varying status are presented in a spatial field, where a fly may eclipse a star, or a dust-grain·a galaxy. The field

178

does not swell to take the higher object; instead, the scale or texture of its space is adjusted. But this field is really spatio-temporal, and its time-texture varies with its space-texture to suit its contents.

### 4. The principle of constant velocity

The many-textured space and time of my field come together in a motion whose texture or intension matches theirs. The famous request—give me a lever long enough, and a spot where-on to rest it, and I will move the world—is granted. I never cease using such an instrument. Myself its still fulcrum, the beam of this lever is what used to be called the beam of my eye—my line of sight. And however long this beam is, whether its far end moves amongst cheese mites or stars, its speed is for me the same: the beam takes no longer to cover the distance between two mites than between two stars. Again, the fly crawling over the window, the sparrow flying in the garden, and the plane tearing across the sky, all keep pace in my field.

I go from star to star more quickly than I cross this room, and with less effort. Nor is it enough to say that this motion is sub-jective. It is not a man who sees the stars, and stars do not live as men and animals live. Thus, at low hierarchical levels, mo-tion is taken to be chiefly the object's over there, while at high levels the projection is withdrawn, and motion is taken to be chiefly the subject's here. Stars live a full social life, free and tran-quil and effortless beyond anything possible on Earth: they pass to and fro in their heavenly country at will, unrestrained, with-out need of transport systems. And this is not guesswork: I am only describing what I can do on any star-lit night. It is no acci-dent that as a microscopist studying pond-life (and glued to the eyepiece of my instrument) I attribute nearly all the observed motions to my object; that as a man I share them between my-self and others impartially; and that as star-gazer I claim them. For to climb the hierarchy is to learn, by many Copernican revolutions, that the motion I see is motion here in me, from an unmoving Centre in my object. When I am acting in my stellar capacity, I may no longer overlook this fact.

But whether I project it at low levels, or claim it at high levels, this motion is neither very fast nor very slow; for any great excess of speed is corrected by ascent to a higher level, and any great defect, by descent. We are said to travel much faster than our grandparents, but the planet has shrunk, leaving our virtual speed much the same. In fact, air-travel seems slower than walking. It is geospheric, and no longer human. Again, if space-ships become practicable, their speed will need to be of a planetary order, and still they will seem to their navigators to creep along. Thus hierarchy avoids, not only large numbers and large spaces and large time-spans, but also unseemly haste. But it is only at the extreme levels that this restriction becomes perfectly lucid and mathematically precise, and we have to admit that space and time conspire to set a limit to velocity—in this instance, the velocity of light. And even this limiting velocity is not excessive, for astronomers contemplate star systems conveniently scaled down to fit a field of view in which light moves slowly.

In every way the naturalist of a level is naturalized at that level. Indeed we have only to look up at the stars to be welcomed into their company on equal terms, and to see for ourselves that they are neither large nor wide apart nor lonely.

And the instruments and tackle whereby the scientist hoists himself up the hierarchical ladder (till he comes to regions whose measures are light-years and parsecs) are neither makeshifts nor orthopaedic devices, but the proper furniture of the levels to which they give access. And they are matched by the gear which lowers him into the deepest infrahuman, to levels where current events are wave motions, and where he discriminates intervals reckoned in billionths of a second. His procedure at these extreme heights and depths, the proportion which sense bears to inference there, the mathematics, the apparatus—these are not his clumsy substitutes for the direct experience of a being whose specious present is either ages or Ångström units; but the conditions of that experience itself, which he directly enjoys.

I live by vertical travel, by change of space-scale and time-scale. To find my way about the country at two or three miles an hour, I go over the ground at many thousands of miles an hour—on the map. To learn history, I condense continents to square inches and dynasties to seconds, then expand them again. How can I so much as speak of a red-light wave or a year or a geological era without taking it to be all-at-once, now? How can I do any job, or study any subject, without continually manipulating the spatio-temporal scale of it? Indeed I can scarcely open my mouth without proclaiming my hierarchical mobility: as when I say that ants run like mad yet trains creep along vexatiously at fifteen miles an hour, that a White Dwarf is a star yet a Flemish Giant is a rabbit, that it is a long while to supper time yet all too near quarter-day—and so on indefinitely. Again, this book can be written only by one who is all the while travelling between the regions of the book and the sentence and the word—of *this* word.

### 5. *The specious present and foreknowledge*

And thus to change the capacity of our Now is to change our level. If this were not so, if we could find out as much as we wished about the future of *this* order of things, then we should see the future as determined, and present action would be stultified. In fact, however, the lower levels are nothing if not obscure: the law of hierarchical perspective rules that it is poor visibility in space and time which makes these levels what they are, and to disperse their spatio-temporal fog is merely to rise to other levels where the air is clearer. Consequently there is no danger that our foreknowledge will ever exceed the requirements of our action. A suprahuman being leaves his long time-vistas behind when he comes down to look out of the human window, just as a scientist leaves his moderate time-vistas behind when he goes down still further, to the dark basement with its narrow outlook upon particles whose behaviour a moment hence is unpredictable. And even the supreme and omniscient observer, descending by every hierarchical staircase to the foundations of his universe, cannot take with him the view from the roof-top: he is limited by the observational conditions at each successive level, otherwise his descent would be no descent.

Our freedom, then, requires that we accept each level's limiting horizon, and unite all levels in a system which combines the graduated vagueness that liberty of action demands, with the graduated clarity of the higher specious presents. For the more we know the hierarchy the less we are its tools.

### 6. *Correspondence-time, structure-time, and the specious present*

My time is not my own, but my object's—the time it takes to build up from nothing to its full status. Part IV has described this hierarchical ascent in three ways—as occurring between our two Centres, and as at my object's Centre, and as at mine.

In the first case (Chapter XV) it is said to develop in *our* time, our correspondence-time; in the second case (Chapter XVI) to develop in *its* time, its structure-time; in the third case (this chapter) to develop in *my* time, my specious present. Which description we choose is a matter of convenience.

This does not mean that we are able, without qualification, to attribute to each hierarchical grade a definite time-span. Correspondence-time is subject to delays; structure-time varies between individuals of the same grade, and between different phases and aspects of the same individual; the specious present may hold an object that is solid but still, or just moving, or swift to the point of vanishing. From every point of view there is room for differences and ambiguities, particularly around the middle levels. All we can be sure of is the order of time-span— millions of years for galaxies, tens of years for stars, a day for a planet, and so on down to much less than a millionth of a second for the physicist's particles.

# PART FIVE

## CHAPTER XVIII

# Autobiographical—The Human Phase

*1. My symmetrical human history*

My minimum structure-time at the human level is brief—it does not take my observer long to see that I am a man. But this man is only an episode in a history, and until my observer can get the whole of this life-history—childhood, manhood and old age—into a single field of view, he sees me very inadequately. To be content with one period of this history is to imitate the dramatic critic who hears a few lines in the middle of Act II, and then goes off to write his article. Nobody sees me till he sees me through.

I am concerned, then, in this part of the inquiry, with my total life-span. But I can find no real birthday in the past, no clear-cut beginning from which to set out, and no clear-cut end to it all. Moreover my history, as it is actually given, is all of it at this Central moment, and projected hence symmetrically upon past and future times. It comes to me now from then, and is promptly sent back again.

The fact is that one-way chronology—beginning in the past and working towards the present and the future—is a useful but secondary construction, which relies upon the concentric or symmetrical time-scheme that is the pattern of immediate experience and the basis of all our behaviour. As the business of the detective, for whom the scene of the crime lies here and now, is to find clues leading out from this centre into distant places and times, so it is always some present event which takes us back into the past, or forward into the future, or both together. The present clue is a two-armed signpost pointing to a past criminal and a future plan to catch him. In the living Now the problems of the future are united to memories of the past: only the post-mortem discovers one-directional history.

### 2. *The seven ages of man*

Looking back, I find first adult life, with its full range of experience and responsibilities and powers; then youth, with these restricted in varying degrees; then childhood and infancy with their still narrower functions; and finally the quiescence

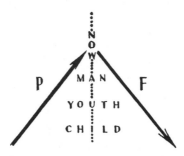

and oblivion of the womb. Looking forward, I find what is, roughly, the same series repeated. Adult working life is followed by the active retirement of second youth, with its partial surrender of responsibilities and powers; then by second childhood and second infancy; and finally the grave.

There is no need to insist upon the distinction between the uphill and the downhill side of the bridge at whose crown I stand, and no danger of confusing them. In any case, it is the immense difference between my past and my future which makes for their need of each other and their organic unity. All the same, the general symmetry is unmistakable. The first basic functions are also the last. Mere animal life is ours from start to finish; the elementary skills of walking and talking and feeding oneself come later and go earlier; most higher functions are briefer still. In short, man is a palindrome.

### 3. *Death into the future and the past*

Both roads lead down to a place of darkness and privation— to a region I acknowledge, yet find quite incredible. When, in the full graveyard, do I envisage as appalling fact what I know in harmless theory—the corruption underfoot? The rotting of this hand is as certain as the fact that it is now recording its own dissolution; yet such certainties are repressed to the end. But it is morbid *not* to think of these things. Unwillingness to think of death is itself a kind of death, for the poignancy of life is inseparable from the knowledge of its encircling decay. Moreover this inquiry has to face the facts.

And my past is no more respectable than my future, and no less hushed up. To see oneself as an infant is easy; as an embryo, very difficult. It is humiliating enough to have to own to such low beginnings: to trace them still further is to make all our remaining pretensions ridiculous. I am not thinking merely of the comic side of sex. What determines that one's parents shall meet at all? Some petty circumstance—a gust of wind, a banged door, a missed train, a dropped newspaper—a trivial chain of trivial events, and upon each silly link this so-important life hangs the whole weight of its being. Here is a microcosm, a universe, fathered by one contemptible accident and dismissed by another. Here is a cosmos poised on a bubble. What could be more absurd? I am not allowed even the dignity of cutting a tragic figure in the world.

*4. Death into society: the individual and the community*

Nor can I claim that, whatever the bathos of my coming and going, I am while here one who can call his soul his own. All that I do, and am, and hope for, derives from society and returns to it. It is not that—if only I could see things for myself— I should at last reach objectivity, a truly individual outlook: it is that a truly individual outlook is no outlook at all. The standards by which I take the world to task are those it kindly lends me for the occasion. Indeed the more insistent my urges and convictions the less likely they are to belong to this solitary man. What I take to be most myself is probably least *my*self.

Discount all that I owe my forbears and my contemporaries, and what is left? And if some loose or underived characteristic were to remain it could never help me to the selfhood I seek, but only reveal me as the habitation of demons accountable to nobody, least of all to myself. Little wonder, then, that I accept society's most fantastic claims without raising an eyebrow. How often (for instance) do I ask the reason for this elaborate pretence that our bodies are deformed, or why organs that are so carefully hushed up in us are in plants specially cultivated, and then amputated and used for table decoration? And are not those of us who think a man is scarcely a man till he can wear (and then come to like wearing, and finally need to wear) a small and very expensive furnace, and can drink the largest possible quantities of dilute but equally expensive poison without altogether collapsing—are not we the very ones to speak condescendingly of native initiation ceremonies that are so much less arbitrary and damaging? In a million ways our conduct is grotesquely self-contradictory and unpractical. And when we debunk one convention it is only in the name of another, which may well strike a future generation as even more comic. There is no escape into objectivity.

And, in case any miserable remnant of disinterestedness or freedom or originality should be left to us, the contemporary psychologist stands ready to dispose of it without residue.

## 5. My physical and psychical continuity

Even my body is always forsaking me, so that I am not the man I was an hour ago or a year ago. I am a continuous meal in which each course is the eater of the next. My success in living is my failure in permanence: I die when I cease dying quickly enough.

Nor will my memories on one hand, and my aims on the other, secure me any real continuity. The facts of amnesia, of ordinary forgetfulness, of multiple personality, of telepathic and mediumistic invasions, of religious conversion and less sudden changes in character, of unstable purposes, of mental conflict of many kinds—these reduce the notion of a continuing soul, or self, or mind, to the emptiest abstraction.

What of the field itself, the specious present or bare screen on to which my changing world is projected? Is this, perhaps, the basis of my continuity? It cannot be. A nothing cannot link two somethings. Besides, there is the certainty that the experience of 'one man' sometimes occupies two or more fields at once (as in cases of automatic writing), and the possibility that dreamless sleep occurs. Indeed it is as if the gods invented sleep and dreams expressly to make final nonsense of my claim to self-continuity, decreeing that to stay conscious I must periodically fall into a deep trance, that to keep my wits I must nightly lose them, that the price of each day's sanity shall be each night's madness.

## 6. Summary, and conclusion so far

Certainly, then, I have not to wait for the death that lies ahead. Driven by urges not of my contriving, ruled by convention even when I defy it, invaded by alien influences which I do not so much as suspect, I am without anything I can call mine. It is not that I lose my life but that I have none to lose; it is not that my continuity is broken but that it was never established. Awareness does not help: it is bad enough to be unreal; to be just real enough to discover my unreality is worse. It is bad enough to be the plaything of silly accident, to be under sentence of idiocy and death, to be without a soul to call my own— but to become aware just to become aware of *this*, and to resent it, is surely an excess of misfortune.

Nothing that I have to add takes away from the force of these remarks. I really am lost, in every sense of the word.

## 7. From the subject's history to the object's

Yet this unflattering conclusion comes as no surprise. Of course I amount to nothing in myself—so much has been plain from the start. Of course the continuing self is elusive—how can that be grasped whose essence is to grasp, or be accommodated whose business is accommodation? Of course I am conformed to the social pattern—I am the screen on which every kind of pattern unfolds, and any intrinsic peculiarity could only be a blemish. Of course I die unceasingly—countless arrows of process find their mark in me, and every one is fatal; the least tremor of remaining vitality would be enough to kill the life of all who live in me. I die, to rise again in my objects. I have no history, so that countless histories may be transacted in me. All my hopes are dashed, and realized in my fellows. In the whole-hearted acceptance of this law of elsewhereness lies the remedy for my state as I have described it.

I need to face the other way, to be converted. Indeed narrowest Hell would be widest Heaven if the Devil could only bring himself to turn round and look out from the Centre instead of in at himself. And in fact self-inspection is impossible. The man whose life-story I told at the beginning of this chapter, the man whose only prospect is decline and death, is not myself. It is always the other man who is mortal: this one is below mortality in himself, and above mortality when he finds an object that cannot die. Indeed I have only to look to see that other men have bodies to die, and I have not. The syllogism *All men are mortal; I am a man; therefore I am mortal* is wrong as to fact in the minor premiss. I am a headless receptacle, not a man; or, if this headless receptacle is a man, then these creatures with heads are not men. In neither case does the conclusion hold that I am mortal. What I have in place of a head is mortal animals and mortal men, mortal stars and mortal galaxies, and the immortal Whole. When I say that all men are mortal (including him who bears my name), I am generalizing from sufficient particular instances; but when I say that *I* am mortal (I who am plainly as different from them as I could well be), I am talking wildly. What is nothing but vacancy for everything is at once too mean and too great to die—it could not be more permanently dead than it is in itself, or more permanently alive than it is in its objects.

Nevertheless these objects come to pass uniquely in me, each of them as a lively act, as a bright spectrum of emotional colouring, as a hierarchy of meanings, which are nowhere else to be found. And so in them, in the unrepeatable and indispensable universe-aspect of which they are the elements, I more than regain the same-personness, the uniqueness, which I fancied I had in my own right. Thus my real and cherished distinction from all others lies in them and not in me; or rather, it lies in what they are to me. And it is not only compact at this Centre of time and space, but turned adrift, broadcast to the ends of the world. The universe that destroys me insists upon it.

## 8. *The resurrection of my past*

The autobiography, then, to which this part of the inquiry is devoted, is really biography, the history of another, of my object. But because I am mobile, and can put myself at my regional observer's Centre as well as my own, I may speak of the history which I have in him as *mine*—provided I remember that he offers me no real escape from my timeless nothingness, which follows me as my shadow. For the price of adopting his estimate of me is that I submit to his nothingness, and know myself as not-myself. And the reward is that, as my observer-self retires through my regions, the time-wounds and space-wounds of my observed-self are progressively healed. In particular, more and more of my past is brought to consciousness.

This recovery takes such diverse forms as religious confession, psychological analysis, the Buddhist's search for emancipation by recollecting the whole of past experience, the Platonic anamnesis, and our own history, archaeology, palaeontology, and the cosmogonic aspects of astronomy. All these are ways of warming the cold expanses of our long history, of claiming the unconscious for consciousness, of reviving by a kind of natural respiration that great body of ours whose extremities are always being drowned in time. Indeed it is only in so far as we succeed in such work upon other times that this time holds anything for us. And it is only in so far as we bring to light the partially repressed and dark elements in our past that we come to present peace and integrity.

### 9. *My responsibility for Humanity*

I have to admit all that I am, making no excuses. And this means taking responsibility for my pre-individual career, for everything that the past contributes to my present. Whether I speak of karma and metempsychosis, of original sin and the flesh, of chromosomes and genes, of the Id and the trans-individual unconscious, I am confronted with two inescapable notions —past heredity and present responsibility. What I am is rooted in human and biological and cosmic history, yet I am accountable for what I am. Sincerely to deny either of these propositions would be to ask for institutional care. Yet, taken together, they must mean that I am all that makes me what I am, and that I now appoint myself my own responsible agent throughout my long pre-individual history. When I condemn myself for an act arising out of inherited tendencies and socially-conditioned defects, I am answering for mankind. 'I did it' is a lie unless Humanity, at the very least, is speaking.

And this is, after all, concealed in the plain man's opinion. Not what we do individually, but are racially, counts as most ourselves. A king is not expected to add very much to that ancestral achievement for which he is honoured, and a woman gets more credit for her inherited than for her contrived beauty. We are admired for picking the right parents rather than for improving on the wrong ones. The implication of all this is that these two or three score years are a mere moment of my real life-span. If I am held as accountable for my face as for the look on it, that can only be because my body is neither equipment loaned to me nor a rented house of clay, but that work of ages which is my true culmination now in my companions. I cannot accept my brief self and decline my lasting self, or confess to-day's sins while repudiating the millennium's, or confess these while repudiating any man's sin and pain now. And in all this there is no duplication: it is as Greeks that I incur guilt in ancient Greece, and as a twentieth-century Englishman that they are now using these brains and eyes and hands to say so.

## 10. Responsibility and the vicarious

Universal vicarious suffering is a plain fact which can only mean one of two things—either the world is a Hell in which all talk of justice is heartless mocking, or the selves that comprise it are in some manner continuous. So long as we find life worth living we virtually choose the second alternative, implying that in the hierarchy no one is lost—either by being wholly saved from himself or by being wholly left to himself. And evidently our private experiences and peculiarities are neither destroyed nor confused at this level by our unity at higher levels, but rather upheld by it. My headache does not cease to be a *head*ache because a man suffers it, or cease to be distinct from the accompanying stomach pains. Nevertheless all is shared and there is endless displacement. One organ is sick because of the excesses of another, and this we think a very proper arrangement. The old schoolmaster chastising one end of the pupil for the ineptitude of the other did not behave more absurdly than the music-mistress who was careful to rap the knuckles of the hand that stumbled on the keys.

Only hierarchy, by at once making and breaking our separateness, can account for the vicarious; and this is in practice plain enough up to our human level. Thereafter our unity is our task no less than something already accomplished, for it is manifest in spontaneous love and sympathy and self-sacrifice which may be withheld and cannot come from any cold calculation as to the hierarchical nature of things. If goodness is not to decay into prudence and habit, then our doubts about our supra-individual unity need that frequent renewal which indeed is not lacking. But on the other hand, none of our goodness could survive the complete denial of that union which is its source and sanction.

Everything depends upon the level we attain. I do not punish my dog now for what he did last week, for the continuity of the two events would be lost to him. So also I am responsible only to the extent that I accept responsibility. But I come to increase this extent by admitting my behaviour, and tracing it to sources beyond myself, and finally admitting those sources. And there is no limit to the history I can make over in this way, finding in it the meaning and intention which at first it seemed utterly to lack. My amnesia cured, my temporal continuity restored, my sympathies no longer withdrawn from my fellows, my sense of responsibility awakened, I begin to find the health and wholeness which are mine in the hierarchy.

### 11. The interval between the intention and the act

Nor is it absurd to say that I have now to take the blame for acts for which I was not to blame at the time. All responsibility is like that. The awareness and intention of an event, which is never anything in itself, can only be regional to its Centre: they are its own development. Without such a time-lapse there is nothing to intend, for the minded are always absent-minded, and mere presence of mind is mindlessness. Nobody is accountable for his deeds except in prospect and in retrospect. All self-control is remote control. It may be a split second or it may be an age which parts the awareness of the act from its unconscious source, but the principle (unlike the scope and status of the action) is the same.

This displacement is evident throughout our everyday life. When I begin learning to ride a bicycle or to play the piano or to use some new tool, I am all consciousness and no performance; when I have done learning, I am all performance and no consciousness. The act calls for attention—at another time. When I drop a plate and my foot goes out—quicker than thought—to break its fall, or when I have suddenly to dodge a car in the street, the act comes first and the thought after. Simi-

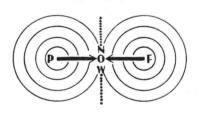

larly, I have again and again during this inquiry found the needed answer to a question coming out of the blue; but only after a long interval of thinking it out do I see why it is the right answer, and what I mean by it, and which way I intend it. I shall not fully claim this work of mine, and lift it out of automatism, till long after it is finished.

We find our careless acts working up to a crisis which demands the attention and intention which are their fulfilment. For instance, leisure comes to require its planned employment; casual meddling with nature makes deliberate interference necessary in the end; sanitation and pestology and peace are together likely to lead either to planned eugenics or to unplanned starvation and war; the economic interdependence of nations cannot go on for long unregulated. Increasingly the situation plagues us till we lift it out of unconsciousness. The fact is that mind is this bringing of the mindless to mind. For the light of our present intention can shine only into the darkness of our unintentional beginnings and endings, and what we call mere matter or energy or mindless mechanism is simply the limit of its beam.

## 12. Intending the future

It is one thing to grant that unlimited present responsibility means responsibility for an unlimited past, and another to grant that it also means responsibility for an unlimited future. Is not much of this present, as a matter of fact, spent in fear of the future?

I foresee my fate as man, species, Life, Earth, and so on; and nowhere is there hope. Not one death awaits me, but many. Yet I live on in this cosmic condemned cell, positively welcoming life on such terms. More than this: it is when I feel most alive and at my best that I endorse my whole future—human, terrestrial, cosmic, with all its deaths. My deepest desire is to live just this kind of life, with its widening circles of death. Once I used to resent being put to bed; now I intend going to bed and to sleep, and the intention is none the less real for the fact that sleep—that first essay in dying—is a necessity of nature. Neither need the fact that I *must* go on dying on an increasing scale, that I can never escape the hierarchy of my deaths, make them any less deliberate than my going to sleep to-night. Few want to live beyond eighty. And when we think of the greater life of this planet or this star or this galaxy, surely the prospect of going on, for ever and ever, is just as dreary and meaningless as the prospect of a human life that does not know when to stop. As we grow up we learn that value means limitation, and we cease wanting anything to last beyond its natural term. Our life-instincts, psychologists have told us, are balanced by death-instincts. In fact, the surprising thing is that I should ever have supposed that my many deaths are forced upon me, and are not my profoundest wish.

But it is easier to talk about dying than to die. Much practice is needed, and my human death is only a five-finger exercise in mortality. There is no avoiding the pain and the bitterness. Yet I do sometimes set foot on that plane where reality, in spite of all its astringent harshness, is what I want. In fact I think it is because nothing less than reality is my true wish-fulfilment that the stages on the way to it must always coerce me, and hold much that I can only (at best) endure with patience.

# CHAPTER XIX

# Autobiographical—From the Human to the Vital Phase

## (I) THE HUMAN PHASE, CONTINUED

### *1. My past descent*

At the start of the previous chapter I stood at the crown of a bridge, looking ahead to my death and back over my shoulder to my birth. I described my history as an ascent on the past side of the Now, matched by an equal descent on the future side. In fact, however, this is only half the view. My hierarchical decline does not begin now, but long ago. I have already fallen half the distance I have to fall.

Tradition is overwhelmingly on the side of man's decline from some higher estate. Certainly his growing up is in important ways a narrowing down, if not actually a kind of degeneration; and even science has its tale of man's descent no less than of his ascent. Which of these two my observer notes depends upon whether, starting from now, he keeps track of me in time

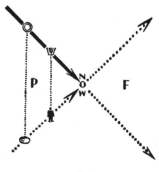

by receding in space or by approaching; for he may do either or both. If he approaches his tale is of a man, a child, a foetus, an embryo, a cell. If he recedes it is of one man, and his two parents, and four grandparents, and eight great-grandparents, and so on, till I vanish into the nation, the race, the species, Life itself. . . . The further back in time and space (or rather, concrete space-time) he takes his researches, the more exalted the hierarchical plane on which he finds himself. Conversely, the birth of Humanity out of Life, of my race out of Humanity, of my tribe and nation out of my race, of my family out of my nation—these successive births of mine are a down-coming, a Fall (or rather many Falls), a loss of status, a narrowing of sympathy, even a kind of dying. And the curious thing is that my Fall into the feeling of self-sufficiency is a Fall from the fact of self-sufficiency: the more I find myself the less there is to find.

### 2. My future ascent

If my ancestry is the ladder by which I come down from Humanity to this particular man, then my progeny is the ladder by which I climb back again. (Indeed some parents are already well on the way, living so much in their children that they are themselves almost defunct.) My future time, like my past, wages war upon every vestige of separate individuality. And if I die childless the case is no different: my gifts to the common life are worked in and worked up till they pervade Humanity.

But it is for me to find *now* my identity with these millions of men in one Species, just as now I find my identity with these billions of cells in one man. I might have kept my cellular self to myself and refused to answer for my fellow cells; and, in fact, that is just what I did do with part of myself, for a cell in me is a mere cell only because it does not feel responsible for its companions. Because of this persistent but fortunate streak of mean-mindedness, I remain cellular. And because I have more generous moods, I am also a man. But my growing sympathy need not stop here: I may go on to Humanity by the same means. I have to take up into myself the battle that I find outside—the clashing temperaments and habits of life, the contradictory philosophies and religious beliefs and political faiths and artistic schools, the struggles of every kind which make our world so lively and so terrible. I have not to wind up, but to claim and incorporate as a going concern all these furiously competing systems of action and feeling and thought, all these heated arguments, without damping them down and without exception. For Humanity is not other than a man's rounding off, the rest of him—just as a man is only a sympathetic cell so Humanity is only a sympathetic man. I can grow beyond a certain limit only by becoming other cells, beyond another limit only by becoming other men. There is no quarrel going on outside me that is not my own indecision thrown on to the world's screen. The immense and indispensable differences between men are organic in me, and their resolution at their own level would be suicidal if it were possible. It is by accepting and containing all this strife, as strife on its own plane, that we come to the remote yet present time and place where it is assuaged. The tranquil one admits the untranquil many.

As the man is the solitary genius and demigod of his cells, that cell who from the start 'loved' his neighbour as himself, so Humanity is the genius and demigod of men. And just as between the cell and the man there is a miniature hierarchy of tissues and organs, so between man and Humanity there is a miniature hierarchy of great and large-hearted souls. Like banknotes of high value, they are few because they stand for so many, or rather are so many. Humanity, the present realization of magnanimous men, is to me, the ordinary selfish human being, exceedingly distant. He is the ancient source and eventual goal, my higher and time-removed self; but linking me with him is this hidden intercession of saints who grasp on my behalf more and more of what I really am.

### 3. My fourfold history

My story, then, is fourfold—a past line of ascent and a past line of descent meeting now, and both prolonged into the future.

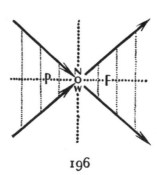

What I must avoid is unbalance, too much insistence upon any one or two of these four arms. My pessimistic preoccupation with the down-pointing arms must be offset against my optimistic preoccupation with the up-pointing; my scientific interest in the two infrahuman arms against my religious interest in the two suprahuman arms; my passive acceptance of the past Pairs against my active realization of their future counterparts. Always symmetry—hierarchical symmetry about the horizontal axis of the Pairs, temporal symmetry about the vertical axis of the Now.

Therefore if my life-span is likened to a bridge, it must be to one which combines an arch and a catenary—one that hangs from two points and rests upon two points: one that is (like a span of the Forth Bridge) roughly symmetrical about a horizontal axis as well as a vertical. Thus it is neither along a level track nor as a single vehicle that I make life's journey: whether I look back or ahead, I find always a Pair of vehicles so roped together that the one goes up while the other goes down.

### 4. My fourfold history—the past Pair

Consider the two past tracks converging to my Now—the upper coming down from Humanity and the lower rising from the infant. Their Paired connection is plain, for in the broad lines of his growth the child repeats the racial history. Of course we cannot find a detailed correspondence between infant babblings and the beginnings of language, between the child's developing skills and primitive craftsmanship, between his love of custom and primitive ritual, between the distressful crises of childhood and adolescence on the one hand and successive racial high-water marks on the other. But about the existence and the meaning of the parallel there is little doubt. Obviously it would be absurd to equate the child's eidetic imagery, his inability to think in abstract terms, his lack of objectivity, his undeveloped sense of separateness and of personal responsibility, his animism, his night fears, and his excited interest in animals and caves and magic and dark forests and fairies and goblins— absurd to equate these with their counterparts in racial history. And equally absurd to deny that they are counterparts, or that any likeness is accidental.

The young are terribly old-fashioned. Born into a pre-human world, I have to catch up with the contemporary world of the human adult, through such intervening worlds as nursery and school and college. Indeed it is not merely that I pass through these stages in the primitive society of my equals, but that whatever company I find myself in is necessarily reduced to my own date. Many of us, in spite of all the short cuts, never reach the present scene, but remain thousands or millions of years behind the times. But our common calendar hides the ample time-depth of society, on which its chief divisions of labour, and in fact its very existence, are based.

As in his mother's womb he grows a backbone and eyes, so in more capacious wombs (ranging from cradle to university) the well-nurtured man grows clothes and appendages for eating and reading and writing and a thousand other functions, till in the end there is born a vast and truly up-to-date human organism. And this development has two Paired aspects—group-racial and individual, or phylogenetic and ontogenetic—neither of which makes sense without the other. The principle is abundantly recognized in our educational methods, if only by implication. Admittedly the historical approach is not the only one, but something of the kind is made inevitable by the expanding capacity and interests of the student. The intricacies of modern knowledge in any subject can be led up to only by degrees, and the historical paths are generally the best, seeing that they link the present multiplicity with its own past unity. Particularly in the arts the true primitiveness of the child's outlook and work is acknowledged. A mass of evidence, supplied by many branches of research, indicates that the child's way lies through the Palaeolithic and the Neolithic, and the Ages of Bronze and of Iron; but the road is so cleared of obstructions, so paved and straightened for fast transit, that we hardly recognize it.

The truth is that a child growing up is a world growing down. We find ourselves always living in the age to which our mental age belongs. Yet we belong to all times and can never finally mature. Clearly we cannot spare our primitive cells and molecules and atoms; less clearly, but not less certainly, we need our savage and infantile past. For my easy goodness, which is not the overcoming of temptation, which rejects without a struggle the selfish alternative, is only lack of imagination; my entirely fearless courage is only stolidity; my temperance, if it never finds excess attractive, is only dullness or timidity. Nothing blooms in my garden but what I have painstakingly grown from the seed. My higher conduct is a joint effort of the beast and the primitive and the adult modern man, working together in creative opposition.

It is the same with my thinking. Wisdom is nothing without its shadow, or unless it is the correction of unwisdom. Propositions do not stay valid: like our homes and bodies they need constant renovation. Habitual truth, truth that does not arise new every morning out of the less true, hardens into dogmatism. For not only are childish errors the muscles and the limbs of adult wisdom: they are organs that need using, and without them we are crippled. Our mistakes are not the rubbish we pitch out of our edifice of truth, but its framework. (To be more precise, truth falls into three layers—the lower through which we think we have advanced, that which engages us now, and the higher that still evades us. The first we dismiss as vulgar error; the second we accept as the whole truth; the third—with which the first is Paired—we dismiss as mere poetry or mysticism; whereas all three are in fact interdependent parts of the whole.)

Similarly in art the merely up-to-date is altogether trivial. The best contemporary work, on the other hand, is the topmost shoot on the tree of an agelong tradition: it could not be new if it were not fed and held aloft by the old. It is as true of great artists as of great saints and thinkers that practice makes imperfect, and that only he learns who never finally learns anything, who is always being driven down to the primeval sources.

## 5. My fourfold history—the future Pair

What of our future—the future which, like our past, forks into a road that goes up to the suprahuman and a road that goes down to the infrahuman? Are its diverging aspects as thoroughly Paired as the converging aspects of our past? Is the old man a citizen of future cities as the child is of past ones?

What is plain is that both roads into the future end in ruin: our racial doom upwards is almost as certain as our individual doom downwards. But this is not the whole story. There still lives the ancient ideal of the sage, of the truly venerable old man who, having discharged his practical duties, links bodily decline with spiritual ascent, and whose growing magnanimity, because it stands far above the tumult and savagery of everyday life, can do much to redeem it. If we respect this ideal, if in falling short of it we fall short of our own completion, then old age's down-going and ungrowth from manhood are only the counterbalancing condition of its arising, of its growth from manhood to greater and more permanent embodiments. The first continues that hierarchical descent which leads down from Life and Humanity to the individual man; and the second continues that ascent which leads up from the cell and the infant. As the child is the foetus of the man, so the man is the foetus of Humanity. The child belongs to the primitive race out of which the nation has still to emerge, and the sage to the same race in its late phases after it has reabsorbed this nation—both are internationalists, living in worlds that for the contemporary man do not exist. They are two of society's necessary anachronisms.

Every seventh year of a man's life used to be called a climacteric or ladder-rung, but for us who have sawn off the top half of the ladder the word necessarily has a very different meaning. Particularly in the West we have forgotten how to grow beyond middle age, how our narrowing activity can make room for widening sympathy, how wisdom can sharpen itself by taking the edge off cleverness, how the valley of humiliation and the delectable mountains of old age imply each other, how the forking of our future (as of our past) guards against spiritual pride on the one hand and mere grovelling on the other. The only antidote for decline into the childish is ascent into the childlike. As we look ahead and behind, earth and heaven are increasingly separated yet increasingly conjoined. And so the second half of our life at least tends to be a blurred mirror-image of the first; and second childhood may, like the first, stand as far above manhood as it stands below.

## (II) THE VITAL PHASE

### 6. From Humanity to Life—past

Looking back again upon my past, and this time looking somewhat further, I find the region between Humanity and Life to be elaborately subdivided. The species leads up and back to the genus *Homo*, and thence to the original primates, the original placentals, the original mammalian stock, and so back and back to primordial Life itself, to that body of which all creatures are the limbs. Each step back in my racial history closes the gaps in this greater body: I come to the spot where I am identical with my species, with all mammals, with all vertebrates, with all animals, with all the living. And, seen in their full historical perspective, each of these increasingly primitive types includes (and therefore surpasses in hierarchical status) all the branches which later spring from it—the vertebrates, for instance, as embracing mammals and men, are higher than both; and Life is by far the most exalted of all biological organisms, even when she is as yet the embryo of herself. In short, ancestor-worship is very appropriate: we have come down in the world.

### 7. *From Humanity to Life—future*

I look out also upon a future which, like my past, more and more transcends this individual man, to a career which by one means or another merges with Humanity's and eventually with Life's. Whether the species, having made its huge and precious gifts to Life, will then die as so many have done; or whether its already profound symbiotic union with other species will reach a point where Humanity will have lost most of its distinctness from the rest of Life—in any case it is the fate of all man's works that they shall not stay human, but shall lose themselves in the vital and terrestrial environment.

But my task is to realize this destiny now. This means going back upon my ancestral decision to cut myself off from other men, other animals, other living things; it means present reunion with all the past selves I had disowned, and the knowledge that without them I am only a piece of myself. No·doubt the order of our reunion, by means of science and sympathy and love, is not always the order of our parting; yet on the whole I find it easier to enclose, in the widening circles of charity, my own kind rather than another. The more distant my relations the less our family likeness; they are increasingly strange, and often repulsive. My need of them is therefore all the greater. Every time I lift a stone I stare across a gulf of ages into a mirror, even though I recoil at the sight of my forgotten faces and limbs.

### 8. *From man to cell—past and prenatal*

These two upper paths of my history, the past and the future roads by which I regain the ancestral wholeness that I have lost, have for inferior counterpart the history of my descent into the world of the individual animal and the cell. The younger I am as a child the more primitive and inclusive my human group, and the younger I am as an embryo the more primitive and inclusive my animal group. Of course I cannot in nine months of womb-history become a full-grown coelomate and fish and reptile and amphibian and primitive mammal (any more than, in the nursery, I can become a troglodite or a savage warrior in earnest). I can only hurry through this long ancestral tale as best I can in the circumstances.

### 9. From man to cell—future and post-mortem

Even more blurred is the story of my future descent. Yet—accidents apart—it is plain enough that I shall die as a man before dying as an animal, and as an animal before dying as cells. I shall go to pieces, in due hierarchical order.

The several layers of my nervous system, constituting a hierarchy in which the later guides the earlier without superseding it, remind me that I am what I was. In a sense, I am the way fish and reptiles and mammals perform their higher tasks. Is it not the merest prejudice to say that the real reptile is the one outside man, the reptile that has failed; and that the reptile at his self-transcending best, in his waking and self-conscious state in me, is of no account? And certainly without this infrahuman filling I am a hollow abstraction, a roof without walls or foundations. Indeed, just as a building may outlast the ruin of the attic but not the basement, so my earlier levels are more permanent and less vulnerable than the human. A fire in a packed theatre, or any disaster that catches us off our guard, and there is no longer any doubt about the beast beneath the skin. Our humanity is the first casualty. We lose our heads before we lose our spinal columns.

There are many descriptions of the way down. The neurologist's tale may be of the anaesthetic or drug (or unassisted degeneration) which puts out our nervous centres in the order (very roughly speaking) of their evolutionary juniority: the last to come is the first to go. The physiologist points to organs which do not cease their vital functions immediately they cease to comprise a living whole, and to cells which are active for some time after the man has died. A third observer may report that I am no longer interested in my fellow men, but only in my private pleasures and pains; and then, no longer caring about

the experience of all my organs and cells, but only in some part
of this experience, I sink to their level.

But the important point is that this future descent is for present realization, as the condition of the linked ascent. To find
renewal in the young lives of my children I have to put off all
adult acquirements; to send up family branches Life-wards I
have to go down to the level of a solitary cell. The higher I
would climb the more drastically I must be remodelled. The
rising weight is securely roped to the sinking counterweight.
My present rebirth, my recognition of what I was and shall be
on suprahuman planes, cannot be separated from my present
dying, my recognition of what I was and shall be as infrahuman.

### 10. Awareness of the 'facts of life'

But this confession of infrahumanity is no easy task. How
often does it come home to me that a few thousand days ago I
was immeasurably the inferior of the fly on the window, that
almost all my life has been spent beneath the level of the kind
of creatures I find in a drop of stagnant water, that my manhood is the last-minute afterthought or appendix of my animal-
ity? When I am eating fish do ever I recollect my own so recent
fish-hood, or consider that I sit down to every meal a cannibal?
When I despair of the future, do I ever remind myself that our
highest and wildest earthly hopes are nothing to what the least
successful of us has already accomplished in his own individual
lifetime?

Nature, it is true, conspires with us to keep our past dark.
Yet it is after all only a biological 'accident' that we do not
grow up as independent larvae in aquariums and zoological
gardens instead of wombs, or at large in sea and swamp and
forest. A slightly different turn in evolution, and a human
mother could scarcely tell her own larval beast-children from
beasts in general—till the day when her pets are at last certified
human by the family physician. But surely the actual story—
the amateur fish (along with its private sea) invading the
human being and turning it into an aquarium-on-legs, and the
ape building his nest in a human belly instead of a tree or a cage
or a baby-carriage—surely this is still more remarkable. Yet it
leaves us cold. We have heard confused rumours of what we are
and have done, but when the facts begin to dawn upon us we
and our world will be transfigured.

The fact is that we would purge our hierarchy of all middle-men, all go-betweens. We contrive at once to acknowledge and deny the infrahuman stairs by which we have climbed from the foot of the pyramid up to the human stage, and the suprahuman stairs by which we have come down from the summit. Supposing ourselves to be electrons in the universe-Atom, we jump in one bound from the Centre and the Circumference to the middle orbit without ever crossing the intervening regions. We like to pretend that at birth we emerge from the deepest Nothing, and at death confront the highest All; and we ask for the mediation neither of embryos nor of angels. Celestial and uterine embryology are equally repressed, and our tails are as embarrassing as our wings.

More than this, we repress man himself—man who is his own bogy-man. Rarely can I face that amazing ninety-nine hnudredths of myself which I share with other men: all I have eyes for is the one hundredth which marks me off from them. The differentiae—these miserable hair-cuttings and nail-parings of a human being—are made to do duty for the whole. But in fact it is not the uncommon but the common in me which is truly marvellous, and my astonishment which is proportional to the scarcity of its object is the vulgarest sensationalism. Just to be a man—never mind what kind of man—that is far to surpass all the wonders of the world, that is wonderfully to sum up the universe's sumless mystery. He walks about in a dream who has never sweated and trembled before the awesome fact of man.

## 11. My fourfold history as a filled concentric system

And I am now all that I was and shall be. These four Now-centred movements of my Life-history—ascending and descending, past and future—make up an organized whole which is both present and projected into time. And this sample of the world in action, rather than the scattered fragments of it which science and common sense attend to, I accept—if I cannot take seriously the sample which I am, what can I take seriously? It discloses a Life whose humble beginnings and endings are the temporal extremities of a concentric whole that embraces Humanity and this man, of a time-whole which is nothing if not organized about this or some similar Now-centre which is Life's own no less than Humanity's and a man's. In time as well as space the vital is the true core of the terrestrial, and the human of the vital; and to consider Earth without the Life at her heart, or Life without the human history enfolded within Life, is to mistake the shell for the shellfish. My human conduct cannot be

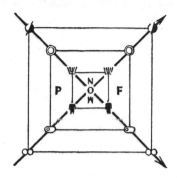

understood by concentrating upon the first peripheral onset of the stimulus and the last peripheral tremor of the response, while ignoring the many-layered body that intervenes and its Central void or synapse; and neither can my vital conduct, or Life-history, or any function of Life, be understood apart from the hierarchical stages by which it is reduced to and built up from nothing now—the Now which is the receptacle and fountain of the entire process.

## 12. The fourfold recapitulation of my Life-history

But this fourfold concentric time-system repeats itself and is really eightfold. That is to say, it presents itself to me now as two versions—a long-term covering probably thousands of millons of years, and a short-term covering probably less than a hundred. (i) My long-term past is a tale of a descending and narrowing ancestral group—the series includes metazoa, fauna, the vertebrates, mammals, Humanity—and of ascending ancestral individuals belonging to these types. And my long-term future history is likely in its own way to reverse this tale, as the human merges again into the vital, and the vital reverts to something like its primitive state before it is at last extinguished on this planet. (ii) My short-term history recapitulates the long-term, swiftly ascending from cell to Life and as swiftly descending from Life to cell, through the man that is now. Nothing less than the Life-cell Pair—busy changing places, busy with their rhythms of vertical interchange—can live. But time is short. Accordingly I must be this Life-cell Pair in its ascending and descending aspects, and with its proper human filling, yet scaled down to workable time-dimensions. My seventy years could not be a life story if it were not the summary of my other life story.

Nevertheless it is the racial tortoise who really sets the pace, for the faster the individual hare runs the longer he must wait while the tortoise steadily comes up with him. My past is a long

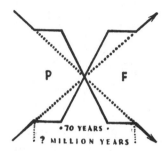

P    F

•70 YEARS •
? MILLION YEARS

arrest followed by a quick advance, my future a quick advance followed by a long arrest. Thus my business is to be as far ahead of the times at death as I am behind them at conception. While in my ancestors I was (at tortoise-pace) evolving into reptiles and mammals and men, I was content to remain in myself mere cells—right up to the last moment forty years ago, when I started (imitating the hare) to catch up. And now, having got the knack of speed, I must anticipate the slow development of later generations, and then await them. Starting as the parasite of man, I must end as his host.

And my downward movement is similarly divided into a steady decline on the one hand, and a long waiting followed by a sudden descent on the other. Until forty years ago I held aloof from Life's divisions and subdivisions; then in quick succession I submitted to them, arriving at Humanity and man; and soon I shall die down to mere cellhood. I am first reminiscent, then contemporary, and at last anticipatory.

### (III) THE LAWS OF DIVARICATION AND FOETALIZATION

*13. My racial past—non-specialization*

Of the many qualifications and elaborations which this concentric schema calls for, I choose two for discussion here. The first points to the fact that each of the four movements of my history takes a zigzag rather than a straight-line route. Like a tacking ship, I get along by pursuing one course for a time, then another. The second points to the fact that I tend to sail too far on each tack, to leave the fairway, and run aground.

When a creature hits upon a new expedient which makes for survival, it is apt to take it to the limit and so become a narrow specialist—supreme, perhaps, in its own class, but no longer in evolution's navigable channel. The birds, for example, fringing their arms and fingers with gigantic scales, were side-tracked; now they cannot get back to the evolutionary thoroughfare, where the unspecialized five-fingered hand is preserved inviolate against the day when it will grasp a tool, and eventually a joystick controlling detachable aluminium wings. So also the horse, running on one of his fingers and losing the rest, became a speed-expert too soon, instead of waiting till, with unmutilated hands on a steering wheel, he could move far more quickly. It is as if almost every type but man were the victim of some kind of monomania, as if only he and his ancestors were sufficiently non-committal, stopping short at each critical fork of the tree of life and turning back before it was too late to turn.

Or rather, a part of him did again and again run off into dead ends, leaving the rest of him to his zigzagging journey. The vegetable and animal worlds are full of his bright ideas pushed to their logical conclusions. In fact the whole system with all its branches is indivisible, and the specialized and unspecialized types imply and need each other in Life's total economy. In uncommitted man the committed creatures went on to self-consciousness; in them he remained as the content of that self-consciousness.

## 14. My individual past—foetalization

My ancestral and long-term refusal to become prematurely expert is repeated even more emphatically in the short-term version of my history: as embryo I sail closer to the wind, more directly to my destination, than ever I did in my ancestors. Avoiding much of their adult specialization, I keep in the main to the recapitulation of their embryonic history; for in the convenient seclusion of the womb I can afford to do without even that moderate degree of professional expertness which, in my grown-up ancestors, I had to cultivate to get a living. Therefore my shorter history is a childlike version of my longer, a tale of incurable amateurishness, of false starts, of ever-renewed plasticity. Nothing succeeds like failure.

Animals are not alien beings, but only too good at their jobs to be quite human. Conversely, men are not exclusively human, but only too restless and too versatile to settle down to any one animal virtuosity. And in so far as we do settle down, ceasing to be the foetalization of the animal, we begin in our behaviour (and even our looks) to resemble one or another type of adult animal. Lesser creatures really do provide the perceptive with a rough index to the endless variety of human character.

## 15. My individual past—postnatal 'foetalization'

We are born into the upper sixth, for our postnatal education gives only the finishing touches to our prenatal, to our long non-vocational training. Liberal education in the womb is continued in the liberal education of school and university, in so far as all premature expertness is resisted. The student does not make straight for his distant goal, but for this mediate object and then that as if it were the real end; and always he changes direction just in time. Thus by divarication, by stopping short of partial goals, he weaves his way towards the real goal which in fact holds much of what they offered but could not give. The victorious lose every battle but the last, while doing their best to win them all. I succeed only by failing, in spite of all my efforts, to become worm, fish, ape, warrior, actor, engineer. . . . Yesterday it was meccano and cubbyholes and bows and arrows in the nursery; the day before it was a tail and gill-slits in the womb. But my childish ineptitude carries the promise of a maturity which is more than compensation.

## 16. My divaricated future ascent

By such drastic means I have compressed into the first half of this little lifetime the past achievements of a thousand million years; and by similar means I have to compress into the second half future achievements no less lengthy. For this life is the womb-version of my longer life, the version in which hours must do duty for millenniums, and where delay is fatal. Therefore while a man ought, indeed, to love his family and country and species, he cannot afford to do so inordinately, at the expense of more inclusive sympathies. The lower loyalty is always threatening to become its own enemy by becoming the enemy of the higher. Fondly we imagine that our real advantage lies in allegiance to our nation right or wrong, in the good of Humanity at the expense of all other creatures, in the improvident satisfaction of Life's day-to-day demands upon the planet's resources, in the cosmic imperialism which is even now planning to impose its own Earth-life upon an inferior universe. The blind alleys are many, and few are those who are not lost in them. Religion, art, science, philosophy—even these when parted become so many dead ends. The higher life does not lack its sabre-toothed tigers and dodos, its doomed monsters of adaptation.

In short, our progress is subject to the law of elsewhereness. Only the oblique approach is an approach. The gain which this hierarchical level seems to offer is only to be had at higher levels which make no such offer overtly. It is only by giving himself up to the supra-individual that each finds individual fulfilment. The great obstacle is self-satisfaction, absence of need. How much that man loses who, because he is so good at being human, is never driven to find out what else he is! He cannot gain even this world if he loses his soul which belongs to all the worlds. It is the worst kind of eccentricity to be so well-balanced that you are never upset in the direction of the Whole.

## 17. My divaricated future descent

The principle of foetalization governs all four arms of my history, including that future descent which is the condition and correlate of my future ascent. Here also are the dead ends, the pseudo-goals. What is wrong with the sensualist, the drug-addict, the imbecile, the suicide, is not that they are rushing down the hierarchical slope too fast, but that each has found a way of halting his descent short of the foot of the hill. Only the one who gets safely past, not only his humanity and vitality, but his materiality also, arrives at the nadir of nothingness whose other aspect is the zenith of allness. Merely to die is not enough. To be redeemed from death I must die at all hierarchical levels, intentionally, in the short time that remains. That is to say, I must realize my present condition. The truly level-headed man sees himself as neither level, nor headed, nor a man.

# CHAPTER XX

# Autobiographical—The Cosmic Phase

*1. The provisional chart of my fourfold cosmic history*

I stand at the mid-point of all my mortal lives, having as many deaths ahead of me as births behind me, having as far to fall as I have climbed and as far to climb as I have fallen. The earlier a function comes the later it goes. A little time on both sides of the Now brings me to my human frontier; more, to the limits of my vital and terrestrial career; more still, to my solar and galactic boundaries. Ultimately I came from the void and shall return to the void. Such, in outline, is my larger history so far as I can now make it out. In this chapter it remains to say something—however provisional and incomplete—about its remoter phases.

I think of my vital boundaries as following the standard fourfold pattern. (i) The more or less homogeneous, primitive Earth

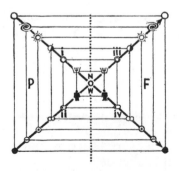

gradually divides into geospheres, and eventually the biosphere or Life emerges; and at the same time (ii) some of Earth's molecules are built up by stages to become cells. But in the dying

Earth all this is presumably reversed—(iii) the distinction between Life and other geospheres is lost, while (iv) Life's cells finally break down into mere molecules. In the beginning there is hierarchical convergence (a differentiation in one superior with an integration of its many inferiors) and in the end hierarchical divergence, restoring something like the original state. And what I must not do is remove any of these four arms from the body as a living time-whole. In particular, I have to remember that Life's tree springs from one planetary 'Seed' no less than from innumerable molecular 'seeds', and that the maturing of the first by differentiation and of the second by integration are one maturing.

This story is seemingly repeated, in its main lines, at the terrestrial and solar levels. The primitive Sun (comprising, perhaps, more than one star) somehow came apart to form the planetary system, while solar atoms came together to form planetary molecules. Just how and when the planet will die back into the Sun is doubtful; but it is reasonable to suppose that all, or nearly all, which now distinguishes the terrestrial (alike in its superior and inferior aspects) from the merely solar, will pass away.

As terrestrial-molecular I am old, as solar-atomic still older. And I take it that (somewhat as the finish of an article soon wears off, while the basic material outlasts all else) my primitive solar-atomic phase is likely to persist long after almost all traces of my less primitive terrestrial-molecular phase have disappeared.

Of the many rival cosmogonies, the more plausible postulate a uniform substratum which develops the Paired aspects of one all-embracing whole that divides, and countless all-excluding parts that join forces. And at the end, it seems, something like the primeval uniformity will be restored—a universal heat-death, in which there will be no local concentrations of energy, and nothing will ever happen. And even if (as some suppose) the physical universe as a whole may avoid this fate, nevertheless our own Galaxy, with every other, is mortal, and destined to run down to virtual extinction.

In summing up the Paired stages of this history, I go back to the figurative language of Chapter XIV. The hierarchical organization opens with a proprietor and a staff of menials. Some of these are promoted to the next grade, which is administered by a new class of very high officials deputizing for the proprietor. Promotions from below to a still higher grade of menials require the appointment of a second grade of supervisory staff, in accordance with the rule of symmetry—the higher the inferior the lower his Paired superior. And this crea-

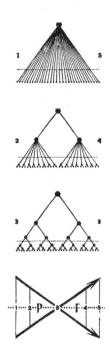

tion of new ranks from above and below goes on till the gap between the two orders is filled, and the business fully staffed. Such is its present state. But, looking ahead, it seems that retrenchment will become necessary. The first to go will be the latest comers; and dismissals will go on in order of juniority till the organization is back where it started. And if this story is not altogether unlike that of some human businesses, that is small wonder, for they are sub-departments of it.

*2. Recapitulation in the cosmic phases of my history*

It is not only the human and vital phases of this history which are governed by the great law of recapitulation. At all levels I fold up my time as if it were my umbrella. My long-term and extended cosmic history is the opened-out state of many shorter histories which cover the same ground in a fraction of the time. Indeed such outlines of history, and outlines of outlines, are my total history's proper filling, without which it is an empty shell. Moreover each main phase of my long-term career has its own means and degree of abbreviation: naturally the protracted earlier and later phases call for more drastic cutting than the compact middle phases.

(i) *Recapitulation—the terrestrial phase*. As I find in the men and the species around me every stage of my human and vital evolution, so I find in Earth the still more remote terrestrial stage—that 'dead' self which I abandoned long ages ago in order to live, yet which I never for a moment abandoned. With one part I narrowed to the Life-cell Pair, and with the other I stayed terrestrial-molecular, biding my time. And now at the very last moment the two streams—inanimate and animate—flow together again: some of the retarded part of me catches up with the rest, coming to vital and human status in a few hours or minutes. Just as to be human is to bring nonhuman creatures to manhood in various ways (notably by feeding upon them) so to live is to raise the dead. My recent living self must live upon my old lifeless self, as I subject planetary material to a lightning process of evolution. The air I breathed and the water I drank this morning were then the property of my backward terrestrial phase; now they have joined my human phase in this account of their adventure.

The planet's life is a nest of self-epitomes. For me to live at this level is to repeat continually my long-term terrestrial ascent-descent—without the hare the tortoise is only a tortoise shell. Of course it would be useless to look for details of the slow journey in the swift one, to expect so brief a synopsis to do perfect justice to such an original—embryonic and dying man have little chance to go into the minutiae of ancestral achievement; anabolic and katabolic man still less. Nevertheless feeding is in a very real sense life's beginning and defecation its end—from soil and water and wind man is always being born; into soil and water and wind he is always dying, leaving behind for witness as it were a string of little corpses.

(ii) *Recapitulation—the solar phase.* It takes thousands of millions of years for the solar to become the human, and it takes a few minutes. Indeed there is no human or vital phase at all except as the solar phase continually issues in them at many rates, and embraces their ascending and descending Paired processes in its own four arms. Thus solar energy is always becoming planetary (as the atmosphere's layers digest it), then vital (as plants further digest it), then animal (as herbivores digest plants), then human and less than human (as we digest our meat). It is only by filling itself out with many such summaries of its life-story that this star has any life-story to summarize.

(iii) *Recapitulation—the galactic phase.* Having produced the living Sun, the Galaxy no more abandons it than the Sun abandons its living planet, or the planet abandons its Life. For (as I have tried to show) our culture is primarily celestial, and an intelligent solitary Sun, with no social life at all, is an impossibility. Once more, then, there has been on the one hand a slow and steady evolution from the non-human to the human, and on the other a long waiting followed by a swift making-up for lost time. In this instance the recapitulatory mode is what we glibly call light. The other star or galaxy evolving region by region from nothing over there to full status here, and this star or galaxy similarly evolving from nothing here to full status in its companions over there—these communicate by re-enacting their long-term history. The excessively protracted fourfold story of my galactic development, scaled down to the workable dimension of a few million years, is involved every time I glance at a spiral nebula; or rather, it *is* the mode of my seeing. Galactic intercourse is abbreviated galactic history.

(iv) *Recapitulation—the final conquest of time.* But even light as a mode of recapitulation leaves much to be desired. It is still too

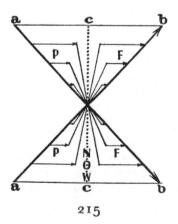

slow; it cannot pierce to the highest and lowest levels; it is no good to me if I go blind. Only the intellectual light which sweeps the universe instantaneously, whose beam shines even to the apex and the base of the hierarchy, whose rays need no retina, can complete and perfect all the lesser modes of recapitulation by finally reducing my wedge-shaped There-now to a mere line. But here is the abolition as well as the climax of recapitulation. For it cannot be said that there exists at the extreme hierarchical levels any time-interval between (a) our original derivation from them, and (b) our eventual return, and (c) our present realization of both—viewed from the middle levels, these three occasions are as temporally remote from one another as they could be, but from their own point of view there is no time to part them. Moreover this culminating means of recapitulation—namely 'consciousness'—is not other than the history it recapitulates; therefore it is in no ordinary sense recapitulatory. It breaks free from the coercive order of history and leaves out what it wishes; yet it leaves out nothing, either of the original history or of its epitomes.

Every mode of recapitulation has its hierarchical ceiling and primary object—in this instance, the highest. The proper study of man, of the mind that is in him, is the Whole: consciousness is to it as light is to heavenly bodies, and growth and decay to biological organisms. But just as light, though shining from heavenly bodies, illuminates all earthly ones, so consciousness is not restricted to the ultimate Pair, but is the ground of all the Pairs. In Earth we feed on what is less than terrestrial; in the Sun we see what is less than solar; in the Whole we know what is less than the Whole. Thus it is not merely the Whole which is present at this Centre: as a result of its presence here all my other objects are present too. For only as accommodation for the Whole am I nothing, and only as nothing am I accommodation for anything. I do not need to see all things in the Whole, so much as to see that there is no other way of having any experience whatever.

### 3. 'Foetalization' in my cosmic history

For me to live is to find myself at the confluence of numerous versions of my history, so that I can claim the universe as mine in short-term practice because it was and shall be mine in long-term fact. The modes of my history are the modes of my maintenance, and what distinguishes them is degree of 'foetalization'.

Man surpasses the animals by letting them all surpass him; the biosphere is little more than a planetary interface, yet it outdoes all other geospheres; Earth is a small planet, the Sun a commonplace star, the Galaxy not the giant it was once thought to be, yet they are great enough to make this record of their ordinariness. The inferior series shows the same tendency to avoid the too-complete, the over-developed. Thus it is not of the higher atoms and their compounds that cells chiefly consist, and not of independent and self-supporting cells that animals chiefly consist. The price of advance to the next level is some degree of failure—or restraint, or abbreviation—at this level. And the swifter the mode of recapitulation the more drastic this abbreviation has to be. For instance, the light that is now leaving me presents to my regional observers the main steps of my evolution—atomic, molecular, cellular, human, and so on—but in summary, with scant attention to the intermediate historical stages. As for consciousness, it is committed to no evolutionary programme whatever, but is free to climb up and down the hierarchical ladder in one stride. It combines the ideal end of recapitulation—perfect respect for historical fact—with the ideal end of 'foetalization'—perfect disrespect for historical fact.

*4. Hierarchical process: the three 'explanations'*

What is the secret of this sheaf of histories tied at the middle, of my simultaneous ascent and descent of the hierarchy by so many and such different vehicles? The 'explanations' may be reduced to three: what I become is determined (i) by what I was at the start, by my original substratum or matter or germ-plasm; or (ii) by what I am now going through, by my circumstances; or (iii) by what I shall be in the end, by my goal. In regional terms, the first gives the credit to the Centre, the second to the radius, the third to the circumference.

And none of them will do. Each points away from itself to the others. The original featureless matter is plainly incompetent to create anything, and we are referred to the finished product. But this is powerless to work back upon its own past. We must look, then, to development. But here we find much that cannot be accounted for in terms of a shaping environment, and we are referred again to the beginning and the end.

Now this reference back and forth is no new thing in this inquiry. Indeed it is not surprising to find that the elsewhere-ness, the processes of projection and reflection which I have seen building me at all levels, should regulate also my total history. In fact they are the essential dynamic. Just as the star is here at the Centre yet a fugitive from here to my star region, so the flower is Central in the seed yet regionally projected; and we call this projection growth. And just as the star I project is not stellar over there in itself, so the flower is not a flower in itself, but on closer inspection is observed to be seeds, and then a single seed—a nucleus from which projective growth may again arise. In short, the true rationale of development unites in a living whole all three 'explanations'.

Consider the chief alternative to this doctrine. It has two quite incompatible versions of our particles or matter: they are the lowest of the low, opaque and senseless—and the divine Original of the highest and best in us. Again, it finds in man two utterly different types of cell—on the one hand the germ cell that creates him and the brain cell that creates his universe, and on the other hand the rest of his cells. The former are supra-human and indeed divine, the godlike joint authors of man and his world and all that he finds valuable in it; the latter are not merely animals, but animals of the humblest grade.

I propose to do without this picturesque modern myth, this most astonishing of all instances of animal worship. For I say that, on the contrary, both these types of cells are lowly animals which, in common with the rest of the hierarchy's members, are in themselves nothing but room for objects of equal rank, which are sent off by various means and at various speeds to their regional destinations. And this dispatching, this projection and reflection between Centres and through regions, includes every type of evolution and growth and hierarchical process, every life-story and every mode of its recapitulation.

CHAPTER XXI

# Autobiographical—Life Beyond Death

*1. Survival and cosmic migration*

What kind of after-life can I reasonably expect? In this chapter three of the various alternatives are considered—survival by identification with an ascending Humanity, survival as a disembodied spirit or something of the kind, and survival which arises out of the supersession of time.

The first of these offers no hope of 'personal' immortality: indeed it is survival by progressively giving up hope of survival as this restricted self. For it is practically certain that all the vehicles of our life—even Earth and Sun and Galaxy—are bound to break down in turn. And the programme is that we shall at each stage develop a technique of survival sufficient to see us through to the next stage, so that accumulated gains are shifted from one celestial conveyance to the next in time to save what is essential. We are offered a vision of Humanity colonizing and taking over other planets and stars, just as already this planet has been taken over.

Nor, if we grant the possibility of some thousands or millions of years of scientific advance comparable with the advance of the past hundred years, is there anything absurd in so ambitious a plan of cosmic expansion. It looks unlikely now, but it is certainly not impossible that we shall save ourselves by promoting ourselves from terrestrial to solar rank, and even higher. And unquestionably our past holds many hints that the price of survival is growth, and that the way to keep what talents we have is to multiply them. Perhaps we may after all be forced to climb the hierarchical ladder, and to find our future where tradition has so often found it—in the skies.

To the objection that such a cosmic future would not be mine,

I reply that I find myself thinking now the thoughts of Earth and Sun and Galaxy, and making their future my concern—this chapter so far is my witness. The decision rests with me: their destiny is mine if I care to make it mine.

## 2. Survival and psychical phenomena

But this is at once far too much and not nearly enough for most of us. We want this particular human mind or view-out to survive at the human level after its body or view-in has vanished. And we point, perhaps, to psychical phenomena which suggest that our hope is not vain.

Death is like a severe and worsening case of schizophrenia; it is a bifurcation in which the superior and inferior elements of the personality pull apart, the first merging with the wholes of which it is part and the second dividing into the parts of which it is the whole. Now though there is obviously much evidence which is neither for nor against such an interpretation of death, I can find some that seems to be for it, but little or none that is indubitably against it. Thus there are accounts, by persons who have been near to dying, of an experienced division into a confused 'lower consciousness' linked with the bodily organs, and a lucid 'higher consciousness' which surveys the scene with calm detachment. Again, many so-called 'communications from the dead' suggest that amongst them the barriers between individual minds are falling, and falling in such a way that some kind of hierarchical order is established.

## 3. Survival and the supersession of time

The two alternatives which I have so far touched upon point to the hierarchy: the third is fully hierarchical from the start. It postulates a lowest grade of individuals for whom all events are either past or future, middle grades for whom some are also present, and a highest grade for whom all are present. And the recipe for survival is that we entertain objects of exalted hierarchical status—objects that give us now the time they take to come to themselves in us. Our survival, coming under the law of elsewhereness, is the enjoyment of others' survival, and our immortality consists in making room now for the immortal Whole. Thus Raleigh's prayer before his decapitation—'Set on my soul an everlasting head'—was granted in the asking, for it was addressed to an everlasting object. I am dead in me, my friend is alive in me, my God is deathless in me. In the earthy darkness of my womb many long-lived heroes are conceived, but only Heaven's Child cannot die: and he is the death of me as well as the resurrection and the life.

Is not such immortality only a euphemism for extinction? Yes, if it were not that the Whole, while removing every hierarchical distinction, ensures that no distinction once made is ever lost. The destruction of time is the preservation of all the things of time. The finished picture conserves as well as completes every brush-mark.

And this is indeed what we want—to be our sole selves yet rescued from ourselves, to be immortal yet relieved of the weariness of time that goes on for ever and ever, to be sure that none of the immense agonies and labours and joys of the past is lost or forgotten, to know that our present striving (however seemingly useless) is not wasted, to be rid of all desire to sacrifice any man upon the altar of some glorious Moloch-future, and above all to enjoy undying life now in the middle of time. No grandiose time-table of cosmic migrations, no unbodied spirit-life however lofty, no version whatever of survival can meet the case, except as it issues in this version. Man is a cat with nine lives: the ninth, being immortal, makes the others immortal, but he can discover this only by dying eight deaths.

If time is taken at its face value, half the good deeds in the world are foolishness, and honesty is more often than not the worst policy. 'All's well that ends well' is the Devil's own motto. On the other hand, to act lovingly towards all creatures without hope of temporal reward is already to live in the timeless kingdom where they are one. Time is the product of our reciprocal distrust: we abolish it to the extent that we love. And to love is to deny the separate self. And to push this denial to the limit is the only way to keep inviolate the separate self. Conversely, insistence upon our 'personal' immortality is itself a demonstration of mortality. The specification of the true time-machine is an open secret: it is self-transcending sympathy and goodness. And the working of this engine is no patent process: to go forward in time we must go back—back to where we broke away from all other creatures, so that we may now go forward in them. Trying to claim the future asymmetrically, without its equal past, is like trying to get a sum right by going on and on, instead of going back to where it went wrong, and only then going forward to the solution. The survival of the living and the resurrection of the dead are the halves of one whole.

Nevertheless immortality is not to be contrived by us but enjoyed as established present fact in the other. Indeed our business is rather to cease breaking up the time-transcending totality than to start building it. Not what our life is, but what it holds for us, is the vital question. Our need is not length of days, but depth, capacity, comprehension, and the death that makes room for the life of those we love.

It is no ordinary culprit that is his own headsman, and no ordinary corpse that thus conducts its own autopsy. For me to witness my death is to survive it—dead men do not practise self-observation. To be present at every one of my cosmic deathbeds is to outlast them all, and by dying to get the better of death. The fact is that death is life's most terrible but least dispensable instrument, the absurdity without which life is absurd indeed. For without the edges of the canvas where there is no painting, there is no painting; and without life's black mourning-border of death there is only death.

Death and time war against all our abstractions, and progressively kill every illusion of wholeness. Our dying is the graduated reversal of our belief that it is we who live and the universe that is dead. And either we acknowledge now that our life, which is eternal, lies only in the Whole, or that fact is forced upon us by slow hierarchical stages, so that by dying on an ever vaster scale we are at last made to discover what really lives. Death is realism about life, and the road to it.

### 4. Quickening the dead past and future

I am as defunct as my universe. But responsibility is a powerful life-saver. It belongs to the essence of the moral subject that he cures a torpor and a creeping paralysis that are equally his world's and his own. For his present accountability makes him liable at once for the widening past that is seen to determine him, and for the widening future that he is seen to determine, till in the limit no time or level remains innocent of him and his intention. And it is the degree of his success in this work of cosmic resuscitation which establishes his rank in the hierarchy.

Accordingly our survival cannot be parted from the survival and revival of the universe that we have done our best to murder: it needs a world that has no room for death or mindless mechanism. In other words, the problem of mortality is in principle the problem of automatism—the main difference being that whereas the first asks how we can do without the past and future universe, the second asks how it can do without us. If we say that in us Earth and Sun and Galaxy happen now to be self-conscious briefly and by accident, and they always have done and will always go on doing very well without us, then indeed our immortality is superfluous: the universe has no use for it. But if we say: this mind, of which we are the vehicles, contains now the whole of our history at these and all other levels, leaving none of it to lifelessness and mindlessness, then it is plain that our immortality arises from the nature of the mind in us, and of the universe which is its content. Then it is no longer any question of entreating the past and future to find room for us, but of seeing that they belong in us, and can no more spare us than we can spare them.

I may say, if I like, that the automatism of the physical universe is both prior and posterior to the mind which discerns automatism—so long as I add that this mind, once arrived, has unlimited retrospective and prospective effect, for known and intended automatism is no longer automatism. As a man reapeth so shall he sow. No doubt we must insist on the mindless, applying our minds to it increasingly, but let us occasionally reflect that our practice is the progressive disproof of our theory, and that the only valid argument for the universe's mindless mechanism is absence of argument. We do not always have to keep a straight face before an order of things whose declared purpose is to show us that it has none. And indeed I cannot appoint myself my own registrar of births and deaths, my own midwife and coroner and sexton, without living a prenatal and a post-mortem life. I cannot tell my greater history, from its remotest pre-galactic beginnings to this moment in which it is all realized, except by tracing innumerable lines of causation which meet here and now—'purposive' converging lines which run counter to the 'non-purposive' diverging lines of 'natural' causation—thereby raising all of it to intentionality. Such a history, by selecting at every turn past material with a view to present outcome, itself supplies the mind it cannot discover.

Nor need I marvel at the expanse of time thus made over to mind: the longer the period the higher the mind—the more comprehensive the specious present—which works upon it.

Thus what really is mechanism from the lower hierarchical viewpoint is intention from the higher. And in fact I find it no more difficult to dissolve and quicken those parts of my higher body—terrestrial and solar and galactic—which are dead in time than those which are dead in space. In my terrestrial capacity I do not feel pot-bellied or lumpish or weighed down by the planet's heavy core, nor in my solar capacity do I find myself perennially encumbered with the great lifeless masses of Jupiter and Saturn—they are lighter than thistledown and clearer than glass, obscured by not so much as a dust-grain. I carry no ballast, no mere passengers, no tare even, on my upward journey; and the more lifeless matter I take on board the more lively I become. What makes me slow to understand this is my abiding illusion that mind is a butter which, when spread over our bun-shaped universe to make it more palatable, gets thinner the further it goes; whereas in fact it gets thicker, till in the end we have all butter and no bread. Indeed it is the absolute brevity and absolute smallness of the Central animating principle which ensures its absolute extension in space and time, and its absolute effectiveness at the Circumference.

Light is not light at its source, but in the zones it irradiates. Similarly present 'spirit' is as empty without past and future 'matter' as this is senseless without present 'spirit'. To shine is not to have but to give light, and to live is not to contain but to confer life. Therefore we must see, in the dead wastelands of space and time that enclose us, our livelihood, our living space and our living, the raw material of our immortality. Only against such resistance can effort be expended. Without such fuel life's fires would go out. The world's torpor sets the measure of the vitality which overcomes it, and part of the greatness of the universe is that it needs to be so great.

## 5. *Beyond history: the timeless*

When all has been said on the subject of my history, it remains a fact that I am an extreme case of arrested development, for I can never leave the Centre which is incapable of any change. The immense surge and sweep of evolution is powerless to shake my grip on the rock of timelessness—the timelessness which is submerged below time, not that other timelessness which rises above time. To realize this instantaneous Now, to live in the present moment, taking no thought for to-morrow or yesterday, must be my first concern. And my second must be to find in this Now all my to-morrows and yesterdays.

The use of time is to call time's bluff. It is like money—the more you respect it the less good it does you: you can do nothing without it, and you can do nothing with it except get rid of it. Time arises out of its partial repression. Admit all of it, and it vanishes. The man who would live well this life in time needs to know that it is based upon that lowest hierarchical level which is timeless by the exclusion of time, and upheld by that topmost hierarchical level which is timeless by the inclusion of time.

# PART SIX

## CHAPTER XXII

# The New Angelology

### *1. The approach from tradition*

Upon what may be called the angelology of this book four different lines of thought, four approaches, converge—the approach from tradition, the approach from present intuition, the theoretical approach and the practical approach.

Though universal tradition favours a hierarchy of beings more or less similar to those which the previous chapters have described, certain qualifications must be made. First, belief in the hierarchy (and particularly in the suprahuman part of it) has often been rejected by individuals and groups, and at times driven underground. Second, pre-scientific hierarchies take many forms, some of which are very fantastic. Third, there is much diversity of belief as to how far the remoter levels of the hierarchy are accessible to man; as a rule, however, he is not altogether shut out from these nonhuman realms, and their influence upon his earthly life and destiny is apt to be reckoned overwhelming.

As to the work and place of the various orders, there is a notable measure of agreement. We find physical height matching real status, so that the hierarchy is eventually strung out along a radius reaching from earth to the remotest encircling heavens. Cosmic space is regionally organized and non-uniform, and the long-range is likely to be divine. And from their stations in the sky the suprahuman orders guide our present life and all earthly events, and they are seen as our homes or our companions or even ourselves in after-life. They take on lofty moral attributes and mark out the stages of the mystic's upward journey. There is a tendency to treat cosmological status and degree of mystical

226

# THE NEW ANGELOLOGY

illumination as exterior and interior aspects of the same state. (It is their enjoyment of the beatific vision which holds Dante's celestial bodies to their circular courses. And indeed his revolving saints and angels and stars are not inextricably bound up together for nothing, or in the interest of merely poetic necessity.) Yet distinctions of level are here sharpened rather than smoothed over, and it is not man as mere man who mounts Heavenwards. Jacob's ladder has double work to do: it is the pillar which holds apart the floors of the universe as well as the staircase which joins them.

Counterbalancing these luminous and beneficent orders is the nether realm of dark and often subterranean powers (or else subcutaneous and physiological ones)—erratic, stupid, malignant, or definitely evil. But here we find a significant contradiction: the higher beings are in certain instances bad, and the lower good. In the language of Chapter XIII, regions may be reversed.

And it is not only, or even chiefly, in the religion of primitive men that we find well-developed hierarchies, but rather in the great civilizations and cults of antiquity, and in the higher religions that have lasted to the present day. These not only put man at the Centre of a system of regions at once physical and moral, but spread him through them all: in this life—and even more in the life to come—the good and the evil, the high and the low in him, find their own hierarchical levels. And at its completest this concentric scheme (this Er-myth pattern, or mandala, as some would say) has for radii the four arms of man's universal history, as he comes down from Heaven and arises from the dust, and then returns to both.

Here indeed is a proper man, a man of depth and stature, vertical man. And here indeed is a cosmos. Instead of our verminous hierarchy of great and little fleas *ad infinitum*, a noble succession, a majestic and godly order. And the contrast between such a universe and our modern cosmic funeral-parlour, or soap-bubble expanding in accordance with the equation $d^2r/ds^2 = \frac{1}{3}\lambda r$, cannot be exaggerated.

## 2. The approach from present intuition

Our knack of quietly dropping a belief, while repeating its phrases with a show of sincerity and indeed fervour that deceives even ourselves, is wonderfully used upon our angels.

Jesus and the Apostles are in no doubt concerning the hierarchy and its power and its place. We know better, but (if we call ourselves Christians) crude denials are out of the question. It is so much easier to preserve the shrunken and fossilized heavenly hosts, along with other decorative relics like the Star of Bethlehem, in the tiny self-contained museum-case world of Christmas carols and greeting cards and stained-glass windows, like celestial bees in amber. Their stings are drawn. Dead angels are harmless and pretty, and we can always solemnly play the game of make-believe with them.

Yet they are not permanently embalmed, but only shamming dead. In fact the hierarchy is perennial. Names and physical aspect and relative stations—these may change again and again, but the thing remains. The divinities which are the superior hierarchical series of one people may become the demons or inferior series of their successors. Star-gods in our own tradition have become angels; angels have become disembodied star-moving intelligences; and these have become natural tendencies and forces. In a machine-driven universe angels are an unemployed aristocracy soon liquidated, for every great scientific advance puts more of them out of work, or rather compels them to wear the workmanlike disguise of Laws of Nature.

Nor are they finally got rid of now that science finds even compulsive laws and forces almost as mythological as their winged precursors. The wise have committed judicial murder upon the universe, but the simple and unlearned quietly revive the body, using the most unorthodox of medicines. They are not for long taken in by the apathetic fallacy, or content to reduce the divine dance to a St. Vitus's dance, to cosmic clockwork. Indeed the more colourless the scientific model of the universe the more outrageously ornate the unscientific, for man will not be cheated of his angels. Of course it is easy to show that in detail most popular mythology—to be found in astrology, theosophy, spiritualism, and scores of cults in the Old World and the New—is childish. But what remains, what is indestructible and held in trust for mankind, is the general insistence upon a sacramental universe, the intuition of illustrious beings, of a magnificence and royalty we seldom dream of, of a vertical or tiered world which cannot be less wildly glorious than our wildest imaginings. Only the poets, and occasional prophets that are half poets, are close enough to the people to speak for them, and to tell us that in our bones we love and fear the hierarchies, that we are of the angels' party without knowing it, and have not lost so much as overlooked them.

### 3. The theoretical approach

Stars are first the players in the heavenly game, then footballs kicked around by indefatigable teams of angels, then mere footballs. Consider the main stages of our estimation of the Sun. First, he is a living being like ourselves, only brighter and more divine. Then gradually his animating genius is distinguished and separated from his body, which becomes mere insensate matter controlled from outside. Corpse and wraith begin to decompose for lack of each other; there is no more particular guidance, but only a carcass adrift in the sky and at the mercy of every current. And the next step, after so thoroughly killing the Sun, is to get rid of the body. This is done by dismembering it. We take its sensible qualities one by one and remove them from the object over there to the perceiving subject here, till even its apparent motion becomes our own: all is transferred from Heaven's eye to the beholder's. To complete the work, we dissolve the Sun's bare matter in the acid-bath of modern physics.

And so we have, in a deed spread over many centuries, killed our Sun by inches and disposed of the body. However the murder story has a sequel. The victim turns up in the least likely place—in us. In taking his life we have taken on his life. And even this is not all. The tail-piece is the discovery that the 'I' that now claims the motion, the warmth and brightness and colour, the science of celestial navigation, the divinity, does not lie outside the 'Thou' from which all this has been removed. The entire transaction, the passage of one quality after another from the object-pole to the subject-pole, lay within the Sun. It was only after all the Sun's own way, by voluntarily dying, of arising in us to fuller self-consciousness and more abundant life.

In such ways all our gods are done to death, to rise again in us; and our social heritage is at once the lethal instrument and the vital outcome of this multiple dying. As the origin of a culture is to be found in its divinities, so its development is their slow destruction. We live by deicide. Our ascent is the gods' down-going. We eat them till the universe is for us almost empty and we are full to bursting. To this dangerous state we have now come. The time is ripe for the rehabilitation of the divine object. We have to see that we are possessed, and that what we thought was our human science is in fact the science of the angels—not all of them good ones—who have made their abode in us.

First we have the living hierarchical universe. Next, physical science slowly drops her iron curtain, leaving on one side the many-levelled graveyard of the gods, and on the other the many-levelled mind that is in man. Finally, psychological science lets down a second safety curtain, dividing the theatre of the mind into a many-levelled conscious and a many-levelled unconscious mind. Thus we have exchanged our one psycho-physical hierarchy for three—a mindless hierarchy in time and space; a bodiless hierarchy which, though it reflects the first hierarchy, is itself out of space; and a third hierarchy which is both bodiless and mindless (mindless in any ordinary sense), an individual and racial unconscious which reflects much of the first two hierarchies, but is itself out of space and in some manner out of time also. And each of the three is a mere relic of the totality. The first is all matter and no consciousness; the second all consciousness and no matter; the third neither matter nor consciousness.

They have now to be put together again. Each department of science has to be seen as the mind of its own subject-matter. Art has to recover its cosmic function, to re-assimilate beauty to cosmic status, so that once again we can hear in our loveliest music the voices of star-angels and the ancient harmony of the spheres; and so that every true artist is once more reverenced as the vessel of divine inspiration. Finally, the structure of religious experience must be joined again to the structure of the universe, uniting Heaven with the heavens, angelic choirs with sidereal systems, the moral order with the physical—till the starry haloes of the saints become something more than sacred millinery, the Ascension something more than a myth or a levitation-fantasy, and the Jacob's ladder of the mystics something more than a fire-escape in a Freudian dream.

We have too many lopsided hierarchies on our hands—hierarchies of physical bodies, of mind conscious and unconscious, of loyalties, of intellectual systems, of the mystical and religious life. To these let us bring the rule of economy, and see if one many-sided hierarchy will not do. Doubtless Occam's is no safety razor, and—even if we are careful not to cut our universe's throat with it—we are still in danger of ending with a face-of-things altogether too tidy and clean-shaven. On the other hand, let us beware of mistaking our mental laziness and intellectual squalor for obeisance to the unsearchable mystery —the angelic mystery that shows itself only to those Jacobs who will not give in to it, but wrestle till the morning.

It is our tragedy to have parted the star-strewn vault above from the moral law within. Yet there was no other way. The order of the conscious mind is the order of nature, but neither can be realized till nature is studied as if it were a stranger to mind. Again, the order of the unconscious is, in the last resort, the order of the conscious mind, but unless they are distinguished all is obscure. Sidereal intellect flowers only under the cold radiance of mindless stars; angelic art needs to be in love with a sternly objective physical datum; the moral law must withdraw from the night skies to become the more heavenly. Such is the natural history of the angels.

*4. The theoretical approach: the science of angels*

Mediaeval man robs the angels of their bodies; renaissance man robs them of their functions; modern man robs them of their existence—he gives the *coup de grâce*. It has taken us a millennium thus to disprove our angels, and we have done so with immense thoroughness. All that was above our heads we have drawn into them. We have changed places with the universe: we who used to be its desert are now the oasis. It is not that we have grown out of our angels but that they have grown into us. Indeed our refutation of them has been altogether too thorough: it has become something like their demonstration. For if this is disproof of the life above us then eating is the disproof of food and learning the disproof of books. Our angels have migrated, not absconded; they have passed from transcendence to immanence, not passed away. If they have been reduced to an absurdity, then we are that absurdity.

But the study of these greater organisms cannot remain much longer neglected. A new and surpassingly wonderful world is about to show itself—a world that is all the more fresh and thrilling for having been so long hidden. We are ready for the universe's April, for a revelation which will be to us all that the solar system and the Americas were to other generations. We are about to look upon the visible gods, the innumerable hosts we are still too clever to see, the hierarchies which are still hiding behind the protective colouring of their own obviousness. Indeed the only real difficulty is that they do not sufficiently try our faith. It is because they are so entirely credible that we are incredulous. In violent contrast to so much of our science, they do not ask us to believe a single impossible thing before breakfast: therefore they are a superstition, a fallacy, nonsense—except in the eyes of poets and intellectual outcasts.

Till the seer lends us his eyes, seeing is disbelieving. Yet it was only when we ceased to believe in angels that angelology advanced beyond Dionysian guesswork. The anatomy of the principalities and powers in the heavens, their physiology, girths, weights, complexions, pulses, body-temperatures, age-groups, expectation of life, taxonomy, and races—all are the concern of a science that entertains angels unawares and on condition that they sham dead. Nor is the psychology of these shining giants neglected: only it is so strictly behaviourist that we are not even tempted to credit them with consciousness. But the truth is that all our science, whatever its hierarchical level, is psychological science, and behaviourist or introspective according to how it is viewed: when we study the stars our science is their behaviourist psychology, and when we study our study of the stars our science is their introspective psychology. Thus astronomy—which is knowledge of the stars by the stars—is of two quite different kinds. The first is the way stars think, and the second is the way stars think they think. But at present both kinds of thought are unnaturally parted from their thinker, and unaware that they are stellar and not human.

Our work is now to distribute vertically and horizontally, in space and in time, this intelligence that is concentrated in us. We have to spread it vertically, by restoring it to its own hierarchical levels in commerce with the human level; horizontally, by attributing it equally to the subject-pole here and the object-pole there in accordance with the rule of elsewhereness; in space and time, by acknowledging its double location at the Central Here-Now and the circumferential There-Then. Briefly, the problem of our angels is the problem of their projection. Without ever leaving us, they must fly to every corner of the space-time world. For the legion that possesses us is so great that nothing less than the universe will serve for its embodiment.

But first we must see to what extent the dying transcendent has been secretly reincarnated as the immanent. According to an ancient teaching, the soul, on its downward way to earth through the heavenly spheres, derives from each its gift; we are more grasping, and claim all the goods that we find on our regional journey, till arriving at the Centre we are replete to the degree that the universe is depleted. As soon, however, as we realize our interesting but perilous condition, and see that this Void to which we have come is a womb big with the hierarchy of Heaven and Earth, then our delivery and the universe's re-population are at hand.

Let me give a particular instance. Only by distributing the unconscious throughout the hierarchy can we make sense of it. Surely this ghostly, run-away, and altogether mysterious mental system of many levels (in part individual and in part trans-individual or racial), this unconscious consciousness or un-attached experience which is somehow not experienced, is more fantastic and baffling than any antique myth. But to what em-bodied minds, sufficiently *en rapport* with my conscious mind, sufficiently graded in quality and age and scope of purpose, can I attribute my unconscious processes? The answer is plain: to the hierarchy. Here are vehicles in abundance and fitted in every way to carry all my unconscious psychical content. What they want, I have too much of: my ghosts fly to their corpses and the world comes to life again. All the nebulous angels and demons of the analyst, his phantom world of Ego and Id and Super-Ego, of the unconscious and preconscious and conscious, of autonomous complexes, censor, libido and the rest, which now drift in mid-air, need to be tied down at every point to the merely physical series. To be studied the two aspects had to be isolated, but the further their separate investigation is pushed the more artificial they become. As for the programme of this reunion, the main lines are already plain. The primitive, amoral, illogical Id; the Ego coping with the present human scene; and the Super-Ego, or severe higher authority from which religions derive—these are only the infrahuman and human and suprahuman hierarchical grades partially conceived and under other names. Even the Pairs—the Id and the Super-Ego working together to bypass the conscious Ego—are recognized. Already the fact is that, however we try to describe the procedure of the hierarchy of Heaven and man and Earth, we find ourselves using most of the analyst's concepts, suitably disguised.

## 5. The practical approach

Many good things have flowed from belief in suprahuman beings: indeed our culture itself is the outcome of such a religious vision and impulse. It is true that divinities do not survive their gifts. Nevertheless needing gods to destroy is still needing gods; and when the last remnant of sanctity has been gathered in from the universe to ourselves the only thing to do is to send it all back again. Something like a new angelology is the condition of our renaissance. In fact the human itself cannot long outlast the suprahuman.

Our real choice is not in the long run between divinities and no divinities, but between reasonable and beneficent ones and their opposites. If official science and religion and philosophy combine to take away our good angels we are terribly apt to turn to bad angels. If we are denied a celestial hierarchy whose office is to join us in glorifying God, we try to make do with a terrestrial hierarchy whose office is to deify the Leader, or Party, or Ism, and physical force, and the elemental powers in matter. What may be called the law of the conservation of Mana ensures that when the gods die their potency passes to baser gods, to man and to the demons beneath man. In their flight from the nine heavens to the depths of the human psyche, our angels have inevitably changed for the worse: there is a smell of brimstone and more than a glimpse of the cloven hoof. It is not the glory but only the power which leaves the skies for man, and man for matter.

The body of our universe is centrifugal, its mind centripetal. And now that their separation in the giant centrifuge of our civilization is nearly complete, the need for reversing the machine becomes daily more apparent. Our future greatness lies in the discovery of Heaven's greatness; our present happiness, and sanity, and perhaps survival, lie in the rediscovery of a hierarchy of life and meaning and bliss that are wholly outside ourselves.

*6. The practical approach: religion to-day*

The trouble with religion unmodified by science is that it is incredible; with religion modified by science, that it is not religion. No wonder the pious grow less intelligent and the intelligent less pious, so that both become fragments of men.

Our many personal and social problems are at bottom cosmological. We suffer from a disease in our universe; all the rest is signs and symptoms. And the cure is a vision of the living hierarchy. Awaiting us is the momentous discovery that science, so far from having destroyed the essentials of the traditional religious view of the universe, has only confirmed them, supplying an immense quantity of empirical detail in place of fantasy. Not new facts, but a change of viewpoint, is all that is now needed to reveal to us in its magnificence the sacramental universe that satisfies head no less than heart. Two things we can do without—on the one hand a sacred Plenum, a museum overflowing with dusty ecclesiastical relics; and on the other a sacred Vacuum, a house of God so emptied and swept and garnished that, if it is not presently occupied by the good suprahuman, will be requisitioned by a less desirable authority. The proper use of the scientific broom is to preserve and not destroy the furniture of religion. And indeed the long retreat of faith before science's relentless advance has a very different look once religion claims science as its own agent and general, who hands back at last each territory, not depopulated, but purged of the forces of superstition. The friend of the essence must sometimes be the enemy of the accident. Science threatens religions, not religion.

A faith that cannot stomach the universe does not deserve to survive. Nor can it, without a cosmos. It is almost impossible to go on believing in God without believing in angels, or in angels without believing in man. If we rediscovered hierarchical man in the hierarchical universe, we should be quite sure of its need of a Head; but our levelled-down universe has little use for one. Even the pious are now for the most part near-atheists: though they spare the king they have executed all his ministers. In truth our self-glorifying war against the Court of Heaven has been aimed at its Sovereign, and our resubmission to it is part of our resubmission to Him.

Certainly it was no high intellectual necessity which led to such an act of cosmic insurgence. Our strange conviction that the hierarchy stops short at man—or, if it goes on, that between him and the Absolute there is nothing—is much more due to defect of imagination than excess of reason, to parochialism than enlightenment, to worship of the human parish pump (or rather of its countless rods and pistons) than of the divine Oneness.

Even when we still have some use for angels our belief in them is so unimaginatively man-centred that it is almost disbelief. How odd that the hierarchy above us should be all mind, that the hierarchy below us should be all body, and that only we (where they overlap) should be both. Is it perhaps a common superstition in the hierarchy that one's own order alone is body-mind—a delicious blend of spirit and matter sandwiched between great uninteresting slabs of mere spirit and mere matter —so that for instance angels have us for engines and archangels for ghosts? Really it is time we suspected that our human view-point is not the only one.

### 7. *The practical approach: art to-day*

As science bleeds the universe of its science, and religion bleeds it of its religion, so art bleeds it of its art—all is transfused to man. Beauty leaves the hierarchical world for the non-hierarchical eye of its beholder. But one-level subjectivity is the death of art. And its rebirth is the revelation of the divinely masterful Other, the tremendous many-levelled universe that compels the artist, and is no longer a convenient horizontal row of pegs on which to hang his feelings, his sacred private experience.

Until the artist and the priest find the universe that the scientist has found, it remains a Frankenstein's monster, an energetic body without a soul. No wonder our world is mad: two-thirds of it are missing. The business of art is now to join religion in (what is from one viewpoint) the recognition of objective values at non-human levels, and (from another) the hierarchical dispersion of the subjective values that have been long accumulating in man. So thoroughly have we insulated the human from the cosmic that when at last they are brought together the effect may well prove overwhelming, as the pent-up energy is discharged in a flash of illumination revealing undreamed-of beauty. We are ready for a great poet to celebrate the marriage of the visible Heaven and the virgin Earth, in an ecstasy proportional to their long separation and continence.

*8. The four approaches: summary and conclusion*

In this chapter I have said (i) that men generally have believed in a living cosmic hierarchy; (ii) that the same belief is widely held to-day by the common people and by the poets who speak for them; (iii) that science not only confirms and purifies this belief, but is an important part of the intellectual procedure of the hierarchy itself; and (iv) that for the sake of our health and happiness, of our art and religion, and even (it may be) of our survival as a species, a sincere belief in the hierarchy is indispensable. More concisely, belief in angels (call them what you will) is supported by tradition, present intuition, science, and practical considerations. Of how many of our most cherished convictions can we say half so much?

But our works are our only eyes. We cannot see the angels as they are till we flood them with the light of our active love and admiration. We have the hierarchy which our behaviour deserves and our charity implies, and we are required to pay in the currency of action for all our insights. The angels still perplex me, but that is because I am so rarely good enough for their company, and because my deeds will not let my thoughts run altogether out of sight.

CHAPTER XXIII

# The Three Stages of the Angels' Descent

*1. The three stages: theological, humanist, scientific*

The incoming flight of our divinities through our regions is necessarily their hierarchical descent; and the story of our civilization is a tale of this descent by three stages, which I shall call the theological, the humanist, and the scientific. In these, the suprahuman and the human and the infrahuman orders are emphasized in turn. And their representative men—their men of prestige—are the saint, the artist, and the scientist, respectively.

During the course of their inward migration, our angels appear first as the suprahuman which is good, and also beautiful and true; then as the human which is beautiful, and also true; and finally as the infrahuman which is true. To grasp their nature we must unite all three stages of their flight in a single vision. That is to say, we need three eyes to see the universe, and they are centuries apart—the telescopic eye of the saint and mystic, the unaided eye of the artist, and the microscopic eye of the scientist. Our universe is out of focus till we see with the eye of goodness that looks beyond everyday things, the eye of beauty that looks at them, and the eye of truth that looks into them.

But regions are reversible. Accordingly the centripetal movement is also, in some degree, centrifugal, and hierarchical ascent and descent have a way of changing places. For example, the ideal of the Middle Ages was saintliness, whereas the reality was too often corruption and cruelty and social injustice; it is left to us, no longer caring about saintliness, to put into partial practice its humanitarian implications. In them the root; in us the flower—though a withered and drooping one. Again, our ideal is science, the truth about the universe, while our reality is a universe from which all meaning has been carefully taken away, leaving a set of abstractions which are as 'untrue' as they could well be; we know less and not more than is good for us: our disasters are due to our growing ignorance. For the unitary vision, the knowledge which our immense but atomized mass of information both conceals and implies, we must go back (as I have done in this book) to something like the mediaeval synthesis of Dante. Here the flower precedes the root. Each epoch points to another. Thus, though the preoccupation of the Middle Ages was that which stands above man, one of its chief effects was to ensure his own importance at the centre of the world, and though the preoccupation of the Renaissance was man, its effect was eventually to reduce him to matter. In making sure that the universe shall contain no principalities and powers to lord it over him, he inadvertently loses himself in it to the point of extinction. As in a man's life story so in society's there is displacement and elsewhereness and time-range: the deed, the working out, is remote from the intention.

## 2. The three stages in philosophy

Till Bacon and Descartes finally handed in her notice, philosophy was notoriously the maid-servant of religion. Indeed she was at first inseparable from theology. But gradually the gap appeared and widened—the gap between the higher and revealed knowledge which, as above reason, became the special province of religion, and the lower rational or natural knowledge which became the special province of philosophy. The result was that philosophers, leaving the more exalted hierarchical levels to theologians, were increasingly at liberty to study the middle levels in abstraction from all that is above them. Even such wholes as Mankind came to be reckoned mere words, and only their parts were real.

And so there emerged the world of mere men, of private individuals. But this familiar scene with its endless variety, its irreducible hard facts, is not the true field of the philosopher. He is interested in generalities. Accordingly his alliance with the Renaissance humanist and artist was briefer and far less productive than his alliance with the mediaeval theologian.

Far less productive, also, than his alliance with the modern scientist. And now it is neither the moral and mystical verities of Heaven, nor the beautiful earthly facts of the middle realm, but the underlying truth of things, which is his passion. Convinced that the jewel of perfect knowledge lies buried at the foot of the pyramid, he pulls down the entire structure to get at it. Universe-dissolving doubt and analysis are his tools, and they do not leave much standing above ground. Cosmology becomes impossible because there is no longer any cosmos to discuss, and the philosopher contents himself with discussing his discussion. But it is dull work for him to go on sharpening his knife long after he has chopped his material so fine that there is nothing left to cut.

Or, if he is of a more practical turn of mind, his thinking is apt to come to something like this: The universe, being dead, is merely the means to terrestrial life; terrestrial life, being blind and infrahuman, is merely the means to human society; society, being no unitary organism, is merely the means to the individual organism; this organism is merely the means of maintaining a central nervous system, and in particular a brain which is the seat of consciousness . . . and so on to the Centre—or rather as near to it as the scientist can take him.

But this is no bad place to come to, if he will now turn round and look at where he has come from. The philosopher in his thousand-year pursuit of truth reduces the old universe to himself and so to nothing—to nothing but a repository for the new universe which is not himself.

### 3. The three stages in science

The growth of science is the dismemberment of the universe by degrees, from the whole down to its ultimate particles. For so long as the body was organic and in one piece the scientist could not get to work: it had first to be chloroformed, then operated upon. Brilliant anaesthetists and surgeons at length isolated a limb for study—the solar system—with notable and familiar results. A second great amputation revealed the Earth —the Cape Route to India, the Americas, Australia, the globe that could at last be mapped and measured and treated as quite distinct from the surrounding universe. The sciences of Life, prominent in the nineteenth century, consider only Earth's skin, and are in fact a kind of planetary dermatology. And then the sciences of man, detaching various scales and corpuscles of this skin, make remarkable progress. But the human being vanishes into the infrahuman just as he is about to be revealed: there is no stopping this cosmic operation half-way through. Having cut away the universe, severing each nerve and artery that unites him with his world-body, man is not left with himself, but with a fast disintegrating series of particles. In the end —so thorough is this surgery—there is almost nothing at all left on the operating table. The key science of to-day is nuclear physics.

And what is true of the object of science is true of its organization: progress is by division and subdivision. It is no accident that the earlier science was a unitary discipline speaking one language and all of it within the capacity of one man, whereas our science goes on splitting itself into departments which find one another incomprehensible. For the science of the lower levels can by no means avoid their limitations. Unity, full understanding between departments, is certainly possible, but not at their level. The higher levels are the unity of the lower, and there is no other. In time we acknowledge both—the details and the plan which is their meaning—but fail to bring them together. For centuries we build our world-house out of too few sticks and stones, arranging them in all ways to make them do; and when at last we see that what we need is more materials, we become so fascinated by each growing pile that the house is forgotten.

Building no longer interests us, but only building materials. But the finer we grind them the more explosive they become: for the dust of our universe is gunpowder, not cement. Humanism is unstable in the direction of materialism, and materialism is instability itself. Science's fragmentation of the universe is the release of growing quantities of energy. We owe this dynamism of the third stage to the potential stored in the first, when at huge cost man withdrew from the infrahuman regions of his object to the suprahuman. The hermit weeping and starving in the desert for love of Heaven, the religious inventing new torments to bring the lower into subjection to the higher, the scholastic theologian and poet driven up through the spheres by their intellectual passion and longing for the everlasting beauty —these learned on our behalf the art of keeping distance. In the language of an earlier chapter, mediaeval man circulates in regions where God and His most exalted angels are facts; but later generations jump to narrower and narrower orbits, where suprahuman beings are fictions. They have gone up in smoke. Our machines are driven by this highly combustible angelic fuel. It was not so much the fission of U235 nuclei which destroyed Hiroshima as the fission of the cosmos, due to our regress from the place where there is a cosmos to the place where there are only protons and electrons. For the world-fabric does not suffer itself to be unravelled without some forcible reminders that the threads we fasten on are not all there is. The pieces are for ever becoming something else and going somewhere else, showing by many madly energetic contradictions that they are self-alienated. Forces are the relics of a universe. Only a fallacious body-mind dualism leads us to suppose that we can shatter the world mentally and leave it physically intact; and only the fallacies of simple location and of inequality deceive us into thinking that we can atomize without being atomized. Really it is unsafe to dismantle a universe. The further we take it down the more dangerous the parts become to handle, till in the end they are nothing but naked, directionless violence.

### 4. The three stages in religion

There are many versions and aspects of the traditional Christian division of history into the era of the Father in Heaven, of the Son on Earth, and of the Spirit in man's heart. And certainly this centripetal movement may be traced in the history of Western mysticism. The contemplatives of the early Middle Ages, under Augustinian and Dionysian influence, were chiefly theo-centric: they spoke the language of ascent and the rejection of the earthly. The second stage, most apparent in St. Francis, is marked by the rediscovery of natural beauty and the importance of the middle hierarchical levels; the tendency is here Christo-centric. The third stage, culminating in the great company of the mystics of the sixteenth and seventeenth centuries, is not so much concerned with the awful otherness of God, or with His incarnation in the sensible realm, as with His presence in the soul. The subtle techniques of the inner life now claim minute attention.

Of course there are many exceptions to this broad centripetal movement. Indeed it is one of the marks of the great mystic that his Object is thoroughly trinitarian, and distributed equally at the Circumference and radius and Centre of his regions: such a mystic gathers up into a unity all three historical stages. It is lesser souls who, as Father-centred, are liable to become coldly moralistic, legal, dogmatic; or, as Son-centred, emotional, literal minded, superstitious; or, as Spirit-centred, antinomian, quietistic, bursting with spiritual pride. And of course each of the three types is to be found at each of the three stages: the question is which is dominant, which recessive. No moment of history is anything without its time-depth, its supporting anachronisms. The Inner Light of the third stage, leading men in all directions and into many perilous places, is blackness itself without the Light beyond the Sun of the first.

The inward flight is necessarily a division and a dispersion and a descent. This is most clearly seen in the external history of religious organization: the religion of the universal church becomes the religion of the national church, of dissenting sects, of the family and the home, of the individual man. His faith and worship are now his private affair, and no more to be inquired into than his sexual life. That is to say, they hardly exist.

## 5. *The three stages in art*

The art of the first of our three stages was not so much religious art as religion itself become visible and tangible and audible. The gothic style is the assertion—in attenuated stone and glass and timber, in metals and fabrics, in the music of bells and the discantus—of the angelic world. It does not soar to Heaven but rather dangle from Heaven, and its slow collapse is the result of letting go rather than of ceasing to mount.

To lose height is always to lose unity. At first there is little individual self-expression in art, and little art that is distinctively secular. But in time the pursuit of virtue and the pursuit of loveliness begin to take men in two very different directions. The artist loses his anonymity. He observes for himself. This world becomes something more than a waiting-room for the next, and eventually it is possible to paint a picture without pointing a moral. The artist develops a new eye for the sensuous facts, and his subject becomes important for what it appears to be rather than for any transcendent meaning that can be read into it. The church's supersensuous mysteries are shelved and the laboratory's subsensuous mysteries are as yet undisclosed, and meantime the unmysterious visible world wears reality's badges of rank, is excitingly and beautifully actual. The Copernican cosmology has undermined the angelic orders by attacking their physical basis, so that man can now throw off parental authority and set out to enjoy himself at his own level. And the fruit of this enjoyment is some of our finest art.

But he cannot rest here. Hierarchical gravity pulls him down. As the suprahuman goodness which is the motive of the first stage issues in the human beauty which is the motive of the second, so this in turn issues in the infrahuman truth which is the motive of the third. In Heaven there is no perspective; its light casts no shadows; its angels have no pectoral muscles; the law of gravitation does not hold. But once the artist starts working from earthly models all this is changed. The history of European painting from Giotto to Monet and Degas is on the whole a story of ever more faithful representation of nature, of the gradual rejection of sacred and then of secular meaning in favour of what is actually given at the time to the senses. In the end a dustbin is as fit a subject as a duchess, and a sore is as paintable as a rose. The artist trains himself to descend from the level of public significance and objective knowledge to the level of his own untutored sense experience, his most fleeting impressions. In fact the long centuries spent in the effort to grasp the external world only end (decrees the law of elsewhereness) in a complete shift of emphasis to the inner world of private experience. For are not our dreams, our automatisms, our most primitive imagery and animal desires, even closer to the heart of nature than our sense impressions can ever be? And are they not therefore the most suitable material for the painter and poet and novelist?

Like philosophy and science, art has achieved its superb successes in the course of its descent of the hierarchy—from the world of angels, through the world of men, to the chaotic world of the demons in man, and to the empty Centre itself. And this is the end of art. When all interest passes from what the external world is to what the artist's reaction is, when his only concern is self-expression without any reference to reality outside himself, he confronts only the inane. He had to take this centripetal path, for his mastery on the way required that he should all the while be making for the end which is utter failure.

(I have referred chiefly to painting, but similar stories could be told of the other arts. It could be shown, for instance, that the gothic architect plans for Heaven, the renaissance architect for man, the modern architect for the machine. And the history of Western architecture is the tale of this collapse, this earth-ward sag. The gothic style is vertical, but its arch slowly flattens for three centuries; the renaissance nobly compromises with vertical column and horizontal entablature; the modern hugs the ground—even its window-panes lie on their sides. The thirteenth-century cathedral is a campaign against gravity; the seventeenth-century *palazzo* is reconciled to earth; the twentieth-century factory grovels—and all our really contemporary architecture is factory-inspired. In short, architecture philosophizes, and the lines of our buildings are as truly diagrams of our universe as those of the ziggurat and the pyramid were of older cosmologies.)

## 6. *The three stages in politics*

Finally, consider the changing structure of society. Europe came out of the Dark Ages with the vision of an earthly hierarchy linked to and sanctioned by the heavenly. Of course the ideal of this many-levelled organic society, though operative even down to this day, was never fully realized. Christendom gave way to kings, kings to their subjects. The age of individualism and of equality arrives, and nearly all hint of divinity departs from governments. But once more there is no halting the downward trend at the second stage. When the upper hierarchical levels go, the middle soon follow. The spotlight now shifts from man to productive forces and techniques, to the means of life, to matter. Thus the revolt against the upper half of the social hierarchy does not end in the perfect democracy; succeeding only too well, it tears down the lower half, and man himself is not spared. He must follow his angels to the guillotine.

The great truth that escapes us is that the politics of the City of God are of a piece with those of the earthly city. In fact, the historical demolition of our social structure and of our universe are two aspects of a single operation—it is an under-statement to say that class distinctions have a basis in cosmology. The first phase of our civilization is predominantly aristocratic and rural as well as religious; thereafter the established church is bound up with the obsolescent landed aristocracy, and with the population of the country rather than the town. The second phase belongs especially to the rising middle class, with their zeal for religious reform and schism, and their interest in a broadening secular and humanist culture. The third phase belongs to the industrialized urban masses, whose culture (so far as its exists) is science-inspired, materialist, and often atheist.

It is true that all three classes—(i) religious, aristocratic, conservative; (ii) humanist, bourgeois, liberal; and (iii) pseudo-scientific, proletarian, socialist—coexist in our present-day society. But the last dominates. And this 'reversal of regions' is the more complete for being so far from merely political: the social revolutions which put first the bourgeoisie and then the masses in power are one with the cosmological revolutions which substitute the human for the divine and then the material for the human.

## 7. *Conclusion*

In the third stage of our civilization's history even history becomes third-stage—patternless, just one damned thing after another, bunk. But this dream cannot last: meaning is coming back into our time and space. Our angels are already trying their wings for their seasonal migration, for that long outward flight which will make them angelic again. At each level the equality—even the superiority—of the Other is dawning upon us. Thus at the human level there is a new insistence upon the I-Thou relationship; the discovery of the bees' language provokes the suspicion that Life's intelligence is not, after all, so exclusively concentrated in man; some find convincing evidence that our atmosphere is as haunted with mysterious non-human life as long ago it was believed to be; we are no longer sure that Martian evolution is not far ahead of Earth's; scientists have begun to speak of millions of solar systems—many of them no doubt inhabited—and it would be odd if none surpassed the Sun, living a life beside which ours is merely vegetative; and finally theologians are now more apt to find God outside than within themselves. In short, there are grounds for believing that though we are at the third stage of one civilization we are moving into the first stage of the next.

How far the story of our own civilization may reflect that of others past and to come (and indeed the story of Humanity itself); how far it is a geographical or rather a chthonic movement from East to West; how far its three stages in philosophy and science and art and religion reflect each other and keep to the same time-table; how far we have now come in the history of the third stage—these are questions I need not take up here. It is enough that our task is plain: namely, to hold fast to the tripartite whole; to stand for the present living unity of all three hierarchical stages, and so to gather up into a viable heritage, from which time has slipped away, the splendid works of the past. Even if we are not thereby planting the seed of the civilization that shall follow, we are at least taking in time instead of being taken in by time; we are at least aware that the meaning of history lies neither in some ever-receding future goal, nor in some golden age long past, but in this present moment which holds all together in living simultaneity. The man who fishes first with a mere rod, then with a mere line, then with a mere hook, has left out nothing, yet is unlikely to catch his dinner. Togetherness is needed. To see the world stereoscopically we have to broaden our time-base, using instruments that are centuries apart yet all at once. Otherwise the planes of our universe collapse, and we collapse with them.

CHAPTER XXIV

# The Angels of Darkness

*1. The evil suprahuman*

The hierarchy above man is evil as well as good. For consider the grounds of belief in the suprahuman. First, there is tradition, and tradition insists almost as much upon bad angels as upon good ones. Second, there is the evidence of introspection: we find in ourselves influences at work .that are more than human, but they are perhaps as often evil as good. Third, when we extrapolate the curve of the infrahuman through the human into suprahuman regions, we find, along with increasing power for good, power for evil: the will is as likely to prove immoral as moral, and knowledge may well be knowledge of how to do more and more harm. Everything suggests that, as we mount the hierarchy, the moral conflict is exacerbated.

*2. Extrapolation: the law of diminishing returns*

Worse than this, there appears to lie at the heart of things a fatal contradiction, a doom which makes all optimism ridiculous. If it were simply a case of the brighter light casting the darker shadow, then on balance there would be no loss; but it seems that the light itself grows dim, and the balance alters in favour of the darkness.

Consider knowledge. Knowing more is wondering less, and wondering less is knowing less. For information without humility, or love, or astonishment, or reverence, becomes the worst kind of misinformation. Nor is there any escape from the evil of being too clever and over-wise but return to the lower levels of comparative ignorance. Mental extensions are just like their bodily counterparts: they are crippling deformities if they cannot be amputated at a moment's notice. The know-all is really an ignoramus, and the suprahuman is by definition a know-all. Is there not then justification for the mediaeval warning that there exists unlawful knowledge that can only be got by intercourse with the powers of evil?

Again, consider will. The growth of consciousness is the growth of care. The more intelligent and responsible a man is, the further he looks ahead, and the more trouble he sees coming. Indeed anxiety is the measure of the man—the casual labourer lives from day to day with few forebodings or regrets; the thrifty, respectable citizen provides for his old age and his children's future, and pays for his forethought in peace of mind; and the intellectual, not content with such a burden, takes on future generations, the destiny of Humanity, of the whole world. The more extensive our plans—even our most praiseworthy ones—the more we are bedevilled by worry. Nor is our care unjustified: the further our goal the less we are likely to get to it. Our merely animal desires are capable of genuine (if transient) satisfaction; but to pursue fame, wealth, power, security, learning, or even virtue, is to chase the rainbow.

It is much the same with our capacity for aesthetic and religious experience. The price of keener sensitivity and awareness is apt to prove altogether too high: the pain becomes more and more disproportionate to the attendant delights. Perhaps we could reconcile ourselves to this if the goods were of the finest quality. But in fact the quality tends to fall off as the expense mounts. The learned are rarely inspired. The virtuous are rarely lovable, spontaneous, or charming. The saint whose life is a masterpiece of self-sacrificing goodness has only to realize as much to become insufferable, and in an important respect worse than the ordinary failing mortal who is only too conscious of his depravity. How to go in for goodness without disclosing to himself what he is after—that is the saint's almost insoluble problem. Only by something of a miracle can more than ordinary self-effacement fail to become more than ordinary spiritual pride.

And all these disquieting consequences of hierarchical ascent are scarcely surprising if the hierarchy is a social structure. For we have reason enough to fear that the organization of communities beyond a certain degree of centralized complexity means the disorganization of the values they enshrine. And we have little reason for believing that social life at the more exalted hierarchical levels is particularly peaceful: if the *odium theologi-cum*, and the persistent tradition of sidereal and angelic warfare are any guide, then it is perhaps even less harmonious than at the human level.

## 3. The failure of extension

We all want to grow. And most of us believe that in bigger organizations lies our social salvation. If only we could sink our differences, and combine in a single super-State or world-State; if only we could rouse everyone to take an enlightened interest in world affairs; if only we were not so small-minded, so wrapped up in our toys and games, so childishly indifferent to the grave and immense issues now at stake—then (it is said or implied) our worst troubles would be over.

This faith in the excellence of the adult and the big and the high is ill-founded. My growth in space and time is more than matched by my environment's, so that it is really shrinkage: indeed as I mount the hierarchy I become increasingly space-time-ridden, and draw away from the spaceless and timeless Whole. When I take my hatred of other men, and my fears for this man, and sink them in my hatred of other nations and my fears for this nation, my national egosim is still egoism and still mine. And if, one day, Earth at last unites against a Martian enemy, we have only involved still more of the universe in our war-mindedness. The news page of my paper is more grown-up than the sports page, but it does a great deal more harm on that account: it ensures that I shall be frightened and resentful on the largest possible scale every breakfast time. One of the delusions of our age is that large and high-level vices are virtues; but in fact the damage done by the grossly sensual and weak-willed is negligible compared with that which the disciplined ascetic, with his suprahuman courage and fortitude and patience and foresight, can so easily commit.

However we set out to climb the hierarchical ladder—whether we seek expansion, knowledge, power, goodness, the welfare of society or of any 'higher self'—we are likely before long to find ourselves falling away from our goal. The rungs which from below look so secure let us down. It is not merely that these heights do not suit us: there is more than a suspicion that they are somehow wrong or haunted. We supposed them to be the region of angels of light but we find angels of darkness.

## 4. A change of direction

Yet the suprahuman is certainly real, and the true shrine of that perfection we cannot help but long for. What then is to be done? We must give up the idea of expansion from this Centre, and find another.

The further apart you and I draw the higher is our mutual status, but the more out of touch we are. I know what you used to be and I have designs on your future; but I am not in your presence, nor are you in mine. Too early and too late, we attend only to each other's time-extremities and leave out all their present filling; therefore we are dead and hollow things that know only how to use each other.

There remains the love which restores the world's life, the quick sympathy which, because it places itself instantaneously at the other's Centre, bridges the time-gulf that widens as we climb. Will, looking to the unsure future, is wholly time-ridden; knowledge, looking to the partially secured past, is half-free of time; love, enjoying the certain present, is wholly free. Heaven is present and Hell future, however hard we try in our Utopian frenzies of planning to reverse this order. But it is because the love which is of Heaven is *now* that it belongs to faith and not sight. For whenever we put ourselves in another's place, feel for him, treat him as the end which we are to serve, then (to use the terms of Chapter XX) we are adopting that ultimate and timeless mode of recapitulation which belongs to the highest level but works in all. To refuse to make this leap, to know and to act towards my brother without loving him, is a kind of fratricide, for I deny him present existence and make of him an appendage of my past and future. The question is: am I content to leave him at my periphery as one of my extensions or outermost limbs, or do I also make myself at once peripheral and Central to him? And indeed till I do so, till I love, I can neither understand nor effectively influence. The arm of past knowledge and the arm of future will are increasingly paralysed as they grow, unless they embrace with present sympathy the thing they hold. For love alone yields reliable inside information and knows how to win.

The good suprahuman, then, instead of merely extrapolating the curves of human knowledge and power, changes direction and makes for a new Centre in respect of which it is content to become infrahuman. Thus each higher region is rectified by union with its inferior counterpart. The ever-widening gap between time-vexed intelligence and activity is filled by converging timeless love in such a way that all three are realized. The bad suprahuman is only itself, and therefore in the last resort not even itself; but the good suprahuman is itself because it is also its opposite, because it has found the suprahuman Other. The saint is above us because he is also beneath us. And the artist has his own vision of the same paradox. The blue end of the spectrum and the high notes of the scale cannot stand for the good suprahuman without the red end and the low notes which stand for the infrahuman: what is truly highest here is also the lowest and all that lies between. The greatest paintings and musical compositions and poems are fully cosmological, hierarchically distributed, exercises in the vertical harmony of the universe, but they reach the heights only by containing the depths.

Like pretentious yet trivial works of art, our evil angels ring hollow. They lack hierarchical depth. They have neither guts nor bowels of compassion; for their insides, their nearer regions, have been thoroughly cleaned out and sterilized. In other words, they keep their distance, running away from disorderly and irksome particular things to neat and comfortable classes of things. If they notice human suffering at all, they do so from a safe theoretic range which ensures that they shall not share it: their charity begins away from home, and ends there. Starry-eyed idealists, far-sighted and broad-minded, adept at philosophy and theology and all manner of generalizing, they look only to horizons, and despise the foreground of the empirical, the sordid, the low-grade. They are cosmic snobs, hierarchical climbers. But for our good angels, who respect the laws of numerical and spatial limitation and see all ranks as in one sense equal, the nearest is dearest. They know that to care at all is to care most for the members of one's own family, for the cities of one's own land, for the races of one's own species. They know that the high and the far is nothing of the kind without the low and the near. And they fill the empty shell of the human (no less than of the suprahuman) by working inwards to the very Centre, finding in each region not myriads but one or two. For good angels have difficulty in counting any higher.

## 5. *Suprahuman and infrahuman evil*

The bad suprahuman has no use for paradoxes. Unwilling to face the complexity of things as they are, the angel of darkness denies that to grow he must shrink, that to know he must forget, that to gain power he must give it up, that to hold he must let go, that to become good he must lose all idea of his own goodness. Even angelic love is not free from the need to contradict itself—to care more, we must also care less. The bad angel is strong-willed and brilliantly clever—whereas the good is also simple and acquiescent—yet in one respect he is disastrously stupid: over-simplifying, he cannot or will not see that there is nothing really worth doing that does not require him to do also its opposite. Even Heaven, if it is only Heaven, is Hell.

Nor is the bad suprahuman far to seek. We really are limbs of Satan. Here, presented for my direct inspection, is not merely a selfish man, but a species ready to sacrifice all others to its own interests, a geosphere at war with its neighbours, a planet dreaming of expansion and conquest, a star without reverence or wonder who treats his companions like dirt—dirt much too hot to live. Of course there is the other side: the suprahuman series to which we have access is not wholly bad. And we cannot do better than take it as a fair sample of the suprahuman in general, which in that case is part angelic and part devilish.

Equally I find working in myself the evil infrahuman—hosts of unruly demons for ever dragging me down to their own level of depravity. The higher tempts me to get above myself, the lower to sink beneath myself. Yet happily they cannot—and this is the true ground of optimism—join forces, for when the evil that is above is Paired in me with the evil that is below they are no longer evil. For evil is a kind of hierarchical asymmetry, a failure to superimpose the pyramid of the not-self upon the inverted pyramid of the self. Thus suprahuman evil denies its infrahuman counterpart and is seen in pride and the sins of the mind, whereas infrahuman evil denies its suprahuman counterpart and is seen in the rejection of higher control and in the sins of the flesh.

Let me give some examples. We learn how to plan for the titillation of some bodily organ, but this new power requires that we learn also how to subject our undisciplined cravings to the welfare of our life as a whole and of the community. Similarly birth-control, which comes into effect at the cellular level, itself needs control from the level of high-principled eugenics if it is not to make for the degeneration of Life. Again, it is clear that to exploit physical particles, while neglecting their concrete suprahuman counterparts, becomes increasingly ruinous: our conquest of the inferior world is really its conquest of us. To use our chemical knowledge well, we need to rise to the unity of the living Earth no less than to go down to the multiplicity of her dead molecules. And still more do we need, as we cultivate the atom, to know that we are all one in that large Atom, the living Sun. Refusal to compensate for our descent by equal and opposite ascent, the harnessing of the low, not to the high, but to the middle-grade—this is catastrophic experimenting in practical evil. My inner regions stripped of my outer regions are a nest of Pandora's boxes. Here is witchcraft and sorcery at its most powerful and most malign. Here also is the medicine which, because it treats the patient's organs and cells and molecules while ignoring his universe—his cosmology, his total view out— is liable to prove worse than futile: Heaven's forgiveness of our sins does in fact make all the difference to our ability to take up our beds and walk here on earth.

The brotherhood of man which denies the fatherhood of God, nuclear fission unbalanced by the mystical union, the laboratory which has nothing to do with the church—of these our world is the undertaker's monument. The low has no unity but the high: the bonds which prevent its explosion are not at its own level. Only the hierarchy's One can pacify the Many; or rather, only the One *is* the peace of the Many.

## 6. Evil and the Whole

To tread underfoot the humble creatures of the world, using them as stepping-stones to higher things, is the way of the bad angel; and in the end it does not work. For he deceives himself who thinks he can get to Heaven unless with and through all others: they are not mere stages on the way, but parts of the goal itself. Indeed the salvation that required us to leave to its fate the feeblest or wickedest of sentient beings would be perdition. Only devils hate devils. God is not love of the lovable but of all, and the only way to get to Him is to let ourselves be caught up in His timeless and universal compassion which heals all the world's wounds. Here, in Him alone, is all our good and our wholeness, and here all our evil is overcome. For only He is generous enough to love all without any reservations, and only He is lofty enough to abase Himself beneath all creatures.

Short of this highest level which is out of time, the battle must go on between the good and the evil that is just as real as the good. But the existence of the highest level leaves no doubt as to the issue. The universe can be made good because in the last resort it is good. Until I am sure that the powers of dar ness are already destroyed I am a frightened and half-hearted champion of the light. Yet to believe the struggle illusory is the worst of illusions. Indeed God Himself, whom we may inadequately think of as the final union of intellect and will in timeless love, is not content to stand eternally above the levels of strife and multiplicity, but comes down through them all. He is more deeply involved in the tragedy than are any of His creatures, if only because His sympathy and humility are absolute. Certainly there is nothing cheap or easy about the delights of Heaven. For them the highest of all prices has been paid.

All of which, it may be said, is powerless to subtract a tear or a groan from the frightful tale of the world's suffering and wickedness. Take a sample of the actual horrors—the crucifixion of six thousand slaves along the highroad from Capua to Rome after the revolt of Spartacus, the ingenious atrocities of Caligula and Nero, the Albigensian Crusade, Torquemada's term of office as Grand Inquisitor, Tilly's sack of Magdeburg in 1630, the slave trade, Belsen, Hiroshima and Nagasaki, and all the other countless iniquities of our inhuman (and indeed largely suprahuman) civilization. And infrahuman nature also is full of what is surely needless pain and squalor. The cat's way with the mouse and the ichneumon's way with the caterpillar, the dental abcesses and arthritis and osteo-myelitis of many wild animals, the liver-fluke's career, the raven pecking out the eyes of the living lamb—these are specimens of what kind Mother Nature carries in her bag. To gloss over these things is a stupid and cowardly evasion, and any adult person who wears a permanently beaming expression is either a fraud or a fool.

It is a bad day for us when we forget these things. Yet it is worse to take them for the whole truth. The question is: shall we trust the mood when our hearts are so torn at the sight of the world's suffering that we would see the whole calamitous system unmade, or the mood when we are so in love with God's universe, so thirsty for its life, so enraptured with its improbable beauty, so taken aback with surprise and admiration, that we would not see the particle of a particle altered? Shall we cheerfully say that the world's evil is the inevitable accompaniment of its division and incompleteness at those relatively unreal levels we live on, while at the highest level of the hierarchy all the parts fall into place and there is now and for ever perfect harmony? Or shall we despairingly admit that attachment is the root of all evil, and the entire pain-racked universe that springs from desire a mistake—a will-product which must be patiently unwilled until at the lowest hierarchical level the primeval harmony of absolute non-existence is restored? That is to say, does the remedy for evil lie in undoing it or in making it good, in repentance or in restitution, in ungrowth or in growth, in going back to the beginning or going on to the end? Still more briefly: is our cure to be found at the base or the apex of the hierarchy?

It can only be found in both together. Both movements at once, ascent and descent held together in a Paired and symmetrical unity, must be ours—not so much in theory as in living practice. Then perhaps we shall begin to understand.

Yet good and evil must remain to us a terrible and fathomless mystery. The only solution that works is a confession of utter ignorance coupled with an act of utter surrender. In one sense the more a question is worth asking the less it is answerable; in another, it is only the ultimate questions which can be answered at all, or settled in a way that does not leave two questions where before there was one. Indeed, if we profess to know in our heads *why* evil is necessary to the divine plan, and precisely *how* it is real yet illusory in the end, then we are unlikely to know in our hearts *that* such is the case. If, all undeserving, we are sometimes granted that overwhelming intuition of a Goodness which neither underestimates nor leaves untransmuted the least grain of the world's evil, then we begin to know what knowledge can be: for here is information in the light of which all the rest is misinformation, the vaguest and most dubious of imaginings.

### 7. *The heavenly community*

Every painter has to resist the temptation to work up and beautify the part as a part. For the only perfection which the part can properly boast belongs to the whole work; its own perfections are more likely to prove blemishes. Only God, our Whole, is the completion, the healing remedy, of the fragments that we are. He is what we want, and we are not ourselves without Him. We are lost till we are lost in Him.

But if this were all, the cure would be in danger of eradicating the patient along with the disease. The fact is that the Absolute which only absorbs, which demands the surrender of every self to itself, is the Devil. For God Himself, more than any creature, subjects Himself to the rule that it is not enough to find oneself in others: the others must be free and in no way coerced, must be independent Centres and not radii extending from one's own Centre. He is the guarantor of our distinctness from Himself and from one another; each of us is eternally unique and inviolable, for He needs every member of His Hierarchy of Heaven and Earth to be itself and no other. Evil is the price of this freedom. Creatures incapable of sin, sustained in every perfection, would be mere projections of Himself, and His love for them would be the self-love which is of the essence of evil. Of necessity love individuates its object. So far from the crowning level of the hierarchy threatening the independence of the others, it stands guard over it as a thing most precious.

Nevertheless our freedom does not consist in denying all that determines us, and asserting our own self-will. On the contrary, its true ground is our willingness to accept every necessity, so that it ceases to be merely external. We are free in so far as we join our will to God's. For He alone is by nature free, because subject to no outside influence; yet He lets us share this freedom by uniting ourselves to Him. We have the choice of His freedom or our bondage. Nor is our independence of Him, seeing that it utterly depends upon Him, illusory. We have all seen the waywardness of our creations—if not of the characters in the novels we write, at least of the actors in our dreams—and we have every reason for supposing that the highest creative level is able to complete the independence of its created objects.

The timeless realm of absolute unity is the realm where no distinction made apparent in time is lost. And here alone are fulfilled the conditions of love. Love demands that the loved one shall be himself and free; and love demands union. In the world of time these requirements are incompatible, and love is always working its own undoing. But in the timeless world they are realized together—the perfection of independence and of oneness do not cancel out, but reinforce each other. In Hell I am bent on finding myself in myself, but time destroys me; in Heaven I am bent on losing myself in Another, but eternity preserves me.

# Epilogue

So ends my attempt at autobiography, my experimental self-portrait. What am I? Have I answered the question? Indeed I have not. I have occurred, but what it is that has occurred is more of a puzzle to itself than ever. For the provisional answers I have set down are only a fraction of the fractional truth about himself that man has so far comprehended, and in comparison with the whole truth his most extravagant speculations could only seem absurdly tame—humdrum milk-and-water stuff, prosy to the point of extinction. There are more and grander systems in the sea of Being than have ever been fished out of it. The mystery extends in every direction to infinity, and in its presence all our snippets of information, all our little guesses about human nature, dwindle out of sight. For, besides the countless particular miracles that we comprise, there is that supreme irregularity—the fact that anything exists at all. Most unnaturally, there is not just Nothing. How adroit of It to happen! How deserving of our congratulations It is, for having arranged its quite impossible existence! After that, what are a few billion universes more or less? What impossibilities may not It or He have up His sleeve? And what may I not be in Him?

If His Being, in which I am allowed to share, does not utterly abase me—making this inquiry absurd, though a needful absurdity—what is left worth my amazed reverence? Indeed my finest and most thrilling discovery is that, because all my roots are in the Undiscoverable, I also am undiscoverable: I will not bear inspection, and can never make head or tail of myself. Self-knowledge is the smouldering wick that is left after the light of wonder has been put out. Once the universe becomes credible, once I seriously suppose I know a thing or two about myself, then I have sunk back into the stupor of the half-dead. Nor is it any consolation that I have escaped from astonishment into thought—wonder and love inspire vast underground systems in which to take cover from wonder and love; but those who, lacking constructional enthusiasm, stay above ground, are exposed to God's weather and liable to feel His wind on their faces. If this book quenches the feeblest flame of awe, of direct awareness, in myself or anyone else, then it were better never to have written it.

# Index

# INDEX

# INDEX

as Living, 88, 91-3
Motion of, 94-6
Past of, 96-7
Pulse of, 89
Social Life of, 73, 93-4
and Vision, 32-3
Earthquakes, Artificial, 90
Education, 198, 208
Ecology, 134
Ego, 233
Eidetic Imagery, 197
Electron, 49-56, 57, 133, 136, 143
Elsewhereness, Law of, and Art, 244
in Atom, 52
in Centre-shifting, 187
and Explanation, 218
in Hierarchy, 48, 77
and History, 218, 239
and Mind, 97
and Pairs, 141
and Progress, 209
in Regional Space, 20-1, 115-16, 232
and Subject-Object, 232
and Time, 161, 232
in Whole and Centre, 120-1
Embryo, 72, 89, 97, 185, 203-4
Embryology, 131, 134, 201-4
Emergence, 60, 61, 64
and Motion, 174
Equality, Law of, 24, 42-4, 65, 81, 121, 152
Er Myth, 227
Euclidean and Non-Euclidean Geometry, 27
Eugenics, 192, 254
Evil, 248-58
Angels, 248, 252-3
and Attachment, 256
Infrahuman, 253-5
Problem of, 255-6
and Repentance, 256
Evolution and Emanation, 143
Explanation, 47, 122, 137, 217-18
Extension, of Body, 67-71, 145
Failure of, 248-50
of Mind, 248-9
Exuberance, 72
Eye, 28-32, 104-5

'Facts of Life', 203-4
Fairies, 197
Fall, The, 195
Family, The, 55, 118-19, 154, 209
Father, God the, 131-2, 141, 242
Feudal System, 245
Fiction, Characters in, 39, 257
Field of View, 60, 65, 186
as Constant, 178-9
Fish, 202, 203
Flowers, 84
'Foetalization', 206-10, 216-17
and Education, 208
Foetus, 103, 203
Force, 145, 234
Forces, and Angels, 228
as Relics of Wholes, 172-3, 242
Francis, St., 242
Freedom, and Foreknowledge, 181
and God, 257-8
at Higher Levels, 96, 116
and Religion, 126
and Self-consciousness, 96, 163
in Society, 185-7

Galaxy, The, 109-19
Life of, 110-15
Necessary to Sun, 109-10
as Star-Society, 109
Structure and Functioning of, 115-17
Galaxies, Recession of, 117, 120, 234
Gamma Rays, 52
Genes, 118, 189
Geocide, 98
Geology, 89, 90, 98, 134-5
Geopsychology, 97
Geospheres, 88-91, 253
Evolution of, 211-12, 214
Germ Cells, 103, 154, 203, 218
Gill-slits, 209
Giotto, 244
Goblins, 197
God, 131-2, 246
and Angels, 234-5
and Freedom, 257-8
and Projection-Reflection, 42
Gods, 42, 226-32
Animal, 85

# INDEX

# INDEX

# INDEX

# INDEX

# INDEX